OXFORD READINGS IN PHILOSOPHY

CAUSATION

Also published in this series

Other volumes are in preparation

CAUSATION

edited by

ERNEST SOSA
and
MICHAEL TOOLEY

OXFORD UNIVERSITY PRESS
1993

Oxford University Press, Walton Street, Oxford OX2 6DP
Oxford New York Toronto
Delhi Bombay Calcutta Madras Karachi
Kuala Lumpur Singapore Hong Kong Tokyo
Nairobi Dar es Salaam Cape Town
Melbourne Auckland Madrid
and associated companies in
Berlin Ibadan

Oxford is a trade mark of Oxford University Press

Published in the United States
by Oxford University Press Inc., New York

British Library Cataloguing in Publication Data
Data available

Library of Congress Cataloging in Publication Data
Causation / edited by Ernest Sosa and Michael Tooley.
p. cm. — (Oxford readings in philosophy)
Includes bibliographical references and index.
1. Causation. 1. Sosa, Ernest. II. Tooley, Michael, 1941–
III. Series.
BD591.C26 1993 122—dc20 92-28442
ISBN 0–19–875093–5
ISBN 0–19–875094–3 (Pbk)

Typeset by Pure Tech Corporation, Pondicherry, India

Printed in Great Britain on acid-free paper by
Bookcraft (Bath) Ltd., Midsomer Norton, Avon

CONTENTS

ACKNOWLEDGEMENTS

The editors and publisher are grateful for permission to include the following copyright material.

I: from *American Philosophical Quarterly*, 2/4 (October 1965), 245–55, and 261–4. Used with permission.

II: from *Philosophical Analysis and History*, ed. W. Dray. © 1966 William H. Dray. Reprinted by permission of HarperCollins Publishers.

III: from *Journal of Philosophy*, 68 (1971), 426–41. Reprinted by permission of the author and the journal.

IV: first published in *Journal of Philosophy*, 64 (1967), 691–703; reprinted in *Essays on Actions and Events* (OUP, 1980; © in this collection Donald Davidson 1980). Reprinted by permission of the author and publisher.

V: from *Causality and Determination* (CUP, 1971). Reprinted by permission of the author and publisher.

VI: from *Logic, Methodology and Philosophy of Science IV*, ed. P. Suppes *et al.* (Amsterdam, North-Holland, 1973). © the author and reprinted by his permission.

VII: from *Journal of Philosophy*, 23 (1926), 57–68. Reprinted by permission of the author and the journal.

VIII: from *Pacific Philosophical Quarterly*, 61 (1980), 50–74. Reprinted by permission of the author and Blackwell Publishers.

IX: from *Proceedings of the 1980 Biennial Meeting of the Philosophy of Science Association*, vol. 2, ed. Peter D. Asquith and Ronald N. Giere, pp. 49–69. Reprinted by permission of the author and the Philosophy of Science Association.

X: from *Philosophy and Phenomenological Research*, 50, Supplement (Fall 1990), 215–36. Reprinted with permission.

XI: from *Journal of Philosophy*, 70 (1973), 556–67. Reprinted by permission of the author and the journal.

XII: from *Journal of Philosophy*, 70 (1973), 570–2. Reprinted by permission of the author and the journal.

XIII: from *Asymmetries in Time: Problems in the Philosophy of Science*, pp. 167–76. © 1987 Massachusetts Institute of Technology. Reprinted by permission of the MIT Press.

XIV: from *Philosophical Perspectives*, 1, *Metaphysics* (1987), ed. James E. Tomberlin (copyright by Ridgeview Publishing Co., Atascadero, Calif.) Reprinted by permission of Ridgeview Publishing Company.

XV: from *Grazer Philosophische Studien*, 11 (1980), 93–103. Reprinted by permission of Editions Rodopi BV and Karl-Franzens Universität Graz.

INTRODUCTION[*]

CAUSATION, conditionals, explanation, confirmation, dispositions, and laws form a cluster of closely related topics in metaphysics, philosophy of language, and philosophy of science. In addition, causation plays an important role in connection with many problems in other areas of philosophy, especially philosophy of mind and epistemology. Here, however, we have had to confine the discussion to the nature of causation itself. For, even having thus delimited the scope of the anthology, we have been able to include only a few of the many excellent papers available.

1. SOME FUNDAMENTAL ISSUES IN THE PHILOSOPHY OF CAUSATION

Causal states of affairs encompass, on the one hand, *causal laws* and, on the other, *causal relations* between events, or states of affairs and two of the basic questions that arise in the philosophy of causation concern, first, the relation between causal laws and causal relations, and secondly, the relation of each of these to non-causal states of affairs.

In the first place, then, which are more basic: causal laws, or causal relations? By far the dominant answer to this question, going back to David Hume's profound and extremely influential discussion,[1] is that causal laws are more basic, with causal relations between events being logically supervenient upon causal laws, together with the non-causal properties of, and relations between, events. However, while most subsequent discussion of causation has taken place against the background of this assumption, this view has certainly not gone unchallenged. For, first of all, some philosophers have defended a singularist approach to causation, according to which individual events can be causally related without falling under causal laws. Secondly, others have argued that, even if causal relations between events always presuppose corresponding causal laws, the thesis of Humean supervenience is still unsound, since one can describe possible worlds where not all of the causal relations between events are logically fixed by the combination of causal laws plus the non-causal properties of, and relations between, events.

* Thanks to David Armstrong, David Braddon-Mitchell, Peter Menzies, and Philip Pettit for helpful comments.

[1] David Hume, *A Treatise of Human Nature* (London, 1739), I. 3, sects. 1–6, 11, 12, 14, and 15, and id., *An Enquiry Concerning Human Understanding* (London, 1748), sects. 4 and 7.

The second fundamental issue mentioned above concerns the relation between causal and non-causal states of affairs. Are all causal relations between events, and all causal laws, reducible to non-causal states of affairs? Or does the existence of causal laws, or of causal relations between events, or both, involve something over and above the totality of non-causal facts?

On this second issue, just as with the first, Hume's influence is very apparent, with the overwhelmingly dominant view being the analytical reductionist position generally thought to have been espoused by him,[2] according to which all causal facts are logically supervenient upon the totality of non-causal facts. But this second supervenience thesis, though very widely accepted indeed, has also been seriously challenged, and in a variety of ways. Most commonly, the challenge has focused upon causal laws, with a number of philosophers recently arguing that the total history of the world does not suffice to determine what laws there are.[3] But the claim that causal relations are logically supervenient upon non-causal states of affairs has also been questioned, and here the objections are of two very different sorts. The one involves the contentions, first, that it is possible, either in perception, or else in introspection, to be directly aware of the relation of causation, and secondly, that such awareness provides one with knowledge of the intrinsic nature of causation, and so enables one to see that causal relations between events are not reducible to any non-causal states of affairs.[4] The other objection involves a thesis mentioned earlier—namely, that causal relations between events are not logically supervenient even upon the totality consisting of non-causal facts *together with causal laws*.

Analytical reductionism is not, however, the only form that reductionism with respect to causation can take. Thus, even if it does turn out to be the

---

[2] Virtually all historians of philosophy have regarded Hume as a reductionist with respect to causal facts. Recently, however, a number have argued that Hume was a realist, rather than a reductionist. See John Wright's *The Sceptical Realism of David Hume* (Manchester, 1983); Edward Craig's *The Mind of God and the Works of Man* (Oxford, 1987); and Galen Strawson's *The Secret Connexion: Causation, Realism, and David Hume* (Oxford, 1989). A careful examination of this issue can be found in Simon Blackburn's 'Hume and Thick Connexions', *Philosophy and Phenomenological Research*, suppl., 50 (1990), 237–50. Blackburn argues, very forcefully, that Hume is best viewed neither as a reductionist nor as a sceptical realist, with respect to causation, but as an anti-realist.

[3] See e.g. Fred I. Dretske, 'Laws of Nature', *Philosophy of Science*, 44 (1977), 248–68; Michael Tooley, 'The Nature of Laws', *Canadian Journal of Philosophy*, 7/4 (1977), 667–98; Sydney Shoemaker, 'Causality and Properties', in Peter van Inwagen (ed.), *Time and Cause* (Dordrecht, 1980), 109–35; Chris Swoyer, 'The Nature of Natural Laws', *Australasian Journal of Philosophy*, 60/3 (1982), 203–23; John Foster, 'Induction, Explanation, and Natural Necessity', *Proceedings of the Aristotelian Society*, 83 (1982–3), 87–101; David M. Armstrong, *What Is a Law of Nature?* (Cambridge, 1983).

[4] See e.g. G. E. M. Anscombe, 'Causality and Determination', repr. below (Ch. V); David M. Armstrong, *A Materialist Theory of the Mind* (New York, 1968), 97; and Evan Fales, *Causation and Universals* (London and New York, 1990), 11–25.

case that causal facts are not logically supervenient upon non-causal ones, there is still the possibility of an *a posteriori* identification of causal and non-causal facts, and indeed, this idea of a non-analytic reduction of causation has been advanced over the past few years by a number of philosophers. Thus David Fair, for example, has proposed that basic causal relations can, as a consequence of our scientific knowledge, be identified with certain physicalistic relations between objects that can be characterized in terms of the transference of either energy or momentum between the objects involved in the cause and those involved in the effect.[5]

What are the prospects for a contingent identification of causation with such physicalistic relations? Perhaps the first point that needs to be made is that once one abandons the view that causal relations are logically supervenient upon non-causal states of affairs, and embraces an *a posteriori* reduction, one is left with the question of how the concept of causation is to be analysed. But does someone who advances a contingent identity thesis really need to grapple with this issue? Can it not be left simply as an open question? Perhaps, but the situation in the case of contingent identity theses concerning the mind suggests that this may very well not be so. For until a satisfactory analysis has been offered, there is the possibility of an argument to the effect that it is *logically impossible* for causal relations to be identical with any physicalistic relations. In particular, might it not plausibly be argued that causation possesses an intrinsic nature, so that causation must be one and the same relation in all possible worlds, just as what it is for something to be a law of nature does not vary from one world to another? But if this is right, then one can appeal to the possibility of worlds that involve causation, but that do not contain the physicalistic relations in question—or, more radically, that contain no physicalistic states at all—in order to draw the conclusion that causation cannot, even in this world, be identical with any physicalistic relation.

What is needed, in short, if an *a posteriori* reduction is to be sustainable, is a satisfactory analysis of the concept of causation according to which causation, rather than having any intrinsic nature, is simply whatever relation happens to play a certain role in a given possible world. But at present, no such analysis seems to be at hand.

A second problem for any contingent identification of causation with a physicalistic relation arises from the fact that one needs to find a physicalistic

[5] David Fair, 'Causation and the Flow of Energy', *Erkenntnis*, 14 (1979), 219–50. Jerrold Aronson, in 'The Legacy of Hume's Analysis of Causation', *Studies in the History and Philosophy of Science*, 7 (1971), 135–56, advocates a very similar view, while quite a different identity thesis concerning causation is advanced by David M. Armstrong and Adrian Heathcote in 'Causes and Laws', *Noûs*, 25 (1991), 63–73.

relation that, like causation, has a direction, but where the direction of the physicalistic relation does not itself need to be cashed out in terms of causation. In Fair's account, for example, the appeal is to the direction of the *transference* of energy and/or momentum, and this is exposed to the immediate objection that the concept of transference itself involves the idea of causation. Fair's response to this problem is that the direction of transference can be explained in temporal terms, rather than causal ones.[6] But this response involves substantial assumptions concerning the relation between the direction of time and the direction of causation. In particular, many philosophers think that the direction of time is itself to be explained in terms of the direction of causation—a view that is precluded by Fair's account.

A third difficulty concerns the relations between temporal parts of an enduring object. One way of putting the objection is in terms of the claim that the correct analysis of identity over time involves the idea that any temporal stage of an enduring entity must be causally dependent upon earlier stages of that object. Another, more modest formulation is that, regardless of how identity over time is to be analysed, it is true of any enduring object in this world that its temporal parts are causally interrelated. Either way, the point is that although the temporal parts of an electron, for example, are causally related, this relation does not involve any transference of energy or momentum from one object to another. So causation cannot be identified with physical relations involving the transference of energy and/or momentum.

The prospects for a physicalistic reduction of causation do not, in short, appear very bright. This means that if analytical reductionism also fails, in the face of the objections mentioned earlier, there is no viable alternative to a realist approach to causation.

Causal realism comes, however, in quite different varieties, with the fundamental choice being between, on the one hand, realist approaches that maintain that the relation of causation is immediately given in experience, and, on the other, those that hold that causation is a theoretical relation, and so not directly observable. According to the first of these, the whole enterprise of attempting to offer an analysis of the concept of causation is mistaken, or, at least, unnecessary, since the concept of causation picks out a relation that can be immediately or non-inferentially perceived, a relation with which one can be directly acquainted. According to the second realist approach, in contrast, Hume was right in maintaining that causation cannot be given in immediate experience, and so in insisting on the need for an analysis of fundamental causal concepts. In attempting to offer an analysis, however, he was labouring under a crucial handicap, for, not having any

---

[6] Fair, 'Causation and the Flow of Energy', 240–1.

account of the meaning of theoretical terms, he had no alternative but to offer a reductionist analysis of causal concepts. But the situation is now very different. For the development, in this century, of satisfactory accounts of the semantics of theoretical terms means that it is possible to agree with Hume's fundamental contentions that causal relations are not given in immediate experience, and that causal concepts therefore stand in need of analysis, while embracing, at the same time, a realist, rather than a reductionist, view of causation.

To sum up, then, the following are some of the fundamental issues that need to be considered in any attempt to formulate a satisfactory account of the nature of causation:

(1) What relationship is there between causal laws and causal relations? In particular, are causal relations between events logically supervenient upon causal laws together with the totality of non-causal states of affairs? If not, do causal relations at least presuppose the existence of corresponding, covering laws, or, on the contrary, is a singularist account of causation correct?

(2) Are causal states of affairs logically supervenient upon non-causal ones?

(3) If not, is an *a posteriori* reduction of causal states of affairs to non-causal ones possible? Or is a realist approach to causation correct?

(4) Is it possible for causal relations to be immediately given, either in perceptual experience, or introspectively?

(5) Do causal concepts need to be analysed, or can they be taken as analytically basic? If they do stand in need of analysis, should the analysis be one that reduces causal states of affairs to non-causal ones, or should it treat causal terms as theoretical, and offer a realist account of the meaning of those terms?

2. THE ANALYSIS OF CAUSATION IN TERMS OF NECESSARY AND/OR SUFFICIENT CONDITIONS

Easily the most favoured line of enquiry into the nature of causation is one which extends back to Mill and on to Hume. A natural place to begin, then, is by discussing two familiar accounts of causation within this tradition. The first, and perhaps the most popular, view is this:

> I. *C* is a cause of *E* if and only if *C* and *E* are actual and *C* is *ceteris paribus* sufficient for *E*.

If we ignore the addition of temporal constraints upon the relation between cause and effect, this answer is essentially equivalent to the views of John

Stuart Mill,[7] R. B. Braithwaite,[8] H. L. A. Hart and A. M. Honoré,[9] C. G. Hempel,[10] and Karl Popper,[11] to mention only a few.

The second account is this:

> II. C is a cause of E if and only if C and E are actual and C is *ceteris paribus* necessary for E.

Ignoring temporal conditions, this answer is essentially that advanced by Ernest Nagel.[12] It is also considered seriously, but rejected, by Michael Scriven,[13] while a very similar view is defended by Raymond Martin.[14]

Another possibility within this general tradition is a combination of answers I and II: C is a cause of E if and only if C is *ceteris paribus* both sufficient and necessary for E—a view that is seriously entertained, but ultimately rejected, by Richard Taylor.[15] But this latter account need not be considered separately, since several of the objections set out below against I and II also apply to this combination of the two.

According to answer I, C is a cause of E if and only if (i) C and E are actual and (ii) there is an actual condition D such that C necessitates E on condition D—where C necessitates E on condition D if and only if there is a law L such that E is logically implied by $(C \& D \& L)$, but not by either $(C \& D)$, or $(D \& L)$, alone. A weakness of this account is now apparent, for it entails that if E has a cause, then every actual state of affairs that satisfies certain minimal independence requirements also causes E. The reason is this. Suppose that C causes E. Then there is some D such that C and D are actual, and C necessitates E on condition D—i.e. there is a law L such that $(C \& D \& L)$ logically implies, or entails, E, but neither $(C \& D)$, nor $(D \& L)$, does so. Assume now that X is actual and satisfies the following minimal independence conditions: (1) $X \& [D \& (X \supset C)]$ does not entail E; (2) $[D \& (X \supset C)] \& L$ does not entail E. Since X, C, and D are all actual, it follows, first, that $(X \supset C)$ is actual, and then, secondly, that $[D \& (X \supset C)]$ is actual. But then we have that X necessitates E on condition $[D \& (X \supset C)]$, since $X \& [D \& (X \supset C)] \& L$ logically implies E, whereas neither $X \& [D \& (X \supset C)]$ nor $[D \& (X \supset C)] \& L$ does so. Therefore, by the present account, X causes

[7]   *A System of Logic* (London, 1879), bk. iii, ch. 5.
[8]   *Scientific Explanation* (Cambridge, 1953), 315–18.
[9]   *Causation in the Law* (Oxford, 1959), 106–7.
[10] *Aspects of Scientific Explanation* (New York, 1965), 349.
[11] *Objective Knowledge: An Evolutionary Approach* (Oxford, 1972), 91.
[12] *The Structure of Science* (New York, 1961), 559–60.
[13] 'Causes, Connections, and Conditions in History', in William H. Dray (ed.), *Philosophical Analysis and History* (New York, 1966), 238–64, esp. sect. 8, pp. 258–62, which is reprinted below (Ch. II).
[14] 'The Sufficiency Thesis', *Philosophical Studies*, 23 (1972), 205–11.
[15] *Action and Purpose* (Englewood Cliffs, NJ, 1966), ch. 3.

E. But no restriction was placed on X save that it be actual and satisfy the minimal independence requirements. So the present account entails, for example, that if a fire causes some smoke, then Antarctica's being cold also causes that smoke.

According to answer II, C is a cause of E if and only if (i) C and E are actual and (ii) there is an actual condition D such that E necessitates C on condition D. This again has a demonstrable weakness. For it also entails that if some event has a cause, then every actual state of affairs that satisfies certain minimal independence requirements is also a cause of that event. For suppose that C causes E. Then there is some actual state of affairs D such that E necessitates C on condition D—i.e. there is a law L such that $(E \& D \& L)$ logically implies, or entails, C, but neither $(E \& D)$ nor $(D \& L)$ does so. Assume now that X is actual and satisfies the following minimal independence conditions: (1) $E \& [D \& (C \supset X)]$ does not entail X; (2) $[D \& (C \supset X)] \& L$ does not entail X. Since X, C, and D are all actual, it follows that both $(C \supset X)$ and $[D \& (C \supset X)]$ are actual. But then we have that E necessitates X on condition $[D \& (C \supset X)]$, since $E \& [D \& (C \supset X)] \& L$ logically implies X whereas neither $E \& [D \& (C \supset X)]$ nor $[D \& (C \supset X)] \& L$ does so. Therefore, according to the second account, X causes E. But no restriction was placed on X save that it be actual and satisfy minimal independence requirements. So the second account also entails, for example, that if a fire causes some smoke, then Antarctica's being cold also causes that smoke.

Perhaps, given sufficiently ingenious modifications, one can escape the above objections. One idea, for example, would be to impose a requirement excluding conditional states of affairs. But even if some such repair is possible, there are also other obstacles that must be overcome.

First, with respect to the sufficient condition account of causation, there is a problem posed by what one might call 'undeterminative sufficiency'.[16] Thus the position of a table top relative to the floor is caused by the length of the legs that support the top, and this seems to be exactly the sort of thing that suggests the first account. For the length of the legs is *ceteris paribus* sufficient for the position of the top relative to the floor. Unfortunately, the position of the top is also *ceteris paribus* sufficient for the length of the legs. Ironically, this makes the present example a refutation of answer I, for according to that answer the position of the top of the table relative to the floor must now be said to be a cause of the legs being the length they are.

With respect to the second account, there is a problem posed by over-determination. If two bullets pierce a man's heart simultaneously, it is

---

[16] On pp. 35–7 of *Action and Purpose*, Richard Taylor offers several interesting examples of such 'undeterminative sufficiency'.

reasonable to suppose that each is an essential part of a distinct sufficient condition of the death, and that neither bullet is *ceteris paribus* necessary for the death, since in each case the other bullet is sufficient. Hence, according to answer II, neither bullet is a cause of the death, neither is a 'causal factor' in the death, neither 'contributes causally' to that event.[17]

Returning to the earlier example, notice that the position of the table top relative to the floor is *ceteris paribus* both necessary and sufficient for the length of the legs. This shows that 'undeterminative sufficiency' is a problem not only for answer, I, but also for answer II, and even for that combination of the two according to which C causes E if and only if C is both necessary and sufficient for E.

It appears, in short, that neither of our opening accounts of causation is satisfactory.

3. CAUSATION AND INUS CONDITIONS

A more sophisticated attempt to analyse causation in terms of necessary and/or sufficient conditions is that proposed by John Mackie:

> III. If C is a cause of E (on a certain occasion) then C is an INUS condition of E, i.e. C is an insufficient but necessary part of a condition which is itself unnecessary but exclusively sufficient for E (on that occasion).[18]

Thus, when experts declare a short-circuit the cause of the fire, they '. . . are saying, in effect, that the short-circuit is a condition of this sort, that it occurred, that the other conditions which, conjoined with it, form a sufficient condition were also present, and that no other sufficient condition of the house's catching fire was present on this occasion'.[19]

Thesis III gives us Mackie's explanation of an INUS condition.[20] According to this thesis, however, an INUS condition differs very little from a condition that is *ceteris paribus* sufficient. For the only significant difference

---

[17] Cf. Michael Scriven's discussion in the selection from 'Causes, Connections, and Conditions in History' which is reprinted below (Ch. II).

[18] John L. Mackie, 'Causes and Conditions', *American Philosophical Quarterly*, 2 (1965), 245–64. See p. 245. (This is Ch. I below.)

[19] Ibid. 245. Essentially similar views are attributed by Mackie to Konrad Marc-Wogau ('On Historical Explanation', *Theoria*, 28 (1962), 213–33) and to Michael Scriven (Review of Ernest Nagel's *The Structure of Science*, *Review of Metaphysics*, 17 (1964), 403–24).

[20] On p. 247 of 'Causes and Conditions', Mackie offers a more explicit and slightly modified version of III—call it III*a*. But III*a* is not essentially different from III in any respect that matters here. For in so far as the present discussion locates difficulties with III, it does so *mutatis mutandis* with respect to III*a*.

is that if C is an INUS condition of E, then C is an essential part of a condition that is *uniquely* sufficient for E on that occasion, whereas C may be *ceteris paribus* sufficient for E in circumstances where there are several sufficient conditions, including some that do not contain E as a part. As a consequence, we are not yet in a better position to surmount the obstacles mentioned earlier.

The INUS condition approach to causation encounters a number of other difficulties as well. First, as Kim shows in his discussion of Mackie's approach in the article reprinted below (Chapter III), the ontology that is implicit in Mackie's account needs to be carefully thought through. For otherwise there is a risk of an obscurity within which dangers lurk.[21] Secondly, as is emphasized by Scriven, both accounts of causation in terms of necessary and/or sufficient conditions, and the more sophisticated account proposed by Mackie, suffer from the defect that they do not distinguish between causes and effects in a satisfactory way, unless temporal constraints are explicitly built in.[22] Finally, there is a crucial difficulty posed by probabilistic laws. For if, as seems very plausible, especially in view of quantum physics, there can be probabilistic causal laws, then an event can have a cause that is not a part of any condition which is sufficient, in the circumstances, for the event in question.

4. ALTERNATIVE APPROACHES

We have touched upon a number of attempts to explain causation in terms of necessary and/or sufficient conditions. The difficulties encountered by such attempts have led some to abandon the whole strategy of looking for an account of causation simply in terms of conditionality or lawfulness. Some philosophers (e.g. Ducasse) have tried to offer an account of causation without relying at all on conditionality or lawfulness. Others (e.g. von Wright) have tried supplementing conditionality with other notions—such as that of agency—in order to explain causation. Others (e.g. Reichenbach, Good, Suppes, and Salmon[23]) have argued in support of accounts of causation in which it is the concept of probability, rather than that of conditionality, which

---

[21] See also Kim's 'Causation, Nomic Subsumption and the Concept of Event', *Journal of Philosophy*, 70 (1973), 217–36.

[22] See the selection from Scriven's 'Causes, Connections, and Conditions in History' which is reprinted below (Ch. II).

[23] Hans Reichenbach, *The Direction of Time* (Berkeley, Calif., and Los Angeles, 1956); I. J. Good, 'A Causal Calculus I–II', *British Journal for the Philosophy of Science*, 11 (1961), 305–18, and 12 (1962), 43–51; Patrick Suppes, *A Probabilistic Theory of Causality* (Amsterdam, 1970); Wesley C. Salmon, *Scientific Explanation and the Causal Structure of the World* (Princeton, NJ, 1984).

plays a central role. Others (e.g. Lewis) have suggested that the analysis of causation needs to be framed in terms of counterfactuals. Still others (e.g. Tooley) have argued that the reason that the problem of finding a satisfactory analysis of causal concepts has proved so intractable is due to the mistaken idea that an analysis of causal concepts must be reductionist in form: causal concepts can be analysed, but only along realist lines. Others (e.g. Anscombe and Fales) have also supported a realist view, but hold, in addition, that causation is, in favourable circumstances, directly observable, and thus does not stand in need of analysis. Finally, some philosophers (e.g. Davidson) have set aside the problem of the analysis of causation, and have addressed themselves to the more modest task of characterizing the logical form of singular causal statements.

5. THE LOGICAL FORM OF SINGULAR CAUSAL STATEMENTS

Before surveying other attempts to offer an account of the nature of causation, let us consider Davidson's attempt, in the article which is re-printed below (Chapter IV), to give the logical form of singular causal statements while avoiding any commitment with respect to the analysis of causation. This programme raises questions concerning Davidson's conception of logical form. For suppose that we conceive of the logical form of a sentence S of a natural language as the form of the correlate of S in canonical notation (in an 'ideal language'). Then it is crucial, if the notion of logical form is to be sound, that all abbreviations or defined terms have been eliminated in favour of primitives. Thus, on the one hand, if we suppose that 'is-a-brother-of' and 'falls' are primitives of our canonical notation, then according to Russell the logical form of 'Jill's brother falls' is *not* Fa, but the form of 'The brother of Jill falls', which (assuming 'Jill' to be a logically proper name) has the form of 'There is an x such that x is a brother of Jill, and x falls, and for every y, if y is a brother of Jill then y is identical with x.' Or, more briefly, in terms of some symbols of the trade:

$(\exists x)$ [x is-a-brother-of Jill & (y) (y is-a-brother-of Jill $\supset y = x$) & x falls].

But if 'is-a-brother-of', rather than being taken as primitive, is to be defined by reference to 'is-male' and 'is-a-sibling-of', the logical form of 'The brother of Jill falls' is *not* that given above, but is presumably of the following form:

$(\exists x)$ [x is-male and x is-a-sibling-of Jill & (y) (y is-male and y is-a-sibling-of Jill $\supset y = x$) & x falls].

Here 'is-male', 'is-a-sibling-of', and 'falls' are counted as canonical primitives. Greater complications would result, of course, if one or more of these were in turn to be considered an abbreviation or a defined term.

The relevance of this to Davidson's approach is as follows. According to Davidson's view, the logical form of 'The short-circuit caused the fire' is that of 'The one and only event that was a short-circuit caused the one and only event that was a fire'; or, more briefly:

($\imath e$) Fe caused ($\imath e$) Ge.

(Perhaps this is to be analysed further *à la* Russell. But this would make no difference to the present point.) But then, on the conception of logical form just set out, if '($\imath e$) Fe caused ($\imath e$) Ge' gives the logical form of 'The short-circuit caused the fire', then 'caused' must be a *primitive* of canonical notation. But then how can 'caused' possibly have an analysis? There appears, in short, to be a problem with Davidson's idea that the inability to set out an analysis of the concept of causation does not prevent one from offering an account of the logical form of causal statements.

6. THE QUESTION OF THE ANALYSABILITY OF CAUSAL CONCEPTS

Let us turn, then, to the more fundamental problem of offering an account of the nature of causation. Most philosophers who have addressed this problem have assumed that what is needed is an analysis of causal concepts. But is it clear that this is so? For are there not at least two other alternatives that need to be canvassed? The one is that causal concepts cannot be *analysed*, but that, though this is so, an adequate explication of them can be given by describing the interrelations between causal concepts and non-causal concepts. The other, and more radical possibility is that the relation of causation is capable of being directly perceived, and directly perceived in such a way that an analysis of the concept of causation is neither necessary, nor even possible.

The first of these possibilities is advanced by Michael Scriven, who argues, in the selection reprinted below, for the conclusion that 'the concept of cause is fundamental to our conception of the world in much the same way as the concept of number: we cannot define it in terms of other notions without conceptual or ostensive circularity'.[24] But there is a problem with this suggestion. On the one hand, if the interrelations between the concept of causation and non-causal concepts do not suffice to identify uniquely the concept of causation, then the resulting explanation of the concept of causation cannot be satisfactory. On the other hand, suppose that they do uniquely

---

[24] 'Causes, Connections, and Conditions in History', repr. below (Ch. II), p. 56

identify the concept of causation, in the sense that it is the only concept that stands in the interrelations specified to the relevant non-causal concepts. The problem in that case is that any method that can be used to define the meaning of theoretical terms—such as that proposed by Frank Ramsey and developed by David Lewis[25]—can then be used to generate a definition of causation. The upshot is that the approach advocated by Scriven is not, in the end, an alternative to the project of providing an analysis of the concept of causation: it is better seen as proposing, instead, a more sophisticated style of analysis.

The second possibility—that causation itself is directly perceived in such a manner as to render analysis neither necessary, nor even possible—is defended by Elizabeth Anscombe in her essay 'Causality and Determination', which is reprinted below (Chapter V). Her defence of this approach to causation involves two main strands. The first involves an attempt to show that causal relations do not presuppose laws, thereby setting aside a crucial objection to the thesis that causation is directly observable. The second then consists of an attempt to establish, in a very direct fashion, that the relation of causation can be immediately perceived.

The first line of argument, and the one that she discusses most fully, involves her attack upon two propositions—namely, that causes necessitate their effects, and that all causal relations must be instances of universally quantified causal generalizations which admit of no exceptions. Here her main appeal is to the transformation in the scientific picture of the world brought about by quantum physics. For unless quantum physics is incoherent—which seems rather unlikely—it makes vivid the possibility of a world that contains causal processes, but where events of type C may, on some occasions, cause events of type E, and yet, on other occasions, fail to do so. So it would seem that causal relations need not fall under causal laws of a universal, non-statistical sort. A fortiori, causes need not necessitate their effects.

A number of other philosophers—Hans Reichenbach, I. J. Good, and Patrick Suppes—had argued earlier for these same conclusions.[26] The moral that they drew was that one needed to develop a probabilistic theory of causation according to which, although causal relations must fall under laws, the laws may be merely probabilistic. Anscombe does not refer to their work, and, partly as a consequence, it is not entirely clear whether she is attempting to defend a stronger conclusion. It appears, however—though her article is,

[25] See David Lewis, 'How to Define Theoretical Terms', *Journal of Philosophy*, 67 (1967), 427–46.

[26] See references in n. 23 above.

perhaps, open to different interpretations on this matter—that she does wish to advance a more radical conclusion, to the effect that causal relations need not fall under any laws at all, even probabilistic ones. One reason for thinking this is that there would seem to be a close relation between a singularist conception of causation and the thesis that causation can be directly perceived—a thesis which she certainly is defending. For if two events could be causally related only if that relation were an instance of some law, to observe that two events were causally related would be to observe that there was some relevant law, and it is not easy to see how a single observation could serve to establish such a conclusion. So it is hard to see how causation could be directly observable if a singularist conception of causation were not true.

The problem, however, is that a singularist conception of causation is certainly not an immediate consequence of the possibility raised by quantum physics. The world of quantum physics is a world of events governed by laws, albeit probabilistic ones; it is not a world containing anomic causal connections.

An argument can be developed, however, that moves from the admission of probabilistic causal laws to the conclusion that it must be possible for events to be causally related without that relation being an instance of any law.[27] But there is no hint of such an argument in Anscombe's discussion.

Anscombe's second main line of thought involves the attempt to show that the concept of causation does not stand in need of analysis because causal relations between events can be directly perceived. The thrust of this argument is that, given our everyday concept of observation, one can certainly observe causal processes: one can see, for example, the knife cutting through the butter. But if causal processes are observable, why should it be necessary to offer any analysis of the concept of causation? Why can it not be treated as basic?

This argument for the unanalysability of the concept of causation would not seem, however, to be satisfactory. For the fact that something is observable in the ordinary, non-technical sense of that term does not imply that it is an object of immediate, or non-inferential, perception, and so does not provide any reason for concluding that the relevant concept can be taken as analytically basic. The fact, for example, that sodium chloride is observable and that one can tell by simply looking and tasting that a substance is sodium

[27] Michael Tooley, 'Laws and Causal Relations', *Midwest Studies in Philosophy*, 9, ed. Peter A. French, Theodore E. Uehling, and Howard K. Wettstein (Minneapolis, 1984), 93–112, and id., 'The Nature of Causation: A Singularist Account', in David Copp. (ed.), *Canadian Philosophers: Celebrating Twenty Years of the CJP*, *Canadian Journal of Philosophy*, suppl. 16 (1990), 271–322.

chloride does not mean that the expression 'sodium chloride' does not stand in need of analysis. Similarly, the fact that one can tell by looking that something is round, or square, does not imply that those concepts are analytically basic.

7. CAUSATION AND AGENCY

The ideas of agency and causation are obviously intimately related, and this suggests the possibility of analysing one in terms of the other. Most philosophers would hold, however, that causation is the more basic notion, and thus that there is no prospect of throwing light on the latter concept by appealing to that of agency. But this view of the matter has been challenged by some writers—perhaps most notably, G. H. von Wright and Douglas Gasking[28]—who have contended that causation can be analysed in terms of agency.[29]

Von Wright's approach, as set out in the article reprinted below (Chapter VI),[30] makes use of the idea of a model of the world that satisfies the requirements of Logical Atomism. There is a set of n basic states, and a state of the world, at a time, is a conjunction with n terms such that each of the basic states or its negation appears as a term. Occasions are locations in time (and space), and, on any given occasion, 2^n different states are logically possible. Over m occasions, then, 2^{mn} different histories are logically possible.

Not everything that is logically possible is physically possible. What is physically possible will be defined by a system which specifies a series of occasions, a set of basic states, and a starting-point, and which contains all the *physically possible* historical ramifications of the world defined in terms of the n basic states, the m occasions, and the given initial state.

As an illustration, suppose that there are two basic states, p and q, and two occasions, #1 and #2, and that the initial state at occasion #1 is p & q. Then there are the following four logically possible histories:

---

[28] For Gasking's approach, see his 'Causation and Recipes', *Mind*, 64 (1955), 479–87. Criticism of Gasking's account can be found in Michael Tooley, *Causation: A Realist Approach* (Oxford, 1987), 239–42.

[29] Other writers, while not holding that causation in general can be analysed in terms of agency, have maintained that some types of causation involve agency as an essential element. See e.g. R. G. Collingwood's *An Essay on Metaphysics* (Oxford, 1940), 285 ff.

[30] A more detailed exposition of von Wright's approach can be found in his book, *Explanation and Understanding* (Ithaca, NY, 1971). Cf. also the review by Jaegwon Kim in the *Philosophical Review*, 82 (1973), 380–8.

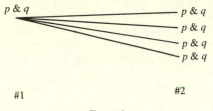

FIG. A

But of these four logically possible histories, it may be that only the first and the last are physically possible. The relevant system will then be this:

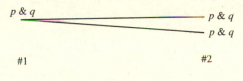

FIG. B

One further point concerning von Wright's model needs to be noted—namely, that von Wright assumes that, at any point in the course of history, there is a natural course of development that things will take following that point, unless some agent intervenes.[31] This natural course of development is represented by the horizontal lines connected with each node. The sloping lines represent what will happen if some agent intervenes.

Consider now a system with four occasions:

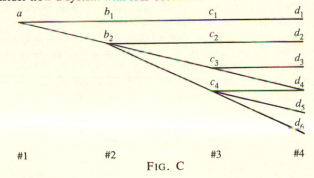

FIG. C

[31] See 'On the Logic and Epistemology of the Causal Relation', Ch. VI below, p. 109.

Here each node is a state of the system with basic states $p_1, \ldots p_n$, and given von Wright's assumption that nature obeys an ironclad determinism but for the interference of agents, the above represents a world where a will be followed by b_1 unless someone acts so as to bring about b_2, while if we are at node b_2, c_2 will follow unless someone acts so as to produce c_3, or c_4, and so on.

Von Wright now proceeds to define causation by reference to the interference of agents: p is a cause relative to q, and q an effect relative to p, if and only if by doing p we could bring about q or by suppressing p we would remove q or prevent it from happening.[32]

One familiar objection to this type of account is that it has the unacceptable consequence that an event has a cause only if there is some agent who either brought about the event or could have prevented it. But if we interpret 'by doing p we could bring about q' as meaning only that 'if we were to do p, we would thus bring about q', then it does not imply that we, or anyone else, actually has the power to do p, and so the reign of causation can extend far beyond the actual reach of agents.

There are, however, at least three serious objections to the above account. In the first place, the proper conceptual order would seem to be reversed. For the idea of bringing about one thing by doing something else would itself seem to presuppose the concept of causation, and this in at least two ways. First, even basic actions would seem to involve a causal relation between certain mental states—such as the relevant beliefs and desires—and other events, such as certain bodily movements, or certain thoughts, if the action is a mental one. Secondly, the notion of bringing about something *by* doing something else also needs to be cashed out, it would seem, in terms of the concept of causation.

In the second place, not all cases of bringing about q by doing p involve a causal relation between p and q. For in some cases one may bring about q by doing p in virtue of the fact that p entails q via relevant conventions.[33] So, as Jaegwon Kim has pointed out, von Wright's analysis is open to the objection that while one may bring it about that one obeys the traffic laws on a given occasion by stopping at a red light, it is not the case that one's obedience of the traffic laws on that occasion is caused by one's stopping at the red light.

Finally, von Wright's analysis of causation is in terms of counterfactual statements about what would have been the case if someone had performed

---

[32] *Explanation and Understanding*, 70.

[33] See Alvin Goldman's discussion of level generation in his book, *A Theory of Human Action* (Englewood Cliffs, NJ, 1970).

a certain action, and the question therefore arises as to what account is to be offered of the truth conditions of counterfactual statements. In particular, the question arises whether a satisfactory account can be given that does not make use of the notion of causation. This is a difficult issue that we cannot discuss here, except to say that some of the objections that are advanced later, in Section 12, against David Lewis's attempt to analyse causation in terms of counterfactual dependence are also objections to his attempt to provide truth conditions for counterfactuals without employing the concept of causation. If those objections are sound, an adequate account of the truth conditions of counterfactuals presupposes the notion of causation,[34] and this means that von Wright's account suffers from a further circularity.

8. A SINGULARIST APPROACH TO CAUSATION

Hume complains about his own first (regularity) definition of causation that it is 'drawn from circumstances foreign to the cause' and 'from something extraneous to it'.[35] Ducasse was impressed by this, and as a consequence offered an account of causation that does not look beyond the actual situation involving the cause and its effect:

Considering two changes, C and K (which may be either of the same or of different objects), the change C is said to have been sufficient to, i.e. to have caused, the change K if:

1. The change C occurred during a time and through a space terminating at the instant I at the surface S.
2. The change K occurred during a time and through a space beginning at the instant I at the surface S.
3. No change other than C occurred during the time and through the space of C, and no change other than K during the time and through the space of K.[36]

An issue that immediately arises concerning this account is why it is formulated only in terms of *changes*. For, as Ducasse himself recognized,[37] it would seem that not only changes, but also non-changes, can be causally

---

[34] For further discussion bearing upon this issue, see Jonathan Bennett, 'Counterfactuals and Temporal Direction', *Philosophical Review*, 93 (1984), 57–91, and Frank Jackson, 'A Causal Theory of Counterfactuals', *Australasian Journal of Philosophy*, 55 (1977), 3–21.

[35] David Hume, *An Enquiry Concerning Human Understanding* (London, 1748), sect. 7.2.

[36] C. J. Ducasse, 'On the Nature and the Observability of the Causal Relation', Ch. VII below, p. 127.

[37] Ibid. 126 and 128.

relevant. If so, this means, within the context of Ducasse's approach, that it is the total complex of changes and non-changes that is the cause.

But are non-changes really causally relevant? For might it not be objected that non-changes can never be sufficient, since, even when the relevant non-changes are present, the effect never takes place until there is a change which triggers the effect? But this claim cannot be sustained. In the first place, it is not in general true that an effect *must* be triggered by a change. There is, for example, a causal explanation of why a pencil lying on a desk remains at rest, but the situation need not involve any relevant change. And in the second place, what Ducasse urges concerning changes is equally applicable to non-changes: 'Step on a man's foot and apologize. Then repeat in precisely the same manner. Then repeat accurately a third time, and so on.'[38] How many times a change has occurred within a certain interval may be causally relevant, and the same applies to how long a non-change has been present.

Ducasse's definition yields, then, the following picture. Take any continuous spatio-temporal volume and slice through it on a plane perpendicular to the time axis. The total complex of events, states, and processes in the earlier part of the volume causes the corresponding totality in the later part. Furthermore, every concrete cause and its effect form the contents of the earlier and later parts, respectively, of such a sliced volume, and that they do so is all that is meant, strictly speaking, when one says that the first *causes* the second.

As Ducasse explicitly recognizes,[39] the definition just given is not true to '. . . the way in which the word "cause" actually is used'. But his avowed principal aim is to give us an account of a concept of causation commonly accepted, and one involved in such ubiquitous ideas as those of breaking, bending, killing, heating, twisting, melting, etc. Accordingly, Ducasse goes on to offer an analysis of ordinary causation in terms of his account of strict causation.

With some minor (but, it would seem, necessary) modifications, Ducasse's analysis of ordinary causation would appear to be this:

> This case of C caused$_o$ (caused in the ordinary sense) this case of E if and only if this case of C caused$_s$ (caused in the strict sense defined above) this case of E, and every case of C causes$_s$ a case of E.[40]

The problem now, however, is that this account seems to differ only terminologically from a Humean account of causation:

---

[38] C. J. Ducasse, *Causation and the Types of Necessity* (Seattle, 1924), 70.

[39] 'On the Nature and the Observability of the Causal Relation', Ch. VII below, p. 133..

[40] For the passage on which this reconstruction is based, see ibid. 133–5.

This case of C caused this case of E if and only if this case of C was spatio-temporally immediately followed by this case of E, and every case of C is thus followed by a case of E.

If this is right, then Ducasse's account is subject to all of the difficulties that attach to such a Humean account.

9. PROBABILISTIC APPROACHES TO CAUSATION

One of the more significant developments in the philosophy of causation in this century has been the emergence of the idea that causation is not restricted to deterministic processes—a conclusion that, as we noted above, appears to be strongly supported by quantum physics. What implications might this conclusion have with respect to the analysis of causal concepts? One suggestion, advanced by philosophers such as Reichenbach, Good, and Suppes, is that probabilistic notions should play a central role in the analysis of causal concepts.

This basic idea of analysing causation in probabilistic terms can be carried out in a variety of ways.[41] At the heart of any such programme, however, is the idea that causes must, in some way, make their effects more likely. The traditional way of attempting to capture this idea, within probabilistic approaches to causation, has been in terms of the notion of *positive statistical relevance*, where an event of type B is positively relevant to an event of type A if and only if the conditional probability of an event of type A relative to an event of type B is greater than the unconditional probability of an event of type A. Thus Suppes, for example, introduces the notion of a prima-facie cause, defined as follows: 'An event B is a prima facie cause of an event A if and only if (i) B occurs earlier than A, and (ii) the conditional probability of A occurring when B occurs is greater than the unconditional probability of A occurring.'[42]

More recently, however, a number of philosophers have argued that the correct way to capture the idea that a cause makes its effect more likely is not in terms of a difference between the conditional and unconditional probabilities of a given type of event, but, rather, in terms of appropriate subjunc-

---

[41] In addition to the references mentioned above in n. 23, see David Lewis, 'Postscript B to "Causation" ', in his *Philosophical Papers*, ii (Oxford, 1986), 175–85, and D. Hugh Mellor, 'Fixed Past, Unfixed Future', in Barry Taylor (ed.), *Contributions to Philosophy: Michael Dummett* (The Hague, 1986), 166–86.

[42] Patrick Suppes, 'Conflicting Intuitions about Causality', *Midwest Studies in Philosophy*, 9, ed. Peter A. French, Theodore E. Uehling, and Howard K. Wettstein (Minneapolis, 1984), 151–68; see p. 151.

tive conditionals concerning the objective chances of the individual event in question.[43] Briefly put, the basic idea is that a sufficient condition of C's being a cause of E is that C and E be actual, individual events such that the objective chance of E's occurring would be greater if C were to occur than if C were not to occur.

Wesley Salmon's article, *Probabilistic Causality*, contains a very careful exposition, and detailed criticisms, of the probabilistic analyses of causation proposed by Suppes, Good and Reichenbach[44]—in all of which the notion of conditional probability plays a pivotal role. But Salmon's central criticisms are not limited in scope to such approaches: they also apply, in general, to the more recent attempts to analyse causation in terms of counterfactuals concerning the objective chances of individual events.

While Salmon argues that purely probabilistic approaches to causation are exposed to serious objections, he is, at the same time, very sympathetic to the idea that the concept of probability enters into the analysis of the concept of causation in a fundamental way. As a consequence, he suggests that the appropriate response to the difficulties in question is not to abandon the attempt to relate causation to probability, but to supplement probabilistic concepts with other ones—and, in particular, with the concept of a causal process.

One of the crucial questions confronting any attempt to relate causation to probability, as Salmon emphasizes, is whether it is true that causes always make their effects more likely, in some appropriate sense. Salmon believes that, properly understood, this dictum is defensible. This conclusion appears difficult to sustain, however, in the face of the following sort of objection to the thesis that causes render their effects more likely. Suppose that there are two types of disease, satisfying the following conditions. First, each disease is potentially fatal within a certain time span, but the first leads to death with probability 0.1, and the second with probability 0.8. Secondly, each disease confers lifelong immunity against the other. Thirdly, at least half of the individuals in question contract the second disease. Finally, there is no other condition that will cause death within the relevant time period. It then follows that both the unconditional probability that one will die within the relevant period, and the probability of death given that one does not have the first disease, must be equal to or greater than 0.4, whereas the probability that one will die if one does contract the first disease is only 0.1. So both the unconditional probability of death, and the probability of death given the absence

---

[43] See e.g. Lewis, 'Postscript B', Mellor, 'Fixed Past', and Peter Menzies, 'Probabilistic Causation and Causal Processes: A Critique of Lewis', *Philosophy of Science*, 56 (1989), 642–63.

[44] In the edited version reprinted below (Ch. VIII), we have had to omit Salmon's discussion of Good's approach.

of the first disease, are greater than the probability of death given the presence of the disease, even though, by hypothesis, the disease does cause death with a certain probability.[45]

This shows that the thesis that causes make their effects more likely cannot be sustained if the thesis is interpreted, in the traditional way, in terms of the difference between conditional and unconditional probabilities of events of the relevant type. But what if the idea that causes make their effects more likely is explicated, instead, in terms of counterfactuals and the relevant objective chances? The answer is that the objection then needs to be reformulated slightly, with references to probabilities replaced by references to corresponding, probabilistic laws. Suppose, then, that there are two types of disease, A and B, satisfying the following conditions. First, it is a law that contracting disease A causes death with probability 0.1, and a law that contracting disease B causes death with probability 0.8. Secondly, it is a law that contracting disease A produces complete immunity to disease B, and a law that contracting disease B produces complete immunity to disease A. Thirdly, it is a causal law that in condition C an individual must contract either disease A or disease B. (Condition C might be a weakening of the immune system.) Fourthly, individual X is in condition C, contracts disease A, and the latter causes his death. Given that these conditions obtain, the question is what would have been the case if X, though being in condition C, had not contracted disease A, and the answer, it would seem, is given by the following counterfactual: if individual X had not contracted disease A, he would have contracted disease B. But if individual X would have contracted disease B if he had not contracted disease A, then his probability of dying had he not contracted disease A would have been 0.8, and so would have been higher than his probability of dying given that he had contracted disease A, since the latter is only 0.1. So, once again, it is not true that causes need make their effects more likely.

The view that causes necessarily make their effects more likely appears to be exposed, in short, to a crucial objection based upon the possibility of there being one or more other causal factors that are incompatible with the given factor, and more efficacious than it. For, given such a possibility, C may be the cause of E even though the probability of E's occurring would have been greater had C not occurred, and even though the conditional probability of an event of type E, given an event of type C, is less than the unconditional probability of an event of type E.

But is there nothing, then, in the rather widely shared intuition that causation is related to increase in probability? The answer is that causation may

---

[45] Cf. Tooley, *Causation*, 234–5.

be related to increase in probability, but not in the way proposed by those who favour a probabilistic analysis of causation. For it would seem to be true, for example, that the logical probability of an event of type E, given only that events of type C *causally necessitate* events of type E, will be higher than the *a priori* logical probability of an event of type E.[46] But this relation cannot be used as part of a probabilistic *analysis* of causation, since the relation itself involves that very concept.

10. CAUSAL PROCESSES AND CAUSAL INTERACTIONS

Salmon's own account of causation is set out in his *Scientific Explanation and the Causal Structure of the World*,[47] and, more concisely, in 'Causality: Production and Propagation', which is reprinted below (Chapter IX). The central elements are as follows. First, Salmon draws a distinction between causal interactions, which involve change, and causal processes, which involve the spatio-temporally continuous transmission of a causal influence from one region to another. Secondly, he argues that causal processes can be distinguished from pseudo-processes in terms of the ability of the former to transmit a mark. Thirdly, Salmon distinguishes three sorts of causal forks—interactive forks, conjunctive forks, and perfect forks—each of which is explained in terms of causal processes plus certain statistical relations. Fourthly, he suggests that the concept of a causal interaction is to be analysed in terms of interactive forks. Finally, Salmon argues that neither causal processes nor causal interactions exhibit any intrinsic directionality. An explanation of the direction of causation must be given, instead, in terms of conjunctive forks.

Salmon's approach enables him to avoid a number of difficulties confronting purely probabilistic analyses of causal concepts. Nevertheless, serious objections remain, most of them connected with his account of what it is that constitutes the direction of causation. First, consider the possibility of a causal process leading from event A to event B, and which does not involve, at any point, a conjunctive fork. What makes it so, in such a case, that A causes B, rather than vice versa? On Salmon's approach, the direction of causation will have to depend upon states of affairs that are external to the causal process linking A to B. But this conflicts with a strong intuition to the effect that the direction of causation is something *intrinsic* to a causal process.

---

[46] Or, at least, this will be so provided that it is not the case either that the logical probability of an event of type E is equal to 1, or that the logical probability of an event of type C is equal to 0. For a proof, see Tooley, *Causation*, 277–8 and 325–8.

[47] Princeton, 1984.

Secondly, if the direction of causation is logically determined by the direction of conjunctive forks, it is essential that all conjunctive forks exhibit the same direction. But what reason is there for believing that this is so? It is not, as Salmon himself points out, a fact that is guaranteed by the laws of nature. Moreover, given that the world does not appear to be a deterministic one, it would seem that it cannot be guaranteed by the combination of laws of nature plus boundary conditions. Accordingly, it would seem, first, that, for any spatio-temporal region, however limited, there must be some non-zero probability of its containing a conjunctive fork whose direction is opposite to that of most conjunctive forks, and secondly, that it is therefore extremely improbable that *no* such oppositely directed conjunctive forks are to be found anywhere in space-time.

A third objection is that, regardless of what is the case in our world, it is surely possible for there to be worlds, either with the same laws of nature as ours, but different boundary conditions, or with different laws of nature, in which not all conjunctive forks exhibit the same direction. Salmon's account implies that, in such worlds, causal processes would have no direction.

Fourthly, it would also seem possible for there to be worlds where there are no conjunctive forks at all. This might be so, for example, because the world was an extremely simple one. Alternatively, the world might be very complex, but deterministic. For in a deterministic world, the probability of any effect, given its complete cause, must be equal to 1, and this fact precludes the existence of conjunctive forks.[48] Such worlds are further counter-examples to Salmon's account.

11. OBJECTIONS TO REDUCTIONIST APPROACHES TO CAUSATION

Why has the problem of finding a satisfactory analysis of causal concepts proved so intractable? Is it merely that no one has yet succeeded in getting all of the details right, or is there some deeper problem? In 'Causation: Reductionism versus Realism', reprinted below (Chapter X), Michael Tooley argues that the latter is the case. He contends that the source of the difficulty is that philosophers have tried to construct reductionist accounts of causation, and that reductionist approaches, both to causal laws and to causal relations, are necessarily exposed to very serious objections.

In the case of laws, Tooley mentions a number of familiar problems. First, there is the following epistemological argument. Suppose that laws were

---

[48] It is crucial to the definition of conjunctive forks that certain probabilities not be equal to 1. See Salmon's discussion in 'Causality: Production and Propagation', Ch. IX below, pp. 158–9 and 166–8.

simply cosmic regularities that did not obtain in virtue of some deeper
fact—such as a second-order atomic state of affairs consisting of an irreducible relation among universals. If laws were simply regularities that lacked
any such backing, would it not be likely that, at some time and place, a
counter-instance would arise? Secondly, there is the difficulty of drawing a
distinction between those regularities that are laws, and those that, though
universal, are merely accidental. Thirdly, it would seem to be possible even
for basic laws of nature to fail to be instantiated at any time, due to an
accident with regard to the 'boundary conditions' of the universe. But this
possibility would appear to be precluded by a reductionist approach. Finally,
there is the problem posed by probabilistic laws, and connected with the fact
that worlds with slightly different probabilistic laws might nevertheless not
differ at any point throughout their histories.

With regard to causal relations, Tooley advances three main lines of argument. The first claims that there are very simple possible worlds that, though
causal, exhibit no temporal asymmetry, and so contain no states of affairs
that can, on a reductionist approach, serve to fix the direction of causation.
The second claims that, in the case of at least some worlds, there can be an
inverted counterpart that differs only with respect to the direction of time and
the direction of causation. A reductionist account of causation will necessarily assign the wrong direction to causation for one member of each pair of
temporally inverted, twin worlds. Finally, Tooley's third argument involves
an attempt to show that, once probabilistic causal laws are admitted, situations can arise where the causal connections between events are not
logically fixed by the totality of non-causal facts, together with causal laws,
even when the direction of causation in all potential causal processes is taken
as given.

That there are serious obstacles that must be overcome if a reductionist
approach to laws is to be sustained is, as was noted in Section 1, a point that
has been developed at length by a number of recent writers—though it is
surely an open question whether those difficulties are insurmountable. But
what about the arguments directed against reductionist accounts of causal
relations? Do they also pose serious problems, or are there satisfactory
answers available to the reductionist?

Consider, for example, the argument which appeals to the possibility of
certain very simple worlds that exhibit no asymmetry with respect to events
in time. Could it be contended that such worlds would not really contain
causal processes? Or, in the case of the 'inverted universes' argument, is it
really clear that there could be a world that was just like ours, except for the
direction of time, and the direction of causation? Or, finally, and as Tooley
himself points out, the third line of argument can apparently be extended into

an argument in support of a singularist conception of causation. But if this is so, then the question of whether one can make sense of a singularist account becomes crucial for an evaluation of that third line of argument.[49]

12. CAUSATION AND COUNTERFACTUAL DEPENDENCE

How are causal statements related to counterfactuals? The traditional view on this matter is that an account of the truth conditions of counterfactuals must involve reference to causal laws. Consider, for example, a situation involving a match that is dry and in the presence of oxygen, but not struck, at time t, and that is not lit thereafter. Of the following two counterfactuals:

(1) If the match had been struck at time t, it would have lit;
(2) If the match had been struck at time t, it would not have been dry at time t

it is surely plausible to accept the first and reject the second, and the rationale traditionally offered involves reference to the fact that, on the one hand, there is a causal law that entails that the striking of a dry match made of material M with velocity V and pressure P against a surface of type S, in the presence of oxygen, at time t, *causes* the match to ignite at a time slightly later than t, while, on the other, there is no causal law that entails that the striking of a match made of material M with velocity V and pressure P against a surface of type S, in the presence of oxygen, at time t, together with the match's not being lit at a time slightly later than t, *causes* the match not to be dry at time t.

On this view of the relation between causation and counterfactuals, the concept of causation is more basic than that of counterfactual dependence, and so there is no possibility of analysing the former in terms of the latter. But there are alternative views concerning the truth conditions of counterfactuals. In particular, there is the view developed by Robert Stalnaker[50] and David Lewis,[51] according to which the truth conditions of counterfactuals are to be given in terms of relations of similarity between relevant possible worlds. According to one version of that alternative approach, a counterfactual of the form, 'If p were the case, then q would be the case' is true if and only if there is a possible world in which both p and q are true which is more similar to the actual world than any possible world in which p is true but q is false.

[49] In 'The Nature of Causation', Tooley attempts to show that one can make sense of a singularist conception of causation.
[50] Robert C. Stalnaker, 'A Theory of Conditionals', in N. Rescher (ed.), *Studies in Logical Theory* (Oxford, 1968), 98–112.
[51] David Lewis, *Counterfactuals* (Cambridge, Mass., 1973).

Given this alternative approach, is it possible to analyse causal concepts in terms of counterfactuals? The answer depends upon what sorts of states of affairs are basic. If a realist view of causation is correct, so that causal states of affairs are not logically supervenient upon non-causal ones, then the degree of similarity of one world to another will depend, among other things, upon the causal structure of the two worlds, and so, once again, any attempt to analyse causal concepts in counterfactual terms will necessarily be circular. But if, on the other hand, causal facts are not basic, then judgements concerning the similarity of one world to another will not presuppose information about the causal structures of the two worlds, and so the door will in principle be open to a counterfactual analysis of causal statements.

In 'Causation', reprinted below (Chapter XI), and in subsequent papers,[52] David Lewis has set out and defended such an approach to causation. His basic idea is to analyse causation in terms of a narrower notion of causal dependence, and then to analyse causal dependence in terms of counterfactual dependence. Thus, if we restrict attention to the case where C and E are actual events, to say that E is causally dependent upon C is, on Lewis's account, just to say that if C had not occurred, then E would not have occurred. Causation can then be defined as the inverse of the relation which is the ancestral of causal dependence, so that to say that C causes E is to say that there is an appropriate chain of causally dependent events linking E with C.

A crucial task in the philosophy of causation is to provide an account of the direction of causation. How does the above approach fare with regard to this problem? Given Lewis's account, the direction of causation is the opposite of counterfactual dependence. But what is it that fixes the latter? On the traditional view of the truth conditions of counterfactuals, it is the direction of causation that does so. Precluded from offering this answer, Lewis appeals instead to the idea that, in our world, events typically have many effects, but rarely have many causes: witness the frequency of outgoing spherical wavefronts, produced, for example, by sources of light, in contrast to that of incoming wavefronts. The idea then is that, given this fact, one can argue that, if p is any proposition that is false in our world, the closest worlds in which p is true will almost always be worlds that differ from ours with respect to the future, rather than with respect to the past. For if events typically have many more effects than causes, a world in which p is true will involve more violations of laws of nature if it is its future, rather than its past, which agrees with that of the actual world.

---

[52] 'Counterfactual Dependence and Time's Arrow', *Noûs*, 13 (1979), 455–76, and 'Postscripts to "Causation"', in his *Philosophical Papers*, ii (Oxford, 1986), 172–212.

There are at least two problems with this account of the direction of counterfactual dependence, and so of causation. The first is that this approach makes it impossible to accept the very appealing idea that the direction of causation is an intrinsic property of individual causal processes. For, on Lewis's approach, the direction of the causal process linking two events, C and E, is not fixed by features of that single causal process itself. It is determined, rather, by other causal processes into which C and E enter.

The second objection turns upon the fact that it is not a necessary truth that any world containing causally related events is one where events typically have more effects than causes. The world could well have been an inverted one, where the opposite was true. Or it could have been a very simple one, where there were no causal forks at all. Lewis's analysis cannot be sound, therefore, since there are logically possible causal worlds for which it yields the wrong results with respect to the direction of causation.

Underlying the second of these objections is the fact that Lewis's account is a reductionist one, and, as such, it is necessarily exposed to all of the objections that tell against non-realist approaches to causation, including the arguments which appeal to the logical possibilities of inverted worlds, and of very simple worlds. But there are also several other objections that have been directed against Lewis's account, and that are completely independent of the reductionism versus realism issue. One such objection, for example, is that developed by Jaegwon Kim in his article, 'Causes and Counterfactuals' (Chapter XII below). Kim argues that counterfactual dependence is not a sufficient condition for causal dependence, since causation is only one among a heterogeneous group of dependency relations that give rise to counterfactuals.

The selection, reprinted below (Chapter XIII), from Paul Horwich's recent book[53] contains a number of other objections to Lewis's approach. One, which is especially important, and which Kim also mentions briefly, involves cases of causal over-determination. This objection can be developed in two slightly different ways. Horwich, in his discussion, formulates the objection in terms of macroscopic events in the actual world. Thus put, however, the objection may be problematic, since, first, the thesis that, in the actual world, causal relations between macroscopic events are logically supervenient upon causal relations between submicroscopic events, plus the laws of nature, seems very appealing, and secondly, a consideration of physics, as it has developed so far, strongly suggests that causal over-determination at the most fundamental level may be precluded by the basic laws of nature.

---

[53] Paul Horwich, *Asymmetries in Time* (Cambridge, Mass., 1987). For Lewis's responses to a number of these objections, see his 'Counterfactual Dependence' and 'Postscripts to "Causation" '.

Since, however, Lewis is offering an analysis of the concept of causation, and not merely an account of what causation is in the actual world, one can appeal instead to what is logically possible. The thrust of the argument will then be that, regardless of what may be so in the actual world, it is surely logically possible for there to be cases where there are two causally independent events, C and D, each of which is not only a causally sufficient condition for the occurrence of event E, but an *immediate* cause of E. In such a case, however, it would not be true either that if C had not occurred, then E would not have occurred, or that if D had not occurred, then E would not have occurred, so E would not be counterfactually dependent upon either C or D, and from this it follows that neither C nor D could, given Lewis's analysis, be an immediate cause of E.

Lewis's counterfactual approach to causation is also the focus of Jonathan Bennett's article, 'Event Causation: The Counterfactual Analysis' (reprinted below, Chapter XIV). In his essay, Bennett focuses upon causation viewed as a relation between events, rather than as a relation between facts, and he attempts to show that any counterfactual analysis of event causation must be unacceptable.

The argument which Bennett develops turns upon the claim that our ordinary concept of causation involves an asymmetry with respect to those events that hasten a given type of event, and those that delay it: if an event hastens the occurrence of an event of a certain type, then it is a cause of that event, whereas if it delays the occurrence of an event of a certain type, then it is not a cause of that event. Given this asymmetry thesis, Bennett argues that a counterfactual analysis of event causation leads to unacceptable consequences concerning the identity of events.

Bennett's argument is subtle and original, and carefully set out. But can it be sustained? One ground for doubting that it can is that Bennett's argument, if sound, would tell against *all* current accounts of event causation, since none of the accounts on offer are sensitive to the distinction between hasteners and delayers. As a consequence, it would seem that an advocate of a counterfactual analysis of causation can reply to Bennett's argument by simply adding an additional requirement which will ensure that while hasteners get classified as causes, delayers do not. For while the employment of what may seem to be an *ad hoc* modification would, other things being equal, count against a counterfactual approach, it will not do so if alternative approaches to causation must incorporate parallel clauses in order to deal with the distinction between hasteners and delayers.

But if current accounts of causation classify both hasteners and delayers as causes of an event, why not conclude that all current accounts must therefore be defective? The answer is that there is reason for thinking that any satisfactory account of causation must start out with a technical notion of an event, along the lines proposed by Jaegwon Kim, and according to which a monadic event, for example, is the exemplifying of a property by a particular at a time, or the instantiation of a property at a space-time point or region.[54] Utilizing that notion, one can offer an analysis that will deal, in a satisfactory way, with sentences such as 'The April rains were part of the cause of the occurrence of a forest fire *at a specific time*.' That analysis in itself will not, of course, provide one with satisfactory truth conditions for ordinary language sentences such as 'The April rains caused the forest fire', since sentences of the latter sort are sensitive to the distinction between hasteners and delayers, while those of the former sort are not. But then one should be able, it would seem, simply to build upon the analysis of the regimented causal sentences, with their technical notion of an event, and, by incorporating a clause that, directly or indirectly, brings in the relevant asymmetry, arrive at a satisfactory account of the truth conditions of ordinary language sentences concerning event causation.

In short, there appears to be a plausible, and perfectly general strategy for dealing with the problem that Bennett raises, and, given that that is so, it is not at all clear why an advocate of a counterfactual analysis of event causation should be unable to avail himself of that strategy.

13. THE METAPHYSICS OF CAUSATION

If *B* is caused by *A*, it is natural to say that *B* occurred *because of A*, or that it was *a consequence of A*, or that it happened *as a result of A*. But it is usually held that not all cases where one state of affairs obtains because of some other state of affairs, or as a consequence of, or as a result of, another state of affairs, are cases of causation. Consider, for example, the fact that the existence of a table in a certain room at a specific time is a consequence of there being a certain arrangement of molecules in the relevant location at that very time, or the fact that certain apples are good because they are crisp and juicy. Such facts, most philosophers would say, do not involve causal relations between the states of affairs in question.

This view has recently been challenged, however, by Ernest Sosa, who argues in 'Varieties of Causation', which is reprinted below (Chapter XV), that the relations in question are causal relations. For, Sosa suggests, 'the root causal relation is being a "source", whose converse is being a result or consequence',[55] and if this is right, then facts such as those just cited do

---

[54] Jaegwon Kim, 'Causes and Events: Mackie on Causation', Ch. III below, pp. 71–2.
[55] Ernest Sosa, 'Varieties of Causation', Ch. XV below, pp. 240–1.

involve causal relations. Those causal relations will not be, of course, precisely the same as the relation that obtains between a match's being struck and its igniting—a relation that Sosa refers to as nomological causation—but they do, Sosa argues, belong to the same family.

The basic conclusion to which Sosa is led, in short, is that there is a variety of causal, or source–consequence, relations. Nomological causation is the most familiar, but there are also others—including what Sosa refers to as material causation, consequentialist causation, and inclusive causation.

One immediate objection to this thesis is that while nomological causation seems to involve a contingent relation between states of affairs, the other source–consequence relations that Sosa discusses appear to be necessary relations. In response, however, Sosa points out that if one thinks of nomological causes as consisting not merely of the earlier states of affairs, but also of the relevant laws of nature, then the relation in the case of nomological causation will also be one of logical necessitation.[56]

If this view can be sustained, then it may be possible to hold that what is common to all forms of causation is necessitation. But there are serious obstacles that must be surmounted if the idea that necessitation lies at the heart of ordinary causation is to be acceptable. First, the idea of direction seems essential to causation, and it seems unlikely that this idea can be explicated in terms of logical necessitation. For in a Newtonian world, for example, the occurrence of later states of affairs, together with the relevant laws of nature, logically necessitate, but do not cause, earlier states of affairs. One is therefore left with the problem of what it is that explains the direction of causation, and with the question of whether this additional element is also present in the other source–consequence relations. Secondly, the idea that logical necessitation is essential to causation presupposes that a singularist conception of causation is incoherent, and, while this view has been, and still is, very widely accepted, some serious arguments in support of the intelligibility of a singularist approach have recently emerged. Finally, there is the difficulty posed by the idea of probabilistic causal laws. If, as many philosophers are inclined to believe, such laws are possible, then logical necessitation cannot be an essential feature of causal relations.

14. ARISTOTLE AND HUME ON CAUSATION

Systematic discussion of the topic of causation began with Aristotle, and with his idea that one can distinguish between four kinds of cause—often referred

---

[56] An alternative response would be to argue that laws of nature are logically necessary. For expositions of this view, see Shoemaker, 'Causality and Properties', and Swoyer, 'The Nature of Natural Laws'.

to as the material cause, the formal cause, the efficient cause, and the final cause.[57] But although Aristotle's approach was the dominant one in philosophy for almost 2,000 years, and although it contains useful distinctions and insights, it is rarely referred to in present-day discussions. There are various reasons for this. One is that Aristotle's conception of causation, and, in particular, his idea of final causes, has a strongly teleological orientation. Another is that Aristotle did not think of causation, as present-day philosophers do, as a relation between events or states of affairs. Perhaps the most important reason, however, is that Aristotle was apparently unaware that there are very serious difficulties concerning the concept of causation.

The realization that the concept of causation is deeply problematic, and very difficult to analyse, begins with David Hume, and it is for this reason that his work represents a decisive turning-point. But Hume did much more than point to a serious problem. He also advanced arguments of great depth and originality—so much so that many present-day philosophers still hold that, as regards the central metaphysical issues that arise concerning causation, Hume was essentially right.

The fact that we have not included any selections from Hume's writings is not due, therefore, to any feeling that Hume's contribution was mainly one of raising an important problem. On the contrary, Hume's arguments are still among the most crucial in the area, and the reductionist approach that he advanced—or, at least, that he has generally been thought to have advanced—remains one of the most important views on the nature of causation. But, precisely because of this, the inclusion of a selection from Hume's writings on causation would not be satisfactory. One needs to approach the topic of causation with a *thorough* understanding of Hume's arguments, and this would involve, at a minimum, the reading of sections 1–6, 11, 12, 14, and 15 of book I, part 3, of Hume's *Treatise of Human Nature*, plus sections 4 and 7 of his *Enquiry Concerning Human Understanding*.

More than 250 years have passed since the publication of Hume's *Treatise*. But although Hume's arguments remain crucial, and although the fundamental issues are as yet unresolved, there has been progress, and subsequent discussions have contributed to our understanding in a variety of ways. First, a number of reductionist accounts which are important alternatives to Hume's own have gradually emerged. Secondly, recent developments in semantics have shown that it is possible to make sense of the idea of a realist approach to causation. Thirdly, reasons have even been advanced for thinking that a singularist approach to causation may not be incoherent. Finally, the

---

[57] Aristotle, *Physics*, II. 3. Discussion of Aristotle's views on causation can be found in W. D. Ross, *Aristotle* (New York, 1959), 74–8, and in A. E. Taylor, *Aristotle* (New York, 1955), 50–5.

difficulties to which various accounts of the nature of causation are exposed have now become much clearer. There are, then, grounds for optimism concerning the problem that Hume posed, in spite of the fact that even the general form that the solution is likely to take remains very much an open question.

I

CAUSES AND CONDITIONS

JOHN L. MACKIE

Asked what a cause is, we may be tempted to say that it is an event which precedes the event of which it is the cause, and is both necessary and sufficient for the latter's occurrence; briefly that a cause is a necessary and sufficient preceding condition. There are, however, many difficulties in this account. I shall try to show that what we often speak of as a cause is a condition not of this sort, but of a sort related to this. That is to say, this account needs modification, and can be modified, and when it is modified we can explain much more satisfactorily how we can arrive at much of what we ordinarily take to be causal knowledge; the claims implicit within our causal assertions can be related to the forms of the evidence on which we are often relying when we assert a causal connection.

1. SINGULAR CAUSAL STATEMENTS

Suppose that a fire has broken out in a certain house, but has been extinguished before the house has been completely destroyed. Experts investigate the cause of the fire, and they conclude that it was caused by an electrical short-circuit at a certain place. What is the exact force of their statement that this short-circuit caused this fire? Clearly the experts are not saying that the short-circuit was a necessary condition for this house's catching fire at this time; they know perfectly well that a short-circuit somewhere else, or the overturning of a lighted oil stove, or any one of a number of other things might, if it had occurred, have set the house on fire. Equally, they are not saying that the short-circuit was a sufficient condition for this house's catching fire; for if the short-circuit had occurred, but there had been no inflammable material near by, the fire would not have broken out, and even given both the short-circuit and the inflammable material, the fire would not have occurred if, say, there had been an efficient automatic sprinkler at just the right spot. Far from being a condition both necessary and sufficient for the fire, the short-circuit was, and is known to the experts to have been, neither necessary nor sufficient for it. In what sense, then, is it said to have caused the fire?

At least part of the answer is that there is a set of conditions (of which some are positive and some are negative), including the presence of inflammable material, the absence of a suitably placed sprinkler, and no doubt quite a number of others, which combined with the short-circuit constituted a complex condition that was sufficient for the house's catching fire—sufficient, but not necessary, for the fire could have started in other ways. Also, of *this* complex condition, the short-circuit was an indispensable part: the other parts of this condition, conjoined with one another in the absence of the short-circuit, would not have produced the fire. The short-circuit which is said to have caused the fire is thus an indispensable part of a complex sufficient (but not necessary) condition of the fire. In this case, then, the so-called cause is, and is known to be, an *insufficient* but *necessary* part of a condition which is itself *unnecessary* but *sufficient* for the result. The experts are saying, in effect, that the short-circuit is a condition of this sort, that it occurred, that the other conditions which conjoined with it to form a sufficient condition were also present, and that no other sufficient condition of the house's catching fire was present on this occasion. I suggest that when we speak of the cause of some particular event, it is often a condition of this sort that we have in mind. In view of the importance of conditions of this sort in our knowledge of and talk about causation, it will be convenient to have a short name for them: let us call such a condition (from the initial letters of the words italicized above) an INUS condition.[1]

This account of the force of the experts' statement about the cause of the fire may be confirmed by reflecting on the way in which they will have reached this conclusion, and the way in which anyone who disagreed with it would have to challenge it. An important part of the investigation will have consisted in tracing the actual course of the fire; the experts will have ascertained that no other condition sufficient for a fire's breaking out and taking this course was present, but that the short-circuit did occur and that conditions were present which in conjunction with it were sufficient for the fire's breaking out and taking the course that it did. Provided that there is some necessary and sufficient condition of the fire—and this is an assumption that we commonly make in such contexts—anyone who wanted to deny the experts' conclusion would have to challenge one or another of these points.

We can give a more formal analysis of the statement that something is an INUS condition. Let '*A*' stand for the INUS condition—in our example, the

---

[1] This term was suggested by D. C. Stove, who has also given me a great deal of help by criticizing earlier versions of this article.

occurrence of a short-circuit at that place—and let 'B' and '$\overline{C}$' (that is, 'not-C', or the absence of C) stand for the other conditions, positive and negative, which were needed along with A to form a sufficient condition of the fire—in our example, B might be the presence of inflammable material, $\overline{C}$ the absence of a suitably placed sprinkler. Then the conjunction '$AB\overline{C}$' represents a sufficient condition of the fire, and one that contains no redundant factors; that is, $AB\overline{C}$ is a minimal sufficient condition for the fire.[2] Similarly, let $D\overline{E}F$, $\overline{G}\overline{H}I$, etc., be all the other minimal sufficient conditions of this result. Now provided that there is some necessary and sufficient condition for this result, the disjunction of all the minimal sufficient conditions for it constitutes a necessary and sufficient condition.[3] That is, the formula '$AB\overline{C}$ or $D\overline{E}F$ or $\overline{G}\overline{H}I$ or . . .' represents a necessary and sufficient condition for the fire, each of its disjuncts, such as '$AB\overline{C}$', represents a minimal sufficient condition, and each conjunct in each minimal sufficient condition, such as 'A', represents an INUS condition. To simplify and generalize this, we can replace the conjunction of terms conjoined with 'A' (here '$B\overline{C}$') by the single term 'X', and the formula representing the disjunction of all the other minimal sufficient conditions—here '$D\overline{E}F$ or $\overline{G}\overline{H}I$ or . . .'—by the single term 'Y'. Then an INUS condition is defined as follows:

> A is an INUS condition of a result P if and only if, for some X and for some Y, (AX or Y) is a necessary and sufficient condition of P, but A is not a sufficient condition of P and X is not a sufficient condition of P.

We can indicate this type of relation more briefly if we take the provisos for granted and replace the existentially quantified variables 'X' and 'Y' by dots. That is, we can say that A is an INUS condition of P when (A . . . or . . .) is a necessary and sufficient condition of P.

---

[2] The phrase 'minimal sufficient condition' is borrowed from Konrad Marc-Wogau, 'On Historical Explanation', *Theoria*, 28 (1962), 213–33. This article gives an analysis of singular causal statements, with special reference to their use by historians, which is substantially equivalent to the account I am suggesting. Many further references are made to this article, especially in n. 9 below.

[3] Cf. n. 8 on p. 227 of Marc-Wogau's article, where it is pointed out that in order to infer that the disjunction of all the minimal sufficient conditions will be a necessary condition, 'it is necessary to presuppose that an arbitrary event C, if it occurs, must have sufficient reason to occur'. This presupposition is equivalent to the presupposition that there is some (possibly complex) condition that is both necessary and sufficient for C. It is of some interest that some common turns of speech embody this presupposition. To say 'Nothing but X will do,' or 'Either X or Y will do, but nothing else will,' is a natural way of saying that X, or the disjunction (X or Y), is a *necessary* condition for whatever result we have in mind. But taken literally these remarks say only that there is no sufficient condition for this result other than X, or other than (X or Y). That is, we use to mean 'a necessary condition' phrases whose literal meanings would be 'the only sufficient condition', or 'the disjunction of all sufficient conditions'. Similarly, to say that Z is 'all that's needed' is a natural way of saying that Z is a sufficient condition, but taken literally this remark says that Z is the only necessary condition. But, once again, that the only necessary condition will also be a sufficient one follows only if we presuppose that some condition is both necessary and sufficient.

(To forestall possible misunderstandings, I would fill out this definition as follows.[4] First, there could be a set of minimal sufficient conditions of P, but no necessary conditions, not even a complex one; in such a case, A might be what Marc-Wogau calls a moment in a minimal sufficient condition, but I shall not call it an INUS condition. I shall speak of an INUS condition only where the disjunction of all the minimal sufficient conditions is also a necessary condition. Secondly, the definition leaves it open that the INUS condition A might be a conjunct in each of the minimal sufficient conditions. If so, A would be itself a necessary condition of the result. I shall still call A an INUS condition in these circumstances: it is not part of the definition of an INUS condition that it should *not* be necessary, although in the standard cases, such as that sketched above, it is not in fact necessary.[5] Thirdly, the requirement that X by itself should not be sufficient for P ensures that A is a non-redundant part of the sufficient condition AX; but there is a sense in which it may not be strictly necessary or indispensable even as a part of *this* condition, for it may be replaceable: for example KX might be another minimal sufficient condition of P.[6] Fourthly, it *is* part of the definition that the minimal sufficient condition, AX, of which A is a non-redundant part, is not also a necessary condition, that there is another sufficient condition Y (which may itself be a disjunction of sufficient conditions). Fifthly, and similarly, it *is* part of the definition that A is not by itself sufficient for P. The fourth and fifth of these points amount to this: I shall call A an INUS condition only if there are terms which actually occupy the places occupied by 'X' and 'Y' in the formula for the necessary and sufficient condition. However, there may be cases where there is only one minimal sufficient condition, say AX. Again, there may be cases where A is itself a minimal sufficient condition, the disjunction of all minimal sufficient conditions being (A or Y); again, there may be cases where A itself is the only minimal sufficient condition, and is itself both necessary and sufficient for P. In any of these cases, as well as in cases where A is an INUS condition, I shall say that A is *at least an* INUS *condition*. As we shall see, we often have evidence which supports the conclusion that something is *at least* an INUS condition; we may or may not have other evidence which shows that it is *no more than* an INUS condition.)

I suggest that a statement which asserts a singular causal sequence, of such a form as 'A caused P,' often makes, implicitly, the following claims:

---

[4] I am indebted to the referees for the suggestion that these points should be clarified.
[5] Special cases where an INUS condition is also a necessary one are mentioned at the end of sect. 3.
[6] This point, and the term 'non-redundant', are taken from Michael Scriven's review of Nagel's *The Structure of Science*, in *Review of Metaphysics*, 17 (1964), 403–24. See esp. the passage on p. 408, quoted below.

(i) A is at least an INUS condition of P—that is, there is a necessary and sufficient condition of P which has one of these forms: (AX or Y), (A or Y), AX, A.

(ii) A was present on the occasion in question.

(iii) The factors represented by the 'X', if any, in the formula for the necessary and sufficient condition were present on the occasion in question.

(iv) Every disjunct in 'Y' which does not contain 'A' as a conjunct was absent on the occasion in question. (As a rule, this means that whatever 'Y' represents was absent on this occasion. If 'Y' represents a single conjunction of factors, then it was absent if at least one of its conjuncts was absent; if it represents a disjunction, then it was absent if each of its disjuncts was absent. But we do not wish to exclude the possibility that 'Y' should be, or contain as a disjunct, a conjunction one of whose conjuncts is A, or to require that *this* conjunction should have been absent.)[7]

I do not suggest that this is the whole of what is meant by 'A caused P' on any occasion, or even that it is a part of what is meant on every occasion: some additional and alternative parts of the meaning of such statements are indicated below.[8] But I am suggesting that this is an important part of the concept of causation; the proof of this suggestion would be that in many cases the falsifying of any one of the above-mentioned claims would rebut the assertion that A caused P.

This account is in fairly close agreement, in substance if not in terminology, with at least two accounts recently offered of the cause of a single event.

Konrad Marc-Wogau sums up his account thus: 'when historians in singular causal statements speak of a cause or the cause of a certain individual event β, then what they are referring to is another individual event α which is a moment in a minimal sufficient and at the same time necessary condition *post factum* for β.'[9]

He explained his phrase 'necessary condition *post factum*' by saying that he will call an event a_1 a necessary condition *post factum* for x if the

---

[7] See example of the wicket-keeper discussed below.

[8] See sects. 7, 8.

[9] See Marc-Wogau, 'On Historical Explanation', 226–7. Marc-Wogau's full formulation is as follows: 'Let "msc" stand for minimal sufficient condition and "nc" for necessary condition. Then suppose we have a class K of individual events $a_1, a_2, \ldots a_n$. (It seems reasonable to assume that K is finite; however even if K were infinite the reasoning below would not be affected.) My analysis of the singular causal statement: α is the cause of β, where α and β stand for individual events, can be summarily expressed in the following statements: (1) $(EK)(K = \{a_1, a_2, \ldots, a_n\})$; (2) (x) $(x \in K \equiv x \operatorname{msc} \beta)$; (3) $(a_1 \vee a_2 \vee \ldots a_n)\operatorname{nc} \beta$; (4) $(x)(x \in K . x \neq a_1) \supset x$ is not fulfilled when α occurs); (5) α is a moment in a_1. (3) and (4) say that a_1 is a necessary condition *post factum* for β. If a_1 is a necessary condition *post factum* for β, then every moment in a_1 is a necessary condition *post factum* for β, and therefore also α. As has been mentioned before (n. 6) there is assumed to be a temporal sequence between α and β; β is not itself an element in K.'

disjunction 'a_1 or a_2 or a_3 ... or a_n' represents a necessary condition for x, and of these disjuncts only a_1 was present on the particular occasion when x occurred.

Similarly, Michael Scriven has said:

> Causes are *not* necessary, even contingently so, they are not sufficient—but they are, to talk that language, *contingently sufficient.* . . . They are part of *a* set of conditions that does guarantee the outcome, and they are non-redundant in that the rest of *this* set (which does not include all the other conditions present) is not alone sufficient for the outcome. It is not even true that they are relatively necessary, i.e., necessary with regard to that set of conditions rather than the total circumstances of their occurrence, for there may be several possible replacements for them which happen not to be present. There remains a ghost of necessity; a cause is a factor from a set of possible factors the presence of one of which (*any* one) is necessary in order that a set of conditions actually present be sufficient for the effect.[10]

There are only slight differences between these two accounts, or between each of them and that offered above. Scriven seems to speak too strongly when he says that causes are not necessary: it is, indeed, not part of the definition of a cause of this sort that it should be necessary, but, as noted above, a cause, or an INUS condition, may be necessary, either because there is only one minimal sufficient condition or because the cause is a moment in each of the minimal sufficient conditions. On the other hand, Marc-Wogau's account of a minimal sufficient condition seems too strong. He says that a minimal sufficient condition contains 'only those moments relevant to the effect' and that a moment is relevant to an effect if 'it is a necessary condition for β : β would not have occurred if this moment had not been present'. This is less accurate than Scriven's statement that the cause only needs to be non-redundant.[11] Also, Marc-Wogau's requirement, in his account of a necessary condition *post factum*, that only one minimal sufficient condition (the one containing α) should be present on the particular occasion, seems a little too strong. If two or more minimal sufficient conditions (say a_1 and a_2) were present, but α was a moment in each of them, then though neither a_1 nor a_2 was necessary *post factum*, α would be so. I shall use this phrase 'necessary *post factum*' to include cases of this sort: that is, α is a necessary condition *post factum* if it is a moment in every minimal sufficient condition that was present. For example, in a cricket team the

---

[10] Scriven, review of Nagel's *Structure of Science*, 408.

[11] However, in n. 7 on pp. 222–33, Marc-Wogau draws attention to the difficulty of giving an accurate definition of 'a moment in a sufficient condition'. Further complications are involved in the account given in sect. 5 below of 'clusters' of factors and the progressive localization of a cause. A condition which is minimally sufficient in relation to one degree of analysis of factors may not be so in relation to another degree of analysis.

wicket-keeper is also a good batsman. He is injured during a match, and does not bat in the second innings, and the substitute wicket-keeper drops a vital catch that the original wicket-keeper would have taken. The team loses the match, but it would have won if the wicket-keeper had *both* batted *and* taken that catch. His injury was a moment in two minimal sufficient conditions for the loss of the match; either his not batting, or the catch's not being taken, would on its own have ensured the loss of the match. But we can certainly say that his injury caused the loss of the match, and that it was a necessary condition *post factum*.

This account may be summed up, briefly and approximately, by saying that the statement '*A* caused *P*' often claims that *A* was necessary and sufficient for *P* in the circumstances. This description applies in the standard cases, but we have already noted that a cause is non-redundant rather than necessary even in the circumstances, and we shall see that there are special cases in which it may be neither necessary nor non-redundant.

2. DIFFICULTIES AND REFINEMENTS[12]

Both Scriven and Marc-Wogau are concerned not only with this basic account, but with certain difficulties and with the refinements and complica-tions that are needed to overcome them. Before dealing with these I shall introduce, as a refinement of my own account, the notion of a causal field.[13]

This notion is most easily explained if we leave, for a time, singular causal statements and consider general ones. The question 'What causes influenza?' is incomplete and partially indeterminate. It may mean 'What causes influenza in human beings in general?' If so, the (full) cause that is being sought is a difference that will mark off cases in which human beings contract influenza from cases in which they do not; the causal field is then the region that is to be thus divided, *human beings in general*. But the question may mean, 'Given that influenza viruses are present, what makes some people contract the disease whereas others do not?' Here the causal field is *human beings in conditions where influenza viruses are present*. In all such cases, the cause is required to differentiate, within a wider region in which the effect

---

[12] This section is something of an aside: the main argument is resumed in sect. 3.

[13] This notion of a causal field was introduced by John Anderson. He used it, e.g., in 'The Problem of Causality', first published in the *Australasian Journal of Psychology and Philosophy*, 16 (1938), 127–42, and repr. in *Studies in Empirical Philosophy* (Sydney, 1962), 126–36, to overcome certain difficulties and paradoxes in Mill's account of causation. I have also used this notion to deal with problems of legal and moral responsibility, in 'Responsibility and Language', *Australasian Journal of Philosophy*, 33 (1955), 143–59.

sometimes occurs and sometimes does not, the sub-region in which it occurs: this wider region is the causal field. This notion can now be applied to singular causal questions and statements. 'What caused this man's skin cancer?'[14] may mean 'Why did this man develop skin cancer now when he did not develop it before?' Here the causal field is the career of this man: it is within this that we are seeking a difference between the time when skin cancer developed and times when it did not. But the same question may mean 'Why did this man develop skin cancer, whereas other men who were also exposed to radiation did not?' Here the causal field is the class of men thus exposed to radiation. And what is the cause in relation to one field may not be the cause in relation to another. Exposure to a certain dose of radiation may be the cause in relation to the former field: it cannot be the cause in relation to the latter field since it is part of the description of that field, and being present throughout that field it cannot differentiate one sub-region of it from another. In relation to the latter field, the cause may be, in Scriven's terms, 'some as-yet-unidentified constitutional factor'.

In our first example of the house which caught fire, the history of this house is the field in relation to which the experts were looking for the cause of the fire: their question was 'Why did this house catch fire on this occasion, and not on others?' However, there may still be some indeterminacy in this choice of a causal field. Does this house, considered as the causal field, include all its features, or all its relatively permanent features, or only some of these? If we take all its features, or even all of its relatively permanent ones, as constituting the field, then some of the things that we have treated as conditions—for example, the presence of inflammable material near the place where the short-circuit occurred—would have to be regarded as parts of the field, and we could not then take them also as conditions which in relation to this field, as additions to it or intrusions into it, are necessary or sufficient for something else. We must therefore take the house, in so far as it constitutes the causal field, as determined only in a fairly general way, by only some of its relatively permanent features, and we shall then be free to treat its other features as conditions which do not constitute the field, and are not parts of it, but which may occur within it or be added to it. It is in general an arbitrary matter whether a particular feature is regarded as a condition (that is, as a possible causal factor) or as part of the field, but it cannot be treated in both ways at once. If we are to say that something happened to this

---

[14] These examples are borrowed from Scriven, review of Nagel's *Structure of Science*, 409–10. Scriven discusses them with reference to what he calls a 'contrast class', the class of cases where the effect did not occur with which the case where it did occur is being contrasted. What I call the causal field is the logical sum of the case (or cases) in which the effect is being said to be caused with what Scriven calls the contrast class.

house because of, or partly because of, a certain feature, we are implying that it would still have been *this* house, the house in relation to which we are seeking the cause of this happening, even if it had not had this particular feature.

I now propose to modify the account given above of the claims often made by singular causal statements. A statement of such a form as '*A* caused *P*' is usually elliptical, and is to be expanded into '*A* caused *P* in relation to the field *F*.' And then in place of the claim stated in (i) above, we require this:

> (i*a*) *A* is at least an INUS condition of *P* in the field *F*—that is, there is a condition which, given the presence of whatever features characterize *F* throughout, is necessary and sufficient for *P*, and which is of one of these forms: (*AX* or *Y*), (*A* or *Y*), *AX*, *A*.

In analysing our ordinary causal statements, we must admit that the field is often taken for granted or only roughly indicated, rather than specified precisely. Nevertheless, the field in relation to which we are looking for a cause of this effect, or saying that such-and-such is a cause, may be definite enough for us to be able to say that certain facts or possibilities are irrelevant to the particular causal problem under consideration, because they would constitute a shift from the intended field to a different one. Thus if we are looking for the cause, or causes, of influenza, meaning its cause(s) in relation to the field *human beings*, we may dismiss, as not directly relevant, evidence which shows that some proposed cause fails to produce influenza in rats. If we are looking for the cause of the fire in *this house*, we may similarly dismiss as irrelevant the fact that a proposed cause would not have produced a fire if the house had been radically different, or had been set in a radically different environment.

This modification enables us to deal with the well-known difficulty that it is impossible, without including in the cause the whole environment, the whole prior state of the universe (and so excluding any likelihood of repetition), to find a genuinely sufficient condition, one which is 'by itself, adequate to secure the effect'.[15] It may be hard to find even a complex condition which was absolutely sufficient for this fire because we should have to include, as one of the negative conjuncts, such an item as the earth's not being destroyed by a nuclear explosion just after the occurrence of the suggested INUS condition; but it is easy and reasonable to say simply that

---

[15] Cf. Bertrand Russell, 'On the Notion of Cause', *Mysticism and Logic* (London, 1917), 187. Cf. also Scriven's first difficulty, review of Nagel's *Structure of Science*, 409: 'First, there are virtually no known sufficient conditions, literally speaking, since human or accidental interference is almost inexhaustibly possible, and hard to exclude by specific qualification without tautology.' The introduction of the causal field also automatically covers Scriven's third difficulty and third refinement, that of the contrast class and the relativity of causal statements to contexts.

such an explosion would, in more senses than one, take us outside the field in which we are considering this effect. That is to say, it may be not so difficult to find a condition which is sufficient in relation to the intended field. No doubt this means that causal statements may be vague, in so far as the specification of the field is vague, but this is not a serious obstacle to establishing or using them, either in science or in everyday contexts.[16]

It is a vital feature of the account I am suggesting that we can say that *A* caused *P*, in the sense described, without being able to specify exactly the terms represented by '*X*' and '*Y*' in our formula. In saying that *A* is at least an INUS condition for *P* in *F*, one is *not* saying what other factors, along with *A*, were both present and non-redundant, and one is *not* saying what other minimal sufficient conditions there may be for *P* in *F*. One is not even claiming to be able to say what they are. This is in no way a difficulty: it is a readily recognizable fact about our ordinary causal statements, and one which this account explicitly and correctly reflects.[17] It will be shown (in sect. 5 below) that this elliptical or indeterminate character of our causal statements is closely connected with some of our characteristic ways of discovering and confirming causal relationships: it is precisely for statements that are thus 'gappy' or indeterminate that we can obtain fairly direct evidence from quite modest ranges of observation. On this analysis, causal statements implicitly contain existential quantifications; one can assert an existentially quantified statement without asserting any instantiation of it, and one can also have good reason for asserting an existentially quantified statement without having the information needed to support any precise instantiation of it. I can know that there is someone at the door even if the question 'Who is he?' would floor me.

Marc-Wogau is concerned especially with cases where 'there are two events, each of which independently of the other is a sufficient condition for another event'. There are, that is to say, two minimal sufficient conditions,

---

[16] J. R. Lucas, 'Causation', in R. J. Butler (ed.), *Analytical Philosophy* (Oxford, 1962), 57–9, resolves this kind of difficulty by an informal appeal to what amounts to this notion of a causal field: 'these circumstances [cosmic cataclysms, etc.] . . . destroy the whole causal situation in which we had been looking for *Z* to appear . . . predictions are not expected to come true when quite unforeseen emergencies arise'.

[17] This is related to Scriven's second difficulty, review of Nagel's *Structure of Science*, 409: 'there still remains the problem of saying what the other factors are which, with the cause, make up the sufficient condition. If they can be stated, causal explanation is then simply a special case of subsumption under a law. If they cannot, the analysis is surely mythological.' Scriven correctly replies that 'a combination of the thesis of macro-determinism . . . and observation-plus-theory frequently gives us the very best of reasons for saying that a certain factor combines with an unknown sub-set of the conditions present into a sufficient condition for a particular effect'. He gives a statistical example of such evidence, but the whole of my account of typical sorts of evidence for causal relationships in sects. 5 and 7 below [omitted from this volume] is an expanded defence of a reply of this sort.

both of which actually occurred. For example, lightning strikes a barn in which straw is stored, and a tramp throws a burning cigarette butt into the straw at the same place and at the same time. Likewise for a historical event there may be more than one 'cause', and each of them may, on its own, be sufficient.[18] Similarly Scriven considers a case where ' . . . conditions (perhaps unusual excitement plus constitutional inadequacies) [are] present at 4.00 p.m. that guarantee a stroke at 4.55 p.m. and consequent death at 5.00 p.m.; but an entirely unrelated heart attack at 4.50 p.m. is still correctly called the cause of death, which, as it happens, does occur at 5.00 p.m.'.[19]

Before we try to resolve these difficulties let us consider another of Marc-Wogau's problems: Smith and Jones commit a crime, but if they had not done so the head of the criminal organization would have sent other members to perform it in their stead, and so it would have been committed anyway.[20] Now in this case, if 'A' stands for the actions of Smith and Jones, what we have is that AX is one minimal sufficient condition of the result (the crime), but $\bar{A}Z$ is another, and both X and Z are present. A combines with one set of the standing conditions to produce the result by one route; but the absence of A would have combined with another set of the standing conditions to produce the same result by another route. In this case we *can* say that A was a necessary condition *post factum*. This sample satisfies the requirements of Marc-Wogau's analysis, and of mine, of the statement that A caused this result; and this agrees with what we would ordinarily say in such a case. (We might indeed add that there was *also* a deeper cause—the existence of the criminal organization, perhaps—but this does not matter; our formal analyses do not ensure that a particular result will have a unique cause, nor does our ordinary causal talk require this.) It is true that in this case we cannot say what will usually serve as an informal substitute for the formal account, that the cause, here A, was necessary (as well as sufficient) in the circumstances; for $\bar{A}$ would have done just as well. We cannot even say that A was non-redundant. But this shows merely that a formal analysis may be superior to its less formal counterparts.

Now in Scriven's example, we might take it that the heart attack prevented the stroke from occurring. If so, then the heart attack *is* a necessary condition *post factum*: it is a moment in the only minimal sufficient condition that was present in full, for the heart attack itself removed some factor that was a necessary part of the minimal sufficient condition which has the excitement

---

[18] Marc-Wogau, 'On Historical Explanation', 228–33.
[19] Review of Nagel's *Structure of Science*, 410–11: this is Scriven's fourth difficulty and refinement.
[20] 'On Historical Explanation', 232: the example is taken from P. Gardiner, *The Nature of Historical Explanation* (Oxford, 1952), 101.

as one of its moments. This is strictly parallel to the Smith and Jones case. Again it is odd to say that the heart attack was in any way necessary, since the absence of the heart attack would have done just as well: this absence would have been a moment in that other minimal sufficient condition, one of whose other moments was the excitement. Nevertheless, the heart attack was necessary *post factum*, and the excitement was not. Scriven draws the distinction, quite correctly, in terms of continuity and discontinuity of causal chains: 'the heart attack was, and the excitement was not the cause of death because the "causal chain" between the latter and death was interrupted, while the former's "went to completion".' But it is worth noting that a break in the causal chain corresponds to a failure to satisfy the logical requirements of a moment in a minimal sufficient condition that is also necessary *post factum*.

Alternatively, if the heart attack did not prevent the stroke, then we have a case parallel to that of the straw in the barn, or of the man who is shot by a firing squad, and two bullets go through his heart simultaneously. In such cases the requirements of my analysis, or Marc-Wogau's, or of Scriven's, are not met: each proposed cause *is* redundant and not even necessary *post factum*, though the disjunction of them is necessary *post factum* and non-redundant. But this agrees very well with the fact that we *would* ordinarily hesitate to say, of either bullet, that it caused the man's death, or of either the lightning or the cigarette butt that it caused the fire, or of either the excitement or the heart attack that it was the cause of death. As Marc-Wogau says, 'in such a situation as this we are unsure also how to use the word "cause".' Our ordinary concept of cause does not deal clearly with cases of this sort, and we are free to decide whether or not to add to our ordinary use, and to the various more or less formal descriptions of it, rules which allow us to say that where more than one at-least-INUS-condition, and its conjunct conditions, are present, each of them caused the result.[21]

The account thus far developed of singular causal statements has been expressed in terms of statements about necessity and sufficiency: it is therefore incomplete until we have added an account of necessity and sufficiency themselves. This question is considered in sect. 4 below. But the present account is independent of any particular analysis of necessity and sufficiency. Whatever analysis of these we finally adopt, we shall use it to complete the account of what it is to be an INUS condition, or to be at least an INUS condition. But in whatever way this account is completed, we can retain the general principle that at least part of what is often done by a

---

[21] Scriven's fifth difficulty and refinement are concerned with the direction of causation. This is considered briefly in sect. 8 below.

singular causal statement is to pick out, as the cause, something that is claimed to be at least an INUS condition.

3. GENERAL CAUSAL STATEMENTS

Many general causal statements are to be understood in a corresponding way. Suppose, for example, that an economist says that the restriction of credit causes (or produces) unemployment. Again, he will no doubt be speaking with reference to some causal field; this is now not an individual object, but a class, presumably economies of a certain general kind; perhaps their specification will include the feature that each economy of the kind in question contains a large private enterprise sector with free wage-earning employees. The result, unemployment, is something which sometimes occurs and sometimes does not occur within this field, and the same is true of the alleged cause, the restriction of credit. But the economist is not saying that (even in relation to this field) credit restriction is either necessary or sufficient for unemployment, let alone both necessary and sufficient. There may well be other circumstances which must be present along with credit restriction, in an economy of the kind referred to, if unemployment is to result; these other circumstances will no doubt include various negative ones, the absence of various counteracting causal factors which, if they were present, would prevent this result. Also, the economist will probably be quite prepared to admit that in an economy of this kind unemployment would be brought about by other combinations of circumstances in which the restriction of credit plays no part. So once again the claim that he is making is merely that the restriction of credit is, in economies of this kind, a non-redundant part of one sufficient condition for unemployment: that is, an INUS condition. The economist is probably assuming that there is some condition, no doubt a complex one, which is both necessary and sufficient for unemployment in this field. This being assumed, what he is asserting is that, for some X and for some Y (AX or Y) is a necessary and sufficient condition for P in F, but neither A nor X is sufficient on its own, where 'A' stands for the restriction of credit, 'P' for unemployment, and 'F' for the field, economies of such-and-such a sort. In a developed economic theory the field F may be specified quite exactly, and so may the relevant combinations of factors represented here by 'X' and 'Y'. (Indeed, the theory may go beyond statements in terms of necessity and sufficiency to ones of functional dependence, but this is a complication which I am leaving aside for the present.) In a preliminary or popular statement, on the other hand, the combinations of factors may either be only roughly indicated or be left quite undetermined. At one extreme we have the statement that (AX or Y) is a necessary and sufficient condition, where 'X' and 'Y' are given definite meanings; at the other extreme we have the merely existentially quantified statement that this holds for *some* pair X and Y. Our knowledge in such cases ordinarily falls somewhere between these two extremes. We can use the same convention as before, deliberately allowing it to be ambiguous between these different interpretations, and say that in any of these cases, where A is an INUS condition of P in F (A . . . or . . .) is a necessary and sufficient condition of P in F.

A great deal of our ordinary causal knowledge is of this form. We know that the eating of sweets causes dental decay. Here the field is human beings who have some of their own teeth. We do not know, indeed it is not true, that the eating of sweets by any such person is a sufficient condition for dental decay: some people have peculiarly resistant teeth, and there are probably measures which, if taken along with the eating of sweets, would protect the eater's teeth from decay. All we know is that sweet-eating combined with a set of positive and negative factors which we can specify, if at all, only roughly and incompletely, constitutes a minimal sufficient condition for dental decay—but not a necessary one, for there are other combinations of factors, which do not include sweet-eating, which would also make teeth decay, but which we can specify, if at all, only roughly and incompletely. That is, if 'A' now represents sweet-eating, 'P' dental decay, and 'F' the class of human beings with some of their own teeth, we can say that, for some X and Y (AX or Y) is necessary and sufficient for P in F, and we *may* be able to go beyond this merely existentially quantified statement to at least a partial specification of the X and Y in question. That is, we can say that (A . . . or , . .) is a necessary and sufficient condition, but that A itself is only an INUS condition. And the same holds for many general causal statements of the form 'A causes (or produces) P.' It is in this sense that the application of a potential difference to the ends of a copper wire produces an electric current in the wire; that a rise in the temperature of a piece of metal makes it expand; that moisture rusts steel; that exposure to various kinds of radiation causes cancer, and so on.

However, it is true that not all ordinary general causal statements are of this sort. Some of them are implicit statements of functional dependence. Functional dependence is a more complicated relationship of which necessity and sufficiency can be regarded as special cases. Here too what we commonly single out as causing some result is only one of a number of factors which jointly affect the result. Again, some causal statements pick out something that is not only an INUS condition, but also a necessary condition. Thus we may say that the yellow fever virus is the cause of yellow fever. (This statement is not, as it might appear to be, tautologous, for the yellow fever virus and the disease itself can be independently specified.) In the field in question—human beings—the injection of this virus is not by itself a sufficient condition for this disease, for persons who have once recovered from yellow fever are thereafter immune to it, and other persons can be immunized against it. The injection of the virus, combined with the absence of immunity (natural or artificial), and perhaps combined with some other factors, constitutes a sufficient condition for the disease. Beside this, the injection of the virus is a necessary condition of the disease. If there is more than one complex sufficient condition for yellow fever, the injection of the virus into the patient's bloodstream (either by a mosquito or in some other way) is a factor included in every such sufficient condition. If 'A' stands for this factor, the necessary and sufficient condition has the form (A . . . or A . . . etc.), where A occurs in every disjunct. We sometimes note the difference between this and the standard case by using the phrase 'the cause'. We may say not merely that this virus *causes* yellow fever, but that it is *the cause* of yellow fever; but we would say only that sweet-eating *causes* dental decay, not that it is *the cause* of dental decay. But about an individual case we could say that sweet-eating was *the cause* of the decay of this person's teeth, meaning (as in sect. 1 above) that the only sufficient condition present here was the one of which sweet-eating is a non-redundant part. Nevertheless, there will not in general be any one item which has a unique claim to be regarded as *the cause* even of an individual event, and even after the causal field has been determined. Each of the moments in the minimal sufficient condition, or in each minimal sufficient condition, that was present can equally be regarded as the cause. They may be distinguished as predisposing causes, triggering causes, and so on, but it is quite arbitrary to pick out as 'main' and 'secondary', different moments which are equally non-redundant items in a minimal sufficient condition, or which are moments in two minimal sufficient conditions each of which makes the other redundant.[22]

4. NECESSITY AND SUFFICIENCY

One possible account of general statements of the forms 'S is a necessary condition of T' and 'S is a sufficient condition of T'—where 'S' and 'T' are general terms—is that they are equivalent to simple universal propositions. That is, the former is equivalent to 'All T are S' and the latter to 'All S are T.' Similarly, 'S is necessary for T in the field F' would be equivalent to 'All FT are S,' and 'S is sufficient for T in the field F' to 'All FS are T.' Whether

---

[22] Cf. Marc-Wogau's concluding remarks, 'On Historical Explanation', 232–3.

an account of this sort is adequate is, of course, a matter of dispute; but it is not disputed that these statements about necessary and sufficient conditions at least *entail* the corresponding universals. I shall work on the assumption that this account is adequate, that general statements of necessity and sufficiency are equivalent to universals: it will be worth while to see how far this account will take us, how far we are able, in terms of it, to understand how we use, support, and criticize these statements of necessity and sufficiency.

A directly analogous account of the corresponding singular statements is not satisfactory. Thus it will not do to say that 'A short-circuit here was a necessary condition of a fire in this house' is equivalent to 'All cases of this house's catching fire are cases of a short-circuit occurring here,' because the latter is automatically true if this house has caught fire only once and a short-circuit has occurred on that occasion, but this is not enough to establish the statement that the short-circuit was a necessary condition of the fire; and there would be an exactly parallel objection to a similar statement about a sufficient condition.

It is much more plausible to relate singular statements about necessity and sufficiency to certain kinds of non-material conditionals. Thus 'A short-circuit here was a necessary condition of a fire in this house' is closely related to the counterfactual conditional 'If a short-circuit had not occurred here this house would not have caught fire,' and 'A short-circuit here was a sufficient condition of a fire in this house' is closely related to what Goodman has called the factual conditional, 'Since a short-circuit occurred here, this house caught fire.'

However, a further account would still have to be given of these non-material conditionals themselves. I have argued elsewhere[23] that they are best considered as condensed or telescoped *arguments*, but that the statements used as premises in these arguments are no more than simple factual universals. To use the above-quoted counterfactual conditional is, in effect, to run through an incomplete argument: 'Suppose that a short-circuit did not occur here, then the house did not catch fire.' To use the factual conditional is, in effect, to run through a similar incomplete argument, 'A short-circuit occurred here; therefore the house caught fire.' In each case the argument might in principle be completed by the insertion of other premises which, together with the stated premiss, would entail the stated conclusion. Such additional premisses may be said to *sustain* the non-material conditional. It is an important point that someone can use a non-material conditional without completing or being able to complete the argument, without being prepared

---

[23] 'Counterfactuals and Causal Laws', in R. J. Butler (ed.), *Analytical Philosophy* (Oxford, 1962), 66–80.

explicitly to assert premisses that would sustain it, and similarly that we can understand such a conditional without knowing exactly how the argument would or could be completed. But to say that a short-circuit here was a necessary condition of a fire in this house is to say that there is some set of true propositions which would sustain the above-stated counterfactual, and to say that it was a sufficient condition is to say that there is some set of true propositions which would sustain the above-stated factual conditional. If this is conceded, then the relating of singular statements about necessity and sufficiency to non-material conditionals leads back to the view that they refer indirectly to certain simple universal propositions. Thus, if we said that a short-circuit here was a necessary condition for a fire in this house, we should be saying that there are true universal propositions from which, together with true statements about the characteristics of this house, and together with the supposition that a short-circuit did not occur here, it would follow that the house did not catch fire. From this we could infer the universal proposition which is the more obvious, but unsatisfactory, candidate for the analysis of this statement of necessity, 'All cases of this house's catching fire are cases of a short-circuit occurring here,' or, in our symbols, 'All FP are A.' We can use this to represent approximately the statement of necessity, on the understanding that it is to be a consequence of some set of wider universal propositions, and is not to be automatically true merely because there is only this one case of an FP, of this house's catching fire.[24] A statement that A was a sufficient condition may be similarly represented by 'All FA are P.' Correspondingly, if all that we want to say is that $(A \ldots \text{or} \ldots)$ was necessary and sufficient for P in F, this will be represented approximately by the pair of universals 'All FP are $(A \ldots \text{or} \ldots)$ and all $F (A \ldots \text{or} \ldots)$ are P,' and more accurately by the statement that there is some set of wider universal propositions from which, together with true statements about the features of F, this pair of universals follows. This, therefore, is the fuller analysis of the claim that in a particular case A is an INUS condition of P in F, and hence of the singular statement that A caused P. (The statement that A is *at least* an INUS condition includes other alternatives, corresponding to cases where the necessary and sufficient condition is $(A \text{ or} \ldots)$, $A \ldots$, or A).

Let us go back now to general statements of necessity and sufficiency and take F as a class, not as an individual. On the view that I am adopting, at

---

[24] This restriction may be compared with one which Nagel imposes on laws of nature: 'the vacuous truth of an unrestricted universal is not sufficient for counting it a law; it counts as a law only if there is a set of other assumed laws from which the universal is logically derivable' (*The Structure of Science* (New York, 1961), 60). It might have been better if he had added 'or if there is some other way in which it is supported (ultimately) by empirical evidence'. Cf. my remarks in 'Counterfactuals and Causal Laws', 72–4, 78–80.

least provisionally, the statement that Z is a necessary and sufficient condition for P in F is equivalent to 'All FP are Z and all FZ are P.' Similarly, if we cannot completely specify a necessary and sufficient condition for P in F, but can only say that the formula '$(A \ldots$ or $\ldots)$' represents such a condition, this is equivalent to the pair of incomplete universals, 'All FP are $(A \ldots$ or $\ldots)$ and all F $(A \ldots$ or $\ldots)$ are P.' In saying that our general causal statements often do no more than specify an INUS condition, I am therefore saying that much of our ordinary causal knowledge is knowledge of such pairs of incomplete universals, of what we may call elliptical or *gappy* causal laws. . . .

[Sections 5,6, and 7 omitted]

8. THE DIRECTION OF CAUSATION

This account of causation is still incomplete, in that nothing has yet been said about the direction of causation, about what distinguishes A causing P from P causing A. This is a difficult question, and it is linked with the equally difficult question of the direction of time. I cannot hope to resolve it completely here, but I shall state some of the relevant considerations.[25]

First, it seems that there is a relation which may be called *causal priority*, and that part of what is meant by 'A caused P' is that this relation holds in one direction between A and P, not the other. Secondly, this relation is not identical with temporal priority; it is conceivable that there should be evidence for a case of backward causation, for A being causally prior to P whereas P was temporally prior to A. Most of us believe, and I think with good reason, that backward causation does not occur, so that we can and do normally use temporal order to limit the possibilities about causal order; but the connection between the two is synthetic. Thirdly, it could be objected to the analysis of 'necessary' and 'sufficient' offered in sect. 4 above that it omits any reference to causal order, whereas our most common use of 'necessary' and 'sufficient' in causal contexts includes such a reference. Thus 'A is (causally) sufficient for B' says 'If A, then B, and A is causally prior to B,' but 'B is (causally) necessary for A' is not equivalent to this: it says 'If A, then B, and B is causally prior to A.' However, it is simpler to use 'necessary' and 'sufficient' in senses which exclude this causal priority, and to introduce the assertion of priority separately into our accounts of 'A caused

---

[25] As was mentioned in n. 21, Scriven's fifth difficulty and refinement are concerned with this point (review of Nagel's *Structure of Science*, 411–12), but his answer seems to me inadequate. Lucas touches on it ('Causation', 51–3). The problem of temporal asymmetry is discussed, e.g. by J. J. C. Smart, *Philosophy and Scientific Realism* (London, 1963), 142–8, and by A. Grünbaum in the article cited in n. 28 below.

P' and 'A causes P.' Fourthly, although 'A is (at least) an INUS condition of P' is not synonymous with 'P is (at least) an INUS condition of A,' this difference of meaning cannot exhaust the relation of causal priority. If it did exhaust it, the direction of causation would be a trivial matter, for, given that there is some necessary and sufficient condition of A in the field, it can be proved that if A is (at least) an INUS condition of P, then P is also (at least) an INUS condition of A: we can construct a minimal sufficient condition of A in which P is a moment.[26]

Fifthly, it is often suggested that the direction of causation is linked with controllability. If there is a causal relation between A and B, and we can control A without making use of B to do so, and the relation between A and B still holds, then we decide that B is not causally prior to A and, in general, that A is causally prior to B. But this means only that if one case of causal priority is known, we can use it to determine others: our rejection of the possibility that B is causally prior to A rests on our knowledge that our action is causally prior to A, and the question how we know the latter, and even the question of what causal priority is, have still to be answered. Similarly, if one of the causally related kinds of event, say A, can be randomized, so that occurrences of A are either not caused at all, or are caused by something which enters this causal field *only* in this way, by causing A, we can reject both the possibility that B is causally prior to A and the possibility that some common cause is prior both to A and separately to B, and we can again conclude that A is causally prior to B. But this still means only that we can infer causal priority in one place if we first know that it is absent from another place. It is true that our knowledge of the direction of causation in ordinary cases is thus based on what we find to be controllable, and on what we either find to be random or find that we can randomize; but this cannot without circularity be taken as providing a full account either of what we mean by causal priority or of how we know about it.

A suggestion put forward by Popper about the direction of time seems to be relevant here.[27] If a stone is dropped into a pool, the entry of the stone will explain the expanding circular waves. But the reverse process, with contracting circular waves, 'would demand a vast number of distant coherent generators of waves the coherence of which, to be explicable, would have to be shown . . . as originating from one centre'. That is, if B is an occurrence which involves a certain sort of 'coherence' between a large number of separated items, whereas A is a single event, and A and B are causally

---

[26] I am indebted to one of the referees for correcting an inaccurate statement on this point in an earlier version.

[27] Karl R. Popper, 'The Arrow of Time', *Nature*, 177 (1956), 538; also ibid. 178 (1956), 382 and 179 (1957), 1297.

connected, *A* will explain *B* in a way in which *B* will not explain *A* unless some other single event, say *C*, first explains the coherence in *B*. Such examples give us a *direction of explanation*, and it may be that this is the basis, or part of the basis, of the relation I have called causal priority.

9. CONCLUSIONS

Even if Mill was wrong in thinking that science consists mainly of causal knowledge, it can hardly be denied that such knowledge is an indispensable element in science, and that it is worth while to investigate the meaning of causal statements and the ways in which we can arrive at causal knowledge. General causal relationships are among the items which a more advanced kind of scientific theory explains, and is confirmed by its success in explaining. Singular causal assertions are involved in almost every report of an experiment: doing such and such *produced* such and such an effect. Materials are commonly identified by their causal properties: to recognize something as a piece of a certain material, therefore, we must establish singular causal assertions about it, that this object affected that other one, or was affected by it, in such and such a way. Causal assertions are embedded in both the results and the procedures of scientific investigation.

The account that I have offered of the force of various kinds of causal statements agrees both with our informal understanding of them and with accounts put forward by other writers: at the same time it is formal enough to show how such statements can be supported by observations and experiments, and thus to throw a new light on philosophical questions about the nature of causation and causal explanation and the status of causal knowledge.

One important point is that, leaving aside the question of the direction of causation, the analysis has been given entirely within the limits of what can still be called a regularity theory of causation, in that the causal laws involved in it are no more than straightforward universal propositions, although their terms may be complex and perhaps incompletely specified. Despite this limitation, I have been able to give an account of the meaning of statements about singular causal sequences, regardless of whether such a sequence is or is not of a kind that frequently recurs: repetition is not essential for causal relation, and regularity does not here disappear into the mere fact that this single sequence has occurred. It has, indeed, often been recognized that the regularity theory could cope with single sequences if, say, a unique sequence could be explained as the resultant of a number of laws each of which was exemplified in many other sequences; but my account shows how a singular causal statement can be interpreted, and how the corresponding sequence can be shown to be causal, even if the corresponding complete laws are not known. It shows how even a unique sequence can be directly recognized as causal.

One consequence of this is that it now becomes possible to reconcile what have appeared to be conflicting views about the nature of historical explanation. We are accustomed to contrast the 'covering-law' theory adopted by Hempel, Popper, and others with the views of such critics as Dray and Scriven who have argued that explanations and causal statements in history cannot be thus assimilated to the patterns accepted in the physical sciences.[28] But while my basic analysis of singular causal statements in sects. 1 and 2 agrees closely with Scriven's, I have argued in sect. 4 that this analysis can be developed in terms of complex and elliptical universal propositions, and this means that wherever we have a singular causal statement we shall still

[28] See e.g. C. G. Hempel, 'The Function of General Laws in History', *Journal of Philosophy*, 39 (1942), repr. in H. Feigl and W. Sellars (eds.), *Readings in Philosophical Analysis* (New York, 1949), 459–71; C. G. Hempel and P. Oppenheim, 'Studies in the Logic of Explanation', *Philosophy of Science*, 15 (1948), repr. in H. Feigl and M. Brodbeck (eds.), *Readings in the Philosophy of Science* (New York, 1953), 319–52; K. R. Popper, *Logik der Forschung* (Vienna, 1934), trans. as *The Logic of Scientific Discovery* (London, 1959), 59–60, also *The Open Society and its Enemies* (London, 1952), 2. 262; W. Dray, *Laws and Explanation in History* (Oxford, 1957); N. Rescher, 'On Prediction and Explanation', *British Journal for the Philosophy of Science*, 9 (1958), 281–90; various papers in *Minnesota Studies in the Philosophy of Science*, 3, ed. H. Feigl and G. Maxwell (Minneapolis, 1962); A. Grünbaum, 'Temporally-Asymmetric Principles, Parity between Explanation and Prediction, and Mechanism versus Teleology', *Philosophy of Science*, 29 (1962), 146–70. Dray's criticisms of the covering-law theory include the following: we cannot state the law used in a historical explanation without making it so vague as to be vacuous (*Laws and Explanation*, 24–37) or so complex that it covers only a single case and is trivial on that account (p. 39); the historian does not come to the task of explaining an event with a sufficient stock of laws already formulated and empirically validated (pp. 42–3); historians do not need to replace judgement about particular cases with deduction from empirically validated laws (pp. 51–2). It will be clear that my account resolves each of these difficulties. Grünbaum draws an important distinction between (1) an asymmetry between explanation and prediction with regard to the grounds on which we claim to know that the explanandum is true, and (2) an asymmetry with respect to the logical relation between the explanans and the explanandum; he thinks that only the former sort of asymmetry obtains. I suggest that my account of the use of gappy laws will clarify both the sense in which Grünbaum is right (since an explanation and a tentative prediction can use similarly gappy laws which are similarly related to the known initial conditions and the result) and the sense in which, in such a case, we may contrast an entirely satisfactory explanation with a merely tentative prediction. Scriven (in his most recent statement, the review of Nagel's *Structure of Science*) says that 'we often pin down a factor as a cause by excluding other possible causes. Simple—but disastrous for the covering-law theory of explanation, because we can eliminate causes only for something *we know has occurred*. And if the grounds for our explanation of an event *have* to include knowledge of that event's occurrence, they cannot be used (without circularity) to predict the occurrence of that event' (p. 414). That is, the observation of this event in these circumstances may be a vital part of the evidence that justifies the particular causal explanation that we give of this event: it may itself go a long way toward establishing the elliptical law in relation to which we explain it (as I have shown in sect. 5), whereas a law used for prediction cannot thus rest on the observation of the event predicted. But as my account also shows, this does not introduce an asymmetry of Grünbaum's second sort, and is therefore not disastrous for the covering-law theory.

have a covering law, albeit a complex and perhaps elliptical one. Also, I have shown in sect. 5, and indicated briefly, for the functional dependence variants, in sect. 7 [both omitted from this volume], that the evidence which supports singular causal statements also supports general causal statements or covering laws, though again only complex and elliptical ones. Hempel recognized long ago that historical accounts can be interpreted as giving incomplete 'explanation sketches', rather than what he would regard as full explanations, which would require fully stated covering laws, and that such sketches are also common outside history. But in these terms what I am saying is that explanation sketches and the related elliptical laws are often all that we can discover, that they play a part in all sciences, that they can be supported and even established without being complete, and so not serve merely as preliminaries to or summaries of complete deductive explanations. If we modify the notion of a covering law to admit laws which not only are complex but also are known only in an elliptical form, the covering-law theory can accommodate many of the points that have been made in criticism of it, while preserving the structural similarity of explanation in history, and in the physical sciences. In this controversy, one point at issue has been the symmetry of explanation and prediction, and my account may help to resolve this dispute. It shows, in agreement with what Scriven has argued, how the actual occurrence of an event in the observed circumstances—the I_1 of my formal account in sect. 5—may be a vital part of the evidence which supports an explanation of that event, which shows that it was A that caused P on this occasion. A prediction, on the other hand, cannot rest on observation of the event predicted. Also, the gappy law which is sufficient for an explanation will not suffice for a prediction (or for a retrodiction): a statement of initial conditions together with a gappy law will not entail the assertion that a specific result will occur, though of course such a law may be, and often is, used to make tentative predictions the failure of which will not necessarily tell against the law. But the recognition of these differences between prediction and explanation does not affect the covering-law theory as modified by the recognition of elliptical laws.

Although what I have given is primarily an account of physical causation, it may be indirectly relevant to the understanding of human action and mental causation. It is sometimes suggested that our ability to recognize a single occurrence as an instance of mental causation is a feature which distinguishes mental causation from physical or 'Humean' causation.[29] But this suggestion

---

[29] See e.g. G. E. M. Anscombe, *Intention* (Oxford, 1957), esp. 16; J. Teichmann, 'Mental Cause and Effect', *Mind*, 70 (1961), 36–52. Teichmann speaks (p. 36) of 'the difference between them and ordinary (or "Humean") sequences of cause and effect' and says (p. 37) 'it is sometimes in order for the person who blinks to say absolutely dogmatically that the cause is such-and-such, and to say

arises from the use of too simple a regularity account of physical causation. If we first see clearly what we mean by singular causal statements in general, and how we can support such a statement by observation of the single sequence itself, even in a physical case, we shall be better able to contrast with this our awareness of mental causes, and to see whether the latter has any really distinctive features.

This account also throws light on both the form and the status of the 'causal principle', the deterministic assumption which is used in any application of the methods of eliminative induction. These methods need not presuppose determinism in general, but only that each specific phenomenon investigated by such a method is deterministic. Moreover, they require not only that the phenomenon should have some cause, but that there should be some restriction of the range of possibly relevant factors (at least to spatio-temporally neighbouring ones, as explained in sect. 5). Now the general causal principle, that every event has some cause, is so general that it is peculiarly difficult either to confirm or to disconfirm, and we might be tempted either to claim for it some *a priori* status, to turn it into a metaphysical absolute presupposition, or to dismiss it as vacuous. But the specific assumption that this phenomenon has some cause based somehow on factors drawn from this range, or even that this phenomenon has some neighbouring cause, is much more open to empirical confirmation and disconfirmation: indeed, the former can be conclusively falsified by the observation of a positive instance I_1 of P, and a negative case N_1 in which P does not occur, but where each of the factors in the given range is either present in both I_1 and N_1 or absent from both. This account, then, encourages us to regard the assumption as something to be empirically confirmed or disconfirmed. At the same time it shows that there must be some principle of the confirmation of hypotheses other than the eliminative methods themselves, since each such method rests on an empirical assumption.

this independently of his knowledge of any previously established correlations', and again, 'if the noise is a cause it seems to be one which is known to be such in a special way. It seems that while it is necessary for an observer to have knowledge of a previously established correlation between noises and Smith's jumpings, before he can assert that one causes the other, it is not necessary for Smith himself to have such knowledge.'

II

DEFECTS OF THE NECESSARY CONDITION ANALYSIS OF CAUSATION*

MICHAEL SCRIVEN

The foregoing analysis has represented causes as selected on pragmatic grounds from conditions which are (*a*) known to be possible causes, (*b*) known to be present in the case under consideration, and (*c*) not known to operate in a way contra-indicated by known data about the case.

But this only defines 'cause' in terms of 'possible cause'. Can we not proceed further and define 'possible cause' in terms of some combination of necessary and sufficient conditions, these being interpreted as simple regularity notions? The answer appears to be that we cannot. The concept of cause is fundamental to our conception of the world in much the same way as the concept of number: we cannot define it in terms of other notions without conceptual or ostensive[1] circularity.

It is probably best to see the notion of cause, like number, as systematically developed from a simple case which we can exhibit, though not define in non-causal terms. The existence of this developmental sequence does not establish the common idea that later members are simply complex combinations of the earlier ones. (Finding the sum of an infinite series is not done by a complex combination of counting procedures even though the calculus is a development from arithmetic.)

8.1. *Basic Experimental Case.* Suppose that whenever and however we produce C, E occurs, and that E never occurs unless C is produced (so that C is in a sense the only handle by means of which we can manipulate E). Then C is the cause of E. (We assume a normal experimental context throughout. E may also turn out to be a cause of C, e.g. where C and E are alterations in pressure and temperature of a cylinder of gas.)

* From *Philosophical Analysis and History*, ed. W. Dray (New York: Harper and Row, 1966), 258–62. Copyright © 1966 by William H. Dray. Reprinted by permission of HarperCollins, Publishers.

[1] Ostensive circularity afflicts the Russellian definition of a number, which can only be applied by someone with the capacity to count that number of quantifiers, and hence in an important sense presupposes possession of the concept. (Cf. Tarski's definition of truth.) Neither ostensive nor conceptual circularity are fatal to *all* the purposes of definitions, but generally make their use as eliminative or reductive devices unsatisfactory.

8.2. *Basic Observation Case.* Suppose that C just occurs on various occasions and is accompanied by (perhaps followed by) E, and E never occurs on any other occasions. C is the cause of E if (but not only if) we can conclude that C *would* always be accompanied by E, no matter how or when it was produced (i.e. if we can reduce it to Case 8.1). Since we assume that something is responsible for the occurrence of E (determinism) and C is at least always present, the great problem is to eliminate the possibility that some *other* antecedent of C and E, say X, is bringing them both about *independently.*[2] Thus, the correlation between the early and late symptoms of a disease has often been mistakenly identified as a causal connection until it is discovered both are due to a third factor, the infection itself.

Case 8.1 is immune to this difficulty, since when we experimentally control C we produce it at random moments, i.e. moments not determined by[3] any preceding environmental factor that could possibly determine E (we may use a table of random numbers, dice, a roulette wheel, a decimal clock, or an electronic randomizer).

8.3. *Compound Causes.* Suppose that we need to bring about not only C but also D in order to get E (and that D alone is not sufficient). We may call C and D *causal factors* or *co-causes* of E. Neither can be called *the* cause, except when the context changes so that one or the other can be regarded as a standing condition or an irrelevant factor.

8.4. *Multiple Causes.* If C and D are *each* sufficient to bring about E, and nothing else is, then whichever occurs is the cause. If both occur, one of them may not have had any effect on this occasion, a possibility which we check by examining the situation for the presence of known intermediate links which characterize the *modus operandi* of C and D, i.e. any sets of conditions 'C_1 or C_2 or . . .' (or 'D_1 or D_2 or . . .') which are necessary for C (or D) to act as the cause of E. This test does not apply where no such links are known, and since it is not logically necessary that there be any (C and E may be adjacent links in the chain, or differ only from a certain descriptive standpoint, or represent 'action at a distance'), the test is not part of the meaning, of course. But it is the historian's and the coroner's key test.

If one has brought about E before the other could, although it would have in time, we have a case of *independent over-determination* (Case 8.5), but only one cause.

---

[2] Of course, even if C is the cause of E, many antecedents of C bring it about and *hence* bring about E. To say X brings about C and E independently means *roughly* that prevention of C's occurrence will not prevent E's occurrence.

[3] Notice that this definition of 'random' itself involves the causal notion of 'determined by', just as the Case 8.1 description involves the notion of 'producing' C. Both are dispensable only in terms of other causal notions, e.g. those of 'independent and dependent variable', 'free act' (in a technical sense).

If both occur, both may have been effective, bringing about E simultaneously, or essentially simultaneously for the purpose at hand, which gives the case of *simultaneous over-determination* (Case 8.6)—for example, a firing squad—and neither factor can be identified as *the* cause (but cf. the compound cause, Case 8.3).

In any case of an effect for which there are multiple causes we are no longer able to infer to C from E, i.e. C is not a necessary condition for E. However, we can infer from E plus the absence of the other possible causes to C, and since the absence of the other causes is part of the surrounding circumstances, we might still regard the cause as 'necessary in the circumstances' or what Nagel calls 'contingently necessary'. But this situation is complicated by the possibility of over-determination, i.e. any cases of multiple causation where the causes are not mutually exclusive. If a revolution is over-determined, as such events frequently are, there are several factors present which will ensure its occurrence, one of which we may assume gets in first. It will be quite incorrect to say that this factor is contingently necessary for the effect if, *ex hypothesi*, the remaining circumstances are quite adequate to bring about the effect by themselves.

We might try to save the situation for the contingently necessary analysis by invoking the fact that the other factors would not bring about the effect at the same time, and we might argue that the effect we are trying to explain is a revolution at the particular time it took place (i.e. the contrast state is peace at that moment). Unfortunately, this possibility is undermined by a species of over-determination which we may call *linked over-determination*. There the factors are not independent; the circumstances are such that the very act of preventing C from occurring will bring about D which will itself cause E ('Damned if he does and damned if he doesn't'). Suppose a radical group attempts a *coup d'état*; the effort is watched attentively by the army, which will take action if the coup is unsuccessful, but not otherwise. In such a case, where the political coup may be slower moving than the military, we cannot argue that the government's downfall would occur at a different time.

Suppose we argue that the cause is necessary to explain the way in which the collapse occurred, if not the time. But *many* facts about the way the collapse occurred are, in a particular case, such that the cause is not a necessary condition for *their* occurrence, e.g. whether communication of the crisis details between members of the tottering cabinet was telephonic or telegraphic. The necessary condition analyst replies that these facts are not historically significant, not relevant to the contrast in which he is interested. He *is* explaining the *exact* historical occurrence, but only historically, i.e. not with an equal interest in all aspects of it. How do we determine which details are historically relevant—since, after all, the delay involved in telegraphing could well be crucial in some such cases? The answer must be, it seems, that it depends on its consequences for the occurrence of the item of principal interest. Alas, this is a *causal* consideration and so we have not analysed cause in terms of necessary condition but in terms of necessary condition and cause. The attempt is not without value, but it is not a reductive analysis. It reflects the good methodological principle of building up a case by finding clues which in their totality can *only* be explained by the hypothesis that C caused E.[4]

In general, then, the search for an acausal definition of 'cause' turns out to be ultimately as unsuccessful as the search for an amoral definition of 'moral'. It is, however, no less illuminating, and in the present discussion we have uncovered two useful approximations to the notion of cause, formulated in terms of considerations which will at least avoid the common failure to allow for over-determination. It may also be seen from the discussion how historical and psychological analysis proceeds by the development of knowledge of possible causes and their *modus operandi*—a knowledge very unlike explicit knowledge of scientific laws—which is applied to the explanation of particular cases by the process of evidential, formal, and contextual elimination described above.

---

[4] *Technical footnote*: 'C is the only possible cause of E in circumstances C'' is not the same as 'C is a necessary condition for E in C'' not only for the reasons given (which show the first to include cases the second excludes unless made equivalent by circularity) but because, embarrassingly enough, the second description would identify many an *effect* of E as E's cause. For, with a suitable choice of C', there are many effects of E (call them $G_1, G_2, \ldots$) whose occurrence it is possible to infer from the occurrence of E, i.e. the Gs must occur if E does—in other words, their occurrence is necessary, given E's occurrence in C'—which makes the Gs causes of F on the above proposed definition. It is possible to salvage the necessary condition analysis here by using a slightly different and possibly more natural definition of necessary condition—unfortunately, it involves a causal notion. An analogous series of difficulties attends the notion of a cause as a non-redundant member of *some* set of conditions which are jointly sufficient for the effect. This handles linked over-determination nicely, but does less well on independent over-determination, where it requires an accessory stipulation about the presence of intervening links, 'links' being a causal notion. Nor can causes be distinguished from effects on this definition. It is possible to give a proof of the equivalence of these two notions under certain plausible assumptions, e.g. the assumption of the thesis of detectivism—the converse of determinism—which asserts that different causes have different effects. It seems clear that the distinction between cause and effect is linked to the *range* of warranted counterfactual claims; we can't say flatly that if C hadn't occurred then E wouldn't have, but the weaknesses in this are less than and different from those in the claim that if G (one of E's effects) hadn't occurred, E couldn't (wouldn't?) have occurred.

III

CAUSES AND EVENTS:
MACKIE ON CAUSATION

JAEGWON KIM

Any discussion of causation must presuppose an ontological framework of entities among which causal relations are to hold, and also an accompanying logical and semantical framework in which these entities can be talked about. We often take *events* as causes and also as effects; but entities of other sorts (if indeed they are 'other sorts'), such as *conditions, states, phenomena, processes*, and sometimes even *facts*, are also pressed into service when we engage in causal talk, although with these there is some controversy as to their suitability as terms of causal relations. Coherent causal talk is possible only within a coherent ontological and logical framework of events and perhaps also other entities of appropriate categories; and the adequacy of an analysis of causal relations may very much depend on the sort of ontological and logical scheme underlying it. What I propose to do in this paper is to examine, from an ontological and logical point of view, a recent notable contribution by J. L. Mackie[1] to the analysis of causation. Although what we will say is relevant to an evaluation of the substantive contents of Mackie's analysis, our primary concern is with the ontology of events implicit in Mackie's discussion. We begin with a brief exposition of the central points of Mackie's analysis of singular causal statements.

1

The central idea in Mackie's conception of causation is that a cause of an event is neither a necessary nor a sufficient condition of that event, although it is a condition of a sort closely related to it. Briefly, a cause is often 'an *insufficient* but *necessary* part of a condition which is itself *unnecessary* but *sufficient* for the result' (p. 34); Mackie calls a condition of this kind an 'INUS condition'. As an example: A short-circuit is said to be the cause of a

---

[1] 'Causes and Conditions', *American Philosophical Quarterly*, 2/4 (1965), 245–64, repr. in part as Ch. I above. With some exceptions, parenthetical references are to pages of this volume.

fire in a house. But it is neither necessary nor sufficient for that fire, since
the fire might have been caused by a short-circuit elsewhere or the overturning of a lighted oil stove; and also, in the absence of inflammable material
near the short-circuit, the fire would not have occurred. So in what sense is
the short-circuit said to be the cause of the fire?

At least part of the answer is that there is a set of conditions (of which some are positive
and some are negative), including the presence of inflammable material, the absence of
a suitably placed sprinkler, and no doubt quite a number of others, which combined
with the short-circuit constituted a complex condition that was sufficient for the house's
catching fire—sufficient, but not necessary, for the fire could have started in other ways.
Also, of *this* complex condition, the short-circuit was an indispensable part: the other
parts of this condition, conjoined with one another in the absence of the short-circuit,
would not have caused the fire. The short-circuit which is said to have caused the fire
is thus an indispensable part of a complex sufficient (but not necessary) condition of
the fire. (p. 34)

A more general definition of 'INUS condition' is needed. Since the exact
wording of Mackie's formulation is important, I quote again:

Let 'A' stand for the INUS condition—in our example, the occurrence of a short-
circuit at that place—and let 'B' and '$\overline{C}$' (that is, 'not-C', or the absence of C) stand
for the other conditions, positive and negative, which were needed along with A
to form a sufficient condition of the fire—in our example, B might be the presence of inflammable material, $\overline{C}$ the absence of a suitably placed sprinkler. Then
the conjunction $AB\overline{C}$ represents a sufficient condition of the fire, and one that contains no redundant factors; that is, $AB\overline{C}$ is a minimal sufficient condition for the fire.
(pp. 34–5)

Now the disjunction of all the minimal sufficient conditions of a given event,
assuming that there is only a finite number of them, constitutes a necessary
and sufficient condition of it. Mackie defines 'INUS condition' thus:

A is an INUS condition of a result P if and only if for some X and for some Y, (AX or
Y) is a necessary and sufficient condition of P, but A is not a sufficient condition of P
and X is not a sufficient condition of P. (p. 35)

Here, 'X' represents the conjunction of terms (possibly just one) that together
with A constitute a minimal sufficient condition of P; 'Y' stands for the
disjunction of other minimal sufficient conditions; both X and Y must be
non-null.

Before the singular causal judgement 'A caused P' can be analysed,
one more notion is needed. A condition A is said to be *at least an* INUS
condition of P provided there is a necessary and sufficient condition of P
that has one of these forms: (AX or Y), (A or Y), AX, A. That is, A is at least
an INUS condition of P if and only if either A is an INUS condition or A
itself is a minimal sufficient condition or a component in the only minimal

sufficient condition of P or A is by itself a necessary and sufficient condition of P.

Mackie's analysis of 'A caused P' is this:

(i) A is at least an INUS condition of P.

(ii) A was present on the occasion in question.

(iii) The factors represented by the 'X', if any, in the formula for the necessary and sufficient condition were present on the occasion in question.

(iv) Every disjunct in 'Y' that does not contain 'A' as a conjunct was absent on the occasion in question.

Mackie does not claim that the conjunction of these four clauses is a complete analysis of 'A caused P'; his only explicit claim is that this is 'an important part of the concept of causation'; Mackie suggests certain refinements, chiefly by the use of the notion of 'causal field', but these do not concern us here. What is of greater importance to us is Mackie's explanation of 'necessary condition' and 'sufficient condition'.

Thus if we said that a short-circuit here was a necessary condition for a fire in this house, we should be saying that there are true universal propositions from which, together with true statements about the characteristics of this house, and together with the supposition that a short-circuit did not occur here, it would follow that the house did not catch fire. (p. 49)

This explains 'necessary condition'; 'sufficient condition' is to be explained on the same model, which is to say: 'A is a sufficient condition of P' amounts to 'there are true universal propositions from which, together with additional singular premises and the statement that A was present, it follows that P occurred'. As Mackie points out, his approach is to construe statements of necessity and sufficiency on the model of the counterfactual 'If A had not occurred, P would not have occurred' and the factual conditional 'Since A occurred, P occurred.' Mackie has given elsewhere[2] what may be called a 'nomic-inferential model' of counterfactual conditionals; the essence of this analysis is that a counterfactual of the form 'If P, then Q' is a covert assertion of the existence of an argument whose premises include universal laws, the indicative form of P, and other singular statements of 'relevant conditions', and whose conclusion is the indicative form of Q.

To recapitulate: singular causal assertions are explained in terms of the notion of 'at least an INUS condition'; a cause of an event is at least an INUS condition of it. The notion of INUS condition in turn is explained on the basis

---

[2] 'Counterfactuals and Causal Laws', in R. J. Butler (ed.), *Analytical Philosophy* (Oxford, 1962). See also Nicholas Rescher, 'Belief-Contravening Suppositions', *Philosophical Review*, 70/2 (1961), 176–96; Ernest Nagel, *The Structure of Science* (New York, 1961), 68–73.

of 'necessary condition' and 'sufficient condition', and these are analysed in terms of counterfactual conditionals. Finally, counterfactuals are explained on the nomic-inferential model. It is at this point that laws and regularities enter into singular causal judgements; according to Mackie, his analysis can be characterized as a form of the regularity theory of causation.

2

Mackie's chief concern is to analyse singular causal statements, e.g. 'This short-circuit caused this fire.' And the letters he uses, 'A', 'B', 'C', ..., are presumably variables taking as values concrete individual events occurring at specific times and places or, at least, dummy variables standing in place of singular terms (names and descriptions) for individual events. Mackie refers to causes and effects as 'events' and also as 'conditions'; 'event' presumably is being used as a wider term which comprehends 'condition', and moreover it must be understood in the broad sense in which it refers to 'states' and 'standing conditions' as well as events narrowly conceived as involving changes.

What sorts of expression can replace these variables over events? That is to say, what sorts of expression can be used to refer to, describe, or name concrete individual events? The following are some of the expressions Mackie uses to specify individual events:

'A fire broke out in a certain house'
'the cause of the fire'
'this house's catching fire at this time'
'the overturning of a lighted oil stove'
'the presence of inflammable material'
'the absence of a suitably placed sprinkler'

The first is a full sentence, and the rest, with the possible exception of the second, are all nominalized sentences. And with the possible exception of the first, they are to be taken as singular terms referring uniquely or purporting to refer uniquely to individual events; they can flank the identity sign ('the overturning of a lighted oil stove = the cause of the fire') and give way to bound variables. Presumably there would be no theoretical objection to using other kinds of names for individual events; for example, 'the most unforgettable event in Herbert's life', 'Larry', 'event #300', etc.

Now, what is interesting is that Mackie uses such connectives as 'and', 'not', and 'or' to compound event names; for example, a minimal sufficient condition is represented by the 'conjunction' '$AB\bar{C}$', and the bar on 'C' is akin to or is identical with the negation sign. And Mackie represents the necessary and sufficient condition of a given event in 'disjunctive normal form', and this concept presupposes that such truth-functional operations as conjunction, negation, and disjunction are meaningfully defined for event names. Further, Mackie often refers to events represented by such compound expressions as 'ABC' as 'complex events'. Thus, if A, B, and C are 'simple events', then ABC is a complex event; so presumably are $AB\overline{C}$, $\overline{A}BC$, and so on. But precisely how are we to understand these compound event names and the 'complex events' they are supposed to refer to?

Take the simple events A, B, and the complex event AB. What is the nature of the conjunction in 'AB'? One thing certain is that this cannot be understood in the sense of the usual logical conjunction 'and' as in 'Oscar *and* Edith like Mexican food', which is straightforwardly equivalent to 'Oscar likes Mexican food *and* Edith likes Mexican food'. For 'AB is a sufficient condition of P' is not to be taken in the sense of 'A is a sufficient condition of P and B is a sufficient condition of P'. It is perhaps more akin to 'Oscar *and* Edith *together* weigh 260 pounds', where 'Oscar and Edith' denotes a single composite entity (i.e. the 'sum' of Oscar and Edith in the sense of the calculus of individuals). This means that we cannot just depend on the familiar meaning of the sentential connective 'and' to understand what 'AB' means; what seems to be a new mode of linguistic construction is involved here which requires explanation. When we consider disjunction and negation, the situation at first blush is even more puzzling. In the case of ordinary singular terms, e.g. 'Socrates', '$2 + 5$', and 'the husband of Calpurnia', negation makes no sense; consider 'not-Socrates', 'not-$(2 + 5)$', etc. Nor do their disjunctions make sense; there is no object corresponding to such expressions as 'Socrates or Cicero', '7 or the colour blue', etc. The reason disjunction and negation appear to be meaningful for event names may be that event names are often nominalized sentences, although even here we would be hard pressed to attach a meaning to 'the cause of the fire or Socrates' death' or to 'not-the cause of the fire' as a singular term naming a single event.

But perhaps a coherent explanation of these operations is possible. What needs explaining is precisely how the complex events AB, $A \vee B$, and $\overline{A}$ are functionally related to the simple events A and B. And Mackie provides a hint:

If 'Y' represents a single conjunction of factors, then it was absent if at least one of its conjuncts was absent; if it represents a disjunction, then it was absent if each of its disjuncts was absent. (p. 37)

'$\overline{C}$' (that is, 'not-C', or the absence of C . . .). (p. 35)

This suggests a systematic procedure of compounding event names parallel to the truth-functional compounding of sentences. But what precisely is the relationship between the 'complex' events designated by compound event names '$\bar{A}$', 'AB', and '$A \vee B$' on the one hand and the simple events designated by 'A' and 'B'? Following Mackie's hint, we might first try something like this:

$\bar{A} = (Ie)$ [e occurs if and only if A does not occur];[3]

$AB = (Ie)$ [e occurs if and only if both A and B occur];

$A \vee B = (Ie)$ [e occurs if and only if A occurs or B occurs]

One trouble with this way of explaining event composition is that there is no reason to believe that for event A there exists a unique event $\bar{A}$ as defined; given the usual truth-functional meaning of 'if and only if' as a biconditional, there would be too many events satisfying the description; similar comments apply to 'AB' and '$A \vee B$'.

Thus one may wish to strengthen these definitions by introducing some sort of modality in the definiens; an obvious choice would be to insert the qualifier 'necessarily true' or 'logically true' just after the description operator:

$\bar{A} = (Ie)N$ [e occurs if and only if A does not occur];

$AB = (Ie)N$ [e occurs if and only if both A and B occur];

$A \vee B = (Ie)N$ [e occurs if and only if either A occurs or B occurs]

when we use 'N' to abbreviate 'necessarily'. We shall ignore here the familiar difficulties involving the use of modal terms like this to govern open sentences. Assuming provisional adequacy of these definitions, we can go on to define 'disjunctive normal form', 'truth-functional implication', 'truth-functional equivalence', and other notions for event descriptions along the obvious lines. The following would then be a direct consequence of these definitions:

> *Equivalence condition:* Truth-functionally equivalent event names and descriptions designate the same event.[4]

All that needs to be assumed here is that truth-functionally equivalent sentences are interchangeable *salva veritate* in contexts prefixed by the necessity operator 'N'. On this interpretation of event composition it is clear that the complexity of 'complex events' pertains not to events *per se* but to event

---

[3] We use 'I' as the description operator, and 'e' as a variable taking individual events as values. We say 'e occurs' where Mackie would say 'e is present'.

[4] Although Mackie does not explicitly recognize this condition, he seems tacitly to accept it; see e.g. 'Causes and Conditions' (complete article), 255, where he talks about representing the necessary and sufficient condition of an event in disjunctive normal form. We leave aside the interesting and important question whether the stronger form of the equivalence condition to the effect that all and *only* truth-functionally equivalent event descriptions designate the same event is a consequence of these definitions, and if not, what further assumptions are needed to make it one.

descriptions. For the equivalence condition tells us that there is no strict correspondence between the complexity of a given compound event name and the event designated by it; to take a simple example, A is the same event as $A\bar{B} \vee AB$. In general, the orthographic features of an event description are not a reliable guide to the ontological structure of the event it describes; and there is no more reason to expect this than to expect the complexity of the description of an object to be an indication of the complexity of the object described.

3

Does the foregoing provide a workable logical and ontological framework for a theory of causation, and more specifically for Mackie's analysis of causal relations? I believe there is ample reason for thinking that the answer is in the negative; moreover, it is not at all clear that there is any coherent ontological framework underlying Mackie's analysis. In this section we shall bring out some of the problems and difficulties; in the next section we shall propose an alternative scheme in which Mackie's analysis could be restated.

Let us first consider the notion of 'minimal sufficient condition', which plays a crucial role in Mackie's definition of causation. The only explanation we get from Mackie is this: 'Then the conjunction '$AB\bar{C}$' represents a sufficient condition of the fire, and one that contains no redundant factors; that is, $AB\bar{C}$ is a minimal sufficient condition for the fire' (p. 35). This suggests the following definition:

> The event $A_1A_2 \ldots A_n$ is a minimal sufficient condition for an event P if and only if it is a sufficient condition for P, and, for each $i(1 \le i \le n)$, $A_1 \ldots A_{i-1}.A_{i+1} \ldots A_n$ is not a sufficient condition for P.

Assume AB is a minimal sufficient condition for P; we can then show, for almost any event C, that C is an INUS condition for P and, hence, a candidate as a cause of P. For, given that AB is minimal-sufficient for P, it follows that $C(\bar{C} \vee A)B$ is also minimal-sufficient (unless $\bar{C} \vee A$ amounts just to A, or else C alone or together with B is sufficient for P). Now, Mackie might say that, when we consider a conjunction of 'factors' for minimal sufficiency, each conjunct must be a single letter; and, more generally, that the necessary and sufficient condition, if it exists, of an event must be represented by a disjunctive normal form each disjunct of which could then be considered as a minimal sufficient condition for that event.[5]

[5] Mackie writes: 'For some Z, Z is a necessary and sufficient condition for the phenomenon P in the field F, that is, all FP are Z and all FZ are P, and Z is a condition represented by some formula in disjunctive normal form all of whose constituents are taken from the range of possibly relevant factors, A, B, C, D, E, etc.' (ibid.).

If we follow this line, the troublesome $C(\overline{C} \vee A)B$ reduces to CAB and the difficulty vanishes. Taking this course, however, does have disadvantages; for one thing, it prevents us from taking 'disjunctive events' as INUS conditions and hence as causes; for another, it requires us to identify certain events as 'simple events' for which we shall have non-compound event descriptions. The real difficulty with this approach is seen, however, when we reflect that sentences do not generally have unique disjunctive normal forms (unique up to the order of disjuncts and the order of conjuncts within each disjunct); for the following two disjunctive normal expressions are logically equivalent: $A \vee \overline{A}B$ and $B \vee \overline{B}A$. By the equivalence condition, these two represent the same event, and it is natural to assume that if one of them is a necessary and sufficient condition for an event P, then so must be the other. But, according to the expression '$A \vee \overline{A}B$', the event $\overline{A}$ is an INUS condition for P; according to '$B \vee \overline{B}A$', $\overline{B}$ is an INUS condition for P; further, these expressions are equivalent to '$A \vee B$' which sanctions neither $\overline{A}$ nor $\overline{B}$ as an INUS condition of P. Which one of these—or perhaps the complete disjunctive normal form, in this case '$AB \vee \overline{A}B \vee A\overline{B}$'—should be picked, or indeed whether it makes any difference which is picked, is a matter requiring further examination.

For this particular case, however, one might say that '$A \vee B$' is the disjunctive normal form that must be used in determining minimal sufficient conditions; one might say that from '$A \vee B$' we know A and B to be each a minimal sufficient condition for a certain event, from which it follows that neither $\overline{A}B$ nor $\overline{B}A$ is minimal-sufficient. But then are we to require in general that the *shortest* disjunctive normal form be the basis for determining minimal sufficient conditions? Although it is true that any truth-functional formula has a shortest normal equivalent,[6] it is not true that there is a *unique* shortest normal equivalent (up to, of course, the order of disjuncts and the order of conjuncts within each disjunct): e.g. $A\overline{B} \vee \overline{A}B \vee A\overline{C}$ and $A\overline{B} \vee \overline{A}B \vee B\overline{C}$. According to the first of these equivalent normal formulas, $A\overline{C}$ is minimal sufficient; according to the second, $B\overline{C}$ is minimal sufficient. Shall we then say that the disjunction of *all* the minimal sufficient conditions, which in this case might be $A\overline{B} \vee \overline{A}B \vee A\overline{C} \vee B\overline{C}$, must be considered the correct representation? Here, the situation seems too fluid for a definite answer. Much deeper analysis of event discourse would be required before one could state and defend a definite stand on this problem.

Let us briefly return to the original definition of 'minimal sufficient condition'. *Qua* definition it is defective; it does not permit the elimination of

---

[6] See W. V. Quine, 'Cores and Prime Implicants', repr. in Quine, *Selected Logical Papers* (New York, 1966).

the defined predicate 'is a minimal sufficient condition' from all contexts; it permits such elimination only when the event in question is represented in a certain logical form, i.e. conjunction of single-event names with no redundancies; by the use of the definition we cannot eliminate the defined term from, say, 'My most unforgettable event was a minimal sufficient condition for my most embarrassing event.' As stated, whether or not an event is a minimal sufficient condition for another would depend on the logical form of the particular description chosen for it; but the equivalence condition shows that no reliable inference can be made from the logical form of an event name to the ontological structure of the event named by it. A better definition of 'minimal sufficiency' would be something like this:

> An event E is a minimal sufficient condition for P if and only if it is representable (i.e. is named) by an expression of the form '$A_1 \ldots A_n$' containing no redundancies such that $A_1 \ldots A_n$ is sufficient for P and the deletion of any of the As results in a condition not sufficient for P.

This makes the concept of minimal sufficiency very much dependent on the particular language used, and it is likely to make it easy for any sufficient condition of an event to be a minimal sufficient condition of it as well.

It seems to me that the difficulties under discussion are symptomatic of an underlying confusion of events with their descriptions, a confusion which, I believe, stems from our common use of full sentences and nominalized sentences to pick out events. This confusion manifests itself in the uncritical assumption that truth-functional compositions of event names are intelligible without much further ado; it also leads to the talk of 'disjunctive events', 'conjunctive events', and 'complex events'. A comprehensive theory of events would have to have room for the concept of complex event; intuitively, an earthquake or the pitching of a baseball is a *complex* event that has other events as *parts*; but it would be an illusion to count on the sentential connectives applied to event descriptions to yield a clear explanation of these notions.

The sort of ambivalence with respect to events and their descriptions becomes apparent also when we examine Mackie's explanations of 'necessary condition' and 'sufficient condition'. Mackie's analysis of 'necessary condition' comes to this:[7]

> A is a necessary condition of P if and only if there are true universal propositions L and true singular statements S such that L and S together

---

[7] See the quotation at the end of sect. 1, p. 62 above.

with the statement that *A* did not occur logically imply the statement that *P* did not occur.

This involves the unintelligible assumption that for a given event *A* there is *the* statement that *A* occurred. Take as *A* the death of Socrates. What is *the* statement that asserts the occurrence of this event? Is it 'Socrates died' or 'Xantippe's husband died' or perhaps some other statement? Which of these statements is chosen makes a great deal of difference to the question what other statements are implied by it. The source of this difficulty lies in the fact that the definition involves a cross-reference into the context of quotation, since the expressions '*A* did not occur' and '*P* did not occur' in the definiens are in effect as though sealed with quotation marks.[8]

One final point concerning Mackie's framework of events: three of the four classes in Mackie's analysis of '*A* caused *P*' have to do with the existence or non-existence ('presence' or 'absence' in his terminology) of certain events. The first of these clauses (which we may call 'existence conditions') requires that the cause event, *A*, must be 'present on the occasion in question'. What could this mean? The qualification 'on the occasion in question' suggests that *A* perhaps is not an individual event but rather a generic event or a property, and that the clause in effect says that the generic event must be exemplified on the occasion in question, that is, an individual event falling under this generic event must exist on that occasion. If '*A*' is a bona fide singular term denoting a particular individual event, the further requirement that *A* must exist 'on the occasion in question' over and beyond the existence of *A* would seem to be completely otiose. This becomes especially clear when the last clause is considered, to the effect that every minimal sufficient condition other than that in which the cause event figures must *not* exist 'on the occasion in question'. Now, this cannot be construed as meaning that these events must not exist at all, for then it would be hard to see how they could figure as sufficient conditions for any event. But it is also hard to make sense of the requirement that these events must exist *but not on the occasion in question*. If so, where and when? Far enough away from *P* not to have caused it? In that case, why should they figure at all as sufficient conditions of *P*?

[8] Let me briefly mention here what seems to be an incongruity between Mackie's analysis of causation and his analysis of 'necessary condition' and 'sufficient condition'. The point of introducing the notion of INUS condition is just that what is said to be the cause of an event is often not a necessary or a sufficient condition, *when taken alone*, for that event. This implies that a sufficient condition for an event, as Mackie understands it here, is a *fully* sufficient condition even if taken alone by itself; and similarly, for a necessary condition. If this is so, it is difficult to understand why, in his explanation of necessity and sufficiency, Mackie allows the use of auxiliary singular statements of 'relevant conditions' (i.e. *S* in the reconstructed definition in the text above).

It is unclear that the existence conditions make any sense at all if 'A', 'B', etc., are construed as denoting individual events. If 'A' is a genuine singular term, it would seem that the first clause 'A is at least an INUS condition' entails the existence of A, making the second clause requiring the existence of A redundant; a non-existent event cannot be an INUS condition for any event. If, of course, A were taken as a generic event rather than an individual event, good sense could be made of 'A is at least an INUS condition' even in the absence of any individual events falling under A. (But notice that A as a generic event must still exist.) So perhaps $A, B, \ldots$, are best taken as universals, and 'present on the occasion in question' and 'absent on the occasion in question' should be understood in the sense of 'exemplified on the occasion in question' and 'not exemplified on the occasion in question', respectively. In fact, in spite of Mackie's announced aim of analysing singular causal statements, it is doubtful that the entities he is concerned with can consistently be interpreted as spatio-temporally bounded individual events.

To continue a little further in this vein, consider the rule governing the operation of negation on event names. The idea here is that, given an event name 'A', we can construct a compound event name by placing the negation sign over 'A'. But what event does this compound event description '$\bar{A}$' designate? The rule says that it designates that event which necessarily occurs if and only if A does not occur. But if the event A exists, then the event $\bar{A}$ does not exist, and '$\bar{A}$' fails to refer. Thus, the operation of negation as explained is not a well-defined notion; in the usual mathematical sense, it does not qualify as an operation; in this sense it differs from sentential negation, the concept of 'negate' in the calculus of individuals, and set-theoretical complementation. Moreover, given that an event A does not exist, does the event $A \vee B$ just come to B? The scheme we provisionally attributed to Mackie does not entail that it does; in fact, it entails that it does not, unless the occurrence of A is entailed by the occurrence of B. What then is the exact difference in hard cash value between $A \vee B$ and B, when A does not exist? On the other hand, if we adopt a scheme in which $A \vee B$ does not turn out to be identical with B when A does not exist, Mackie's notion of causation faces an imminent danger of collapse; for suppose A is an INUS condition of P which is also a cause of P. According to Mackie's analysis of 'A caused P', this means that Y in the complex necessary and sufficient condition $AX \vee Y$ of P does not exist (unless it happens to contain a disjunct that contains A as a conjunct), and $AX \vee Y$ reduces to AX, from which it follows that A is no longer an INUS condition.

4

It should by now be clear that the logical and ontological foundations of Mackie's discussion of causal relations are in urgent need of repair; in fact, 'repair' is too mild a word, since Mackie does not seem aware of the problem of the underlying logic of event talk for his analysis of causation. And the absence of such ontological awareness is not limited to Mackie; it is common to almost all the recent writings on causation and other related problems involving event talk, although, happily, an explicit recognition has lately been given by some philosophers to the importance of the ontological issues in connection with the problem of analysing causation.[9] In this final section, I shall attempt to restate Mackie's theory of causal relations within a frame-work of events elaborated elsewhere.[10]

The relations of necessity and sufficiency seem best suited for properties and for property-like entities such as generic states and events; and their application to individual events and states seems best explained as being derivative from their application to properties and generic events and states. Typically, we say things like: 'Being an equiangular triangle is a necessary and sufficient condition for being an equilateral triangle,' 'Exposure to sunlight is necessary for the process of photosynthesis,' and so on. Even when we attribute necessity to an 'object', as in 'Oxygen is necessary for combustion,' this is easily paraphrased in terms of generic states and events, as 'The presence of oxygen is necessary for combustion.' But since Mackie's chief objective is to analyse singular causal statements, we must have a way of relating the talk of necessity and sufficiency to individual events that are spatio-temporally localized. Thus, we need entities that possess both an element of generality and an element of particularity; the former is necessary for making sense of the relations of necessity and sufficiency, and the latter for making sense of singular causal judgements.

Such entities are ready at hand, however, since realizations of properties at particular space–time regions or by objects (if one accepts some sort of substance ontology) fill the bill; they are general in that they involve proper-ties, and particular in that they involve particular space–time regions or objects. Thus, we take an event to be the exemplifying of an empirical property by an object at a time (alternatively, at a space–time region, but we

[9] Donald Davidson, 'Causal Relations', *Journal of Philosophy*, 64/21 (1967), 691–703 [repr. as Ch. IV below]; Zeno Vendler, *Linguistics in Philosophy* (Ithaca, NY, 1967), chs. 5, 6. See also my 'Events and their Descriptions: Some Considerations', in Nicholas Rescher *et al.* (eds.), *Essays in Honor of Carl G. Hempel* (Dordrecht, 1969).
[10] 'Causation, Nomic Subsumption, and the Concept of Event', *Journal of Philosophy*, 70 (1973), 217–36.

shall adopt the former approach); as we use it, the term 'event' must be understood in the wider sense in which it refers to states as well as events in the narrower sense involving changes. The approach being advocated here is well entrenched in the ordinary language: the entities we call 'events' are often those referred to by nominalized sentences of English, especially the gerundial nominalizations; e.g. 'the death of Socrates', 'the sinking of the Titanic', 'Brutus's stabbing Caesar', 'Jack's breaking his leg', and so on. We can take these as singular terms referring to individual events (although of course they must further be supplemented by explicit specification of dates); a bit more formally, we shall use the notation '$[x, P, t]$' to refer to the event of x's exemplifying property P at time t; this is obviously generalizable to yield polyadic events, but this further step is not necessary for the purposes of this paper.

Mackie's 'A', 'B', . . . are best taken as referring to properties—or generic events, i.e. properties whose exemplification by an object is an event. Mackie wants to say that a formula like '$ABC \vee CDF \vee \ldots$' specifies a sufficient condition for an event P and that each disjunct, e.g. 'ABC', specifies a minimal sufficient condition for P. This manner of speaking has certain important disadvantages; for one, it assumes (as Mackie is aware) that there are only finitely many minimal sufficient conditions for P, and, what is more important, it presupposes the compounding of property expressions for which we have nothing like an accepted theory. I think we would do better by talking about *sets* of properties rather than about conjunctive and disjunctive properties. Let us say that a set of properties is *realized* or *exemplified* on a given occasion provided each property in the set is exemplified on that occasion. Assuming, then, that the notions of necessity and sufficiency as applied to properties or generic events are understood, we can capture the import of the statement '$ABC \vee CDF$ is a necessary and sufficient condition of P' by the statement 'Whenever the set of properties $[A, B, C]$ or the set $[C, D, F]$ is realized, P is realized, and also conversely.' And we say that a set of properties is a minimal sufficient set for P just in case the set is sufficient for P but no proper subset of it is sufficient for P. More generally, we say that a set of properties is sufficient for a property if and only if, whenever the set is realized, the property is also realized; and similarly for necessity. The notion of INUS condition for properties can be explained thus: A is an INUS property of P if and only if there is some unique family S_{AP} of sets s_i of properties such that, for some $i, A \in s_i$; for each $i, s_i \in S_{AP}$ if and only if s_i is minimal sufficient for P; and S_{AP} is a necessary condition of P (by which we mean that if P is realized some member of S_{AP} must also be realized).

We now come to the all-important notion of INUS condition for individual events:

$[x, A, t_1]$ is an INUS condition of $[y, P, t]$ if and only if

(i) $A(x, t_1), P(y, t)$;

(ii) A is an INUS property of P;

(iii) some set s_i in S_{AP} containing A and at least one other property is realized on the occasion of $[x, A, t_1]$;

(iv) S_{AP} contains at least one set other than s_i;

(v) no set of properties in S_{AP} other than s_i is realized on the occasion of $[y, P, t]$.

The notion of 'at least an INUS condition' is similarly definable. And finally '$[x, A, t_1]$ caused $[y, P, t]$' goes simply into '$[x, A, t_1]$ is at least an INUS condition of $[y, P, t]$'.

There is, however, a gaping hole in the foregoing account which was covered over by the unexplained expression 'on the occasion of'. It should be clear why the proviso 'on the occasion of $[x, A, t_1]$' is necessary in (iii), for the realizations of the properties in s_i in widely separated spatio-temporal regions would be irrelevant; the properties in this set must be 'jointly realized'. Also the import of the qualification 'on the occasion of $[y, P, t]$' in (v) is evident; we do not want to say that these sets are *never* realized; we only want to deny that this particular realization of P followed the realization of one of these sets. This shows that the conditions (i) to (v) are not quite sufficient to capture the definiendum; we must add that $[y, P, t]$ was the realization of P 'on the occasion of' $[x, A, t_1]$; we can think of (i) as modified to incorporate this.[11] So there are two general problems here: first, how do we characterize generally the set of individual events which jointly cause some event? (My striking of the match and the presence of oxygen *in this room*, not my striking of the match and the presence of oxygen in Boise, Idaho, make up such a set.) And, second, how, for each cause event (or set of events), do we generally pick out *its* effect event, and not some other event of the same kind (i.e. whose constitutive property is the same) which happens to occur at the same time? (My striking of the match causes its lighting, not the lighting of Jones's match which he scratched at the same time.)

These are difficult questions which we cannot discuss here, and I do not know of satisfactory general solutions to them. We can try imposing certain temporal and spatial conditions on causes and effects;[12] we can perhaps try complicating the definition of 'the set s of properties is sufficient for the property P' by incorporating into it appropriate relations relating the realiz-

---

[11] Recall Mackie's definition of 'A caused P' quoted earlier: '(ii) A was present *on the occasion in question* . . .' (my italics).

[12] For elaboration of this theme as well as a somewhat more detailed discussion of the problems, see my 'Causation, Nomic Subsumption, and the Concept of Event'.

ations of the properties in s and the realization of P. In any case, these are substantive issues in the analysis of causal relations and not peculiar to the particular ontological scheme I have sketched here for such an analysis; and my objective in this paper has been the limited one of clarifying and restructuring the ontological foundation of Mackie's theory of singular causal statements.

IV

CAUSAL RELATIONS*

DONALD DAVIDSON

What is the logical form of singular causal statements like: 'The flood caused the famine,' 'The stabbing caused Caesar's death,' 'The burning of the house caused the roasting of the pig'? This question is more modest than the question how we know such statements are true, and the question whether they can be analysed in terms of, say, constant conjunction. The request for the logical form is modest because it is answered when we have identified the logical or grammatical roles of the words (or other significant stretches) in the sentences under scrutiny. It goes beyond this to define, analyse, or set down axioms governing, particular words or expressions.

1

According to Hume, 'we may define a cause to be an object, followed by another, and where all the objects similar to the first are followed by objects similar to the second.' This definition pretty clearly suggests that causes and effects are entities that can be named or described by singular terms; probably events, since one can follow another. But in the *Treatise*, under 'rules by which to judge of causes and effects', Hume says that 'where several different objects produce the same effect, it must be by means of some quality, which we discover to be common among them. For as like effects imply like causes, we must always ascribe the causation to the circumstances wherein we discover the resemblance.' Here it seems to be the 'quality' or 'circumstances' of an event that is the cause rather than the event itself, for the event itself is the same as others in some respects and different in other respects. The suspicion that it is not events, but something more closely tied to the descriptions of events, that Hume holds to be causes is fortified

* I am indebted to Harry Lewis and David Nivison, as well as to other members of seminars at Stanford University to whom I presented the ideas in this paper during 1966–7, for many helpful comments. I have profited greatly from discussion with John Wallace of the questions raised here; he may or may not agree with my answers. My research was supported in part by the National Science Foundation.

by Hume's claim that causal statements are never necessary. For if events were causes, then a true description of some event would be 'the cause of b', and, given that such an event exists, it follows logically that the cause of b caused b.

Mill said that the cause 'is the sum total of the conditions positive and negative taken together . . . which being realized, the consequent invariably follows'. Many discussions of causality have concentrated on the question whether Mill was right in insisting that the 'real Cause' must include all the antecedent conditions that jointly were sufficient for the effect, and much ingenuity has been spent on discovering factors, pragmatic or otherwise, that guide and justify our choice of some 'part' of the conditions as the cause. There has been general agreement that the notion of cause may be at least partly characterized in terms of sufficient and (or) necessary conditions.[1] Yet it seems to me we do not understand how such characterizations are to be applied to particular causes.

Take one of Mill's examples: some man, say Smith, dies, and the cause of his death is said to be that his foot slipped in climbing a ladder. Mill would say we have not given the whole cause, since having a foot slip in climbing a ladder is not always followed by death. What we were after, however, was not the cause of death in general but the cause of Smith's death: does it make sense to ask under what conditions Smith's death invariably follows? Mill suggests that part of the cause of Smith's death is 'the circumstance of his weight', perhaps because if Smith had been light as a feather his slip might not have injured him. Mill's explanation of why we don't bother to mention this circumstance is that it is too obvious to bear mention, but it seems to me that if it was Smith's fall that killed him, and Smith weighed 12 stone, then Smith's fall was the fall of a man who weighed 12 stone, whether or not we know it or mention it. How could Smith's actual fall, with Smith weighing, as he did, 12 stone, be any more efficacious in killing him than Smith's actual fall?

The difficulty has nothing to do with Mill's sweeping view of the cause, but attends any attempt of this kind to treat particular causes as necessary or sufficient conditions. Thus Mackie asks, 'What is the exact force of [the statement of some experts] that this short-circuit caused this fire?' And he answers, 'Clearly the experts are not saying that the short-circuit was a necessary condition for this house's catching fire at this time; they know perfectly well that a short-circuit somewhere else, or the overturning of a lighted oil stove . . . might, if it had occurred, have set the house on fire'

---

[1] For a recent example, with reference to many others, see J. L. Mackie, 'Causes and Conditions', *American Philosophical Quarterly*, 2/4 (Oct. 1965), 245–64, repr. in part as Ch. I above.

(ibid. 245). Suppose the experts know what they are said to; how does this bear on the question whether the short circuit was a necessary condition of this particular fire? For a short-circuit elsewhere could not have caused *this* fire, nor could the overturning of a lighted oil stove.

To talk of particular events as conditions is bewildering, but perhaps causes aren't events (like the short-circuit, or Smith's fall from the ladder), but correspond rather to sentences (perhaps like the fact that this short-circuit occurred, or the fact that Smith fell from the ladder). Sentences can express conditions of truth for others—hence the word 'conditional'.

If causes correspond to sentences rather than singular terms, the logical form of a sentence like:

(1) The short-circuit caused the fire.

would be given more accurately by:

(2) *The fact that* there was a short-circuit *caused it to be the case that* there was a fire.

In (2) the italicized words constitute a sentential connective like 'and' or 'if ... then ...'. This approach no doubt receives support from the idea that causal laws are universal conditionals, and singular causal statements ought to be instances of them. Yet the idea is not easily implemented. Suppose, first that a causal law is (as it is usually said Hume taught) nothing but a universally quantified material conditional. If (2) is an instance of such, the italicized words have just the meaning of the material conditional, 'If there was a short-circuit, then there was a fire.' No doubt (2) entails this, but not conversely, since (2) entails something stronger, namely the conjuction 'There was a short-circuit *and* there was a fire.' We might try treating (2) as the conjunction of the appropriate law and 'There was a short-circuit and there was a fire'—indeed this seems a possible interpretation of Hume's definition of cause quoted above—but then (2) would no longer be an instance of the law. And aside from the inherent implausibility of this suggestion as giving the logical form of (2) (in contrast, say, to giving the grounds on which it might be asserted) there is also the oddity that an inference from the fact that there was a short-circuit and there was a fire, and the law, to (2) would turn out to be no more than a conjoining of the premises.

Suppose, then, that there is a non-truth-functional causal connective, as has been proposed by many.[2] In line with the concept of a cause as a condition, the causal connective is conceived as a conditional, though stronger than the

[2] e.g. by: Mackie, 'Causes and Conditions', 254; Arthur W. Burks, 'The Logic of Causal Propositions', *Mind*, 60/239 (July 1951), 363–82; and Arthur Pap, 'Disposition Concepts and Extensional Logic', in *Minnesota Studies in the Philosophy of Science*, 2, ed. H. Feigl, M. Scriven, and G. Maxwell (Minneapolis, 1958), 196–224.

truth-functional conditional. Thus Arthur Pap writes, 'The distinctive property of causal implication as compared with material implication is just that the falsity of the antecedent is no ground for inferring the truth of the causal implication' (p. 212). If the connective Pap had in mind were that of (2), this remark would be strange, for it is a property of the connective in (2) that the falsity of either the 'antecedent' or the 'consequent' is a ground for inferring the falsity of (2). That treating the causal connective as a kind of conditional unsuits it for the work of (1) or (2) is perhaps even more evident from Burks's remark that 'p is causally sufficient for q is logically equivalent to $\sim q$ is causally sufficient for $\sim p$' (p. 369). Indeed, this shows not only that Burks's connective is not that of (2), but also that it is not the subjunctive causal connective 'would cause'. My tickling Jones would cause him to laugh, but his not laughing would not cause it to be the case that I didn't tickle him.

These considerations show that the connective of (2), and hence by hypothesis of (1), cannot, as is often assumed, be a conditional of any sort, but they do not show that (2) does not give the logical form of singular causal statements. To show this needs a stronger argument, and I think there is one, as follows.

It is obvious that the connective in (2) is not truth-functional, since (2) may change from true to false if the contained sentences are switched. Nevertheless, substitution of singular terms for others with the same extension in sentences like (1) and (2) does not touch their truth value. If Smith's death was caused by the fall from the ladder and Smith was the first man to land on the moon, then the fall from the ladder was the cause of the death of the first man to land on the moon. And if the fact that there was a fire in Jones's house caused it to be the case that the pig was roasted, and Jones's house is the oldest building on Elm Street, then the fact that there was a fire in the oldest building on Elm Street caused it to be the case that the pig was roasted. We must accept the principle of extensional substitution, then. Surely also we cannot change the truth value of the likes of (2) by substituting logically equivalent sentences for sentences in it. Thus (2) retains its truth if for 'there was a fire' we substitute the logically equivalent '$\hat{x}(x = x$ & there was a fire$) = \hat{x}(x = x)$'; retains it still if for the left side of this identity we write the coextensive singular term '$\hat{x}(x = x$ & Nero fiddled)'; and still retains it if we replace '$\hat{x}(x = x$ & Nero fiddled$) = \hat{x}(x = x)$' by the logically equivalent 'Nero fiddled'. Since the only aspect of 'there was a fire' and 'Nero fiddled' that matters to this chain of reasoning is the fact of their material equivalence, it appears that our assumed principles have led to the conclusion that the main connective of (2) is, contrary to what we supposed, truth-functional.[3]

[3] This argument is closely related to one spelled out by Dagfinn Føllesdal, 'Quantification into Causal Contexts', in *Boston Studies in the Philosophy of Science*, 2, ed. R. S. Cohen and M. W.

Having already seen that the connective of (2) cannot be truth-functional, it is tempting to try to escape the dilemma by tampering with the principles of substitution that led to it. But there is another, and, I think, wholly preferable way out: we may reject the hypothesis that (2) gives the logical form of (1), and with it the ideas that the 'caused' of (1) is a more or less concealed sentential connective, and that causes are fully expressed only by sentences.

2

Consider these six sentences:

(3) *It is a fact that* Jack fell down.

(4) Jack fell down *and* Jack broke his crown.

(5) Jack fell down *before* Jack broke his crown.

(6) Jack fell down, *which caused it to be the case that* Jack broke his crown.

(7) *Jones forgot the fact that* Jack fell down.

(8) *That* Jack fell down *explains the fact that* Jack broke his crown.

Substitution of equivalent sentences for, or substitution of coextensive singular terms or predicates in, the contained sentences, will not alter the truth value of (3) or (4): here extensionality reigns. In (7) and (8), intensionality reigns, in that similar substitution in or for the contained sentences is not guaranteed to save truth. (5) and (6) seem to fall in between; for in them substitution of coextensive singular terms preserves truth, whereas substitution of equivalent sentences does not. However this last is, as we just saw with respect to (2), and hence also (6), untenable middle ground.

Our recent argument would apply equally against taking the 'before' of (5) as the sentential connective it appears to be. And of course we don't interpret 'before' as a sentential connective, but rather as an ordinary two-place relation true of ordered pairs of times; this is made to work by introducing an extra place into the predicates ('x fell down' becoming 'x fell down at t') and an ontology of times to suit. The logical form of (5) is made perspicuous, then, by:

(5) There exist times t and t' such that Jack fell down at t, Jack broke his crown at t', and t preceded t'.

Wartofsky (New York, 1966), 263–74, to show that unrestricted quantification into causal contexts leads to difficulties. His argument is in turn a direct adaptation of Quine's (*Word and Object* (Cambridge, Mass., 1960), 197–8) to show that (logical) modal distinctions collapse under certain natural assumptions. My argument derives directly from Frege.

This standard way of dealing with (5) seems to me essentially correct, and I propose to apply the same strategy to (6), which then comes out:

(6) There exists events e and e' such that e is a falling down of Jack, e' is a breaking of his crown by Jack, and e caused e'.

Once events are on hand, an obvious economy suggests itself: (5) may as well be construed as about events rather than times. With this, the canonical version of (5) becomes just (6'), with 'preceded' replacing 'caused'. Indeed, it would be difficult to make sense of the claim that causes precede, or at least do not follow, their effects if (5) and (6) did not thus have parallel structures. We will still want to be able to say when an event occurred, but with events this requires an ontology of pure numbers only. So 'Jack fell down at 3 p.m.' says that there is an event e that is a falling down of Jack, and the time of e, measured in hours after noon, is 3; more briefly, $(\exists e)(F(\text{Jack}, e)\ \&\ t(e) = 3)$.

On the present plan, (6) means some fall of Jack's caused some breaking of Jack's crown; so (6) is not false if Jack fell more than once, broke his crown more than once, or had a crown-breaking fall more than once. Nor, if such repetitions turned out to be the case, would we have grounds for saying that (6) referred to one rather than another of the fracturings. The same does not go for 'The short-circuit caused the fire' or 'The flood caused the famine' or 'Jack's fall caused the breaking of Jack's crown'; here singularity is imputed. ('Jack's fall', like 'the day after tomorrow', is no less a singular term because it may refer to different entities on different occasions.) To do justice to 'Jack's fall caused the breaking of Jack's crown' what we need is something like 'The one and only falling down of Jack caused the one and only breaking of his crown by Jack'; in some symbols of the trade, '$(\imath e)\ F$ (Jack, e) caused $(\imath e)\ B$ (Jack's crown, e).'

Evidently (1) and (2) do not have the same logical form. If we think in terms of standard notations for first-order languages, it is (1) that more or less wears its form on its face; (2), like many existentially quantified sentences, does not (witness 'Somebody loves somebody'). The relation between (1) and (2) remains obvious and close: (1) entails (2), but not conversely.[4]

---

[4] A familiar device I use for testing hypotheses about logical grammar is translation into standard quantificational form; since the semantics of such languages is transparent, translation into them is a way of providing a semantic theory (a theory of the logical form) for what is translated. In this employment, canonical notation is not to be conceived as an improvement on the vernacular, but as a comment on it.

For elaboration and defence of the view of events sketched in this section, see my 'The Logical Form of Action Sentences', in Nicholas Rescher (ed.), *The Logic of Action and Preference* (Pittsburgh, 1967).

3

The salient point that emerges so far is that we must distinguish firmly between causes and the features we hit on for describing them, and hence between the question whether a statement says truly that one event caused another and the further question whether the events are characterized in such a way that we can deduce, or otherwise infer, from laws or other causal lore, that the relation was causal. 'The cause of this match's lighting is that it was struck.—Yes, but that was only *part* of the cause; it had to be a dry match, there had to be adequate oxygen in the atmosphere, it had to be struck hard enough, etc.' We ought now to appreciate that the 'Yes, but' comment does not have the force we thought. It cannot be that the striking of this match was only part of the cause, for this match was in fact dry, in adequate oxygen, and the striking was hard enough. What is partial in the sentence 'The cause of this match's lighting is that it was struck' is the *description* of the cause; as we add to the description of the cause, we may approach the point where we can deduce, from this description and laws, that an effect of the kind described would follow.

If Flora dried herself with a coarse towel, she dried herself with a towel. This is an inference we know how to articulate, and the articulation depends in an obvious way on reflecting in language an ontology that includes such things as towels: if there is a towel that is coarse and was used by Flora in her drying, there is a towel that was used by Flora in her drying. The usual way of doing things does not, however, give similar expression to the similar inference from 'Flora dried herself with a towel on the beach at noon' to 'Flora dried herself with a towel', or for that matter, from the last to 'Flora dried herself.' But if, as I suggest, we render 'Flora dried herself' as about an event, as well as about Flora, these inferences turn out to be quite parallel to the more familiar ones. Thus if there was an event that was a drying by Flora of herself and that was done with a towel, on the beach, at noon, then clearly there was an event that was a drying by Flora of herself—and so on.

The mode of inference carries over directly to causal statements. If it was a drying she gave herself with a coarse towel on the beach at noon that caused those awful splotches to appear on Flora's skin, then it was a drying she gave herself that did it; we may also conclude that it was something that happened on the beach, something that took place at noon, and something that was done with a towel, that caused the tragedy. These little pieces of reasoning seem all to be endorsed by intuition, and it speaks well for the analysis of causal statements in terms of events that on that analysis the arguments are transparently valid.

Mill, we are now in a better position to see, was wrong in thinking we have not specified the whole cause of an event when we have not wholly specified it. And there is not, as Mill and others have maintained, anything elliptical in the claim that a certain man's death was caused by his eating a particular dish, even though death resulted only because the man had a particular bodily constitution, a particular state of present health, and so on. On the other hand Mill was, I think, quite right in saying that 'there certainly is, among the circumstances that took place, some combination or other on which death is invariably consequent . . . the whole of which circumstances perhaps constituted in this particular case the conditions of the phenomenon . . .' (*A System of Logic*, 1.5.3.) Mill's critics are no doubt justified in contending that we may correctly give the cause without saying enough about it to demonstrate that it was sufficient; but they share Mill's confusion if they think every deletion from the description of an event represents something deleted from the event described.

The relation between a singular causal statement like 'The short-circuit caused the fire' and necessary and sufficient conditions seems, in brief, to be this. The fuller we make the description of the cause, the better our chances of demonstrating that it was sufficient (as described) to produce the effect, and the worse our chances of demonstrating that it was necessary; the fuller we make the description of the effect, the better our chances of demonstrating that the cause (as described) was necessary, and the worse our chances of demonstrating that it was sufficient. The symmetry of these remarks strongly suggests that in whatever sense causes are correctly said to be (described as) sufficient, they are as correctly said to be necessary. Here is an example. We may suppose there is some predicate '$P(x, y, e)$' true of Brutus, Caesar, and Brutus's stabbing of Caesar and such that any stab (by anyone of anyone) that is P is followed by the death of the stabbed. And let us suppose further that this law meets Mill's requirements of being *unconditional*—it supports counterfactuals of the form 'If Cleopatra had received a stab that was P, she would have died.' Now we can prove (assuming a man dies only once) that Brutus's stab was sufficient for Caesar's death. Yet it was not the cause of Caesar's death, for Caesar's death was the death of a man with more wounds than Brutus inflicted, and such a death could not have been caused by an event that was P ('P' was chosen to apply only to stabbings administered by a single hand). The trouble here is not that the description of the cause is partial, but that the event described was literally (spatio-temporally) only part of the cause.

Can we then analyse 'a caused b' as meaning that a and b may be described in such a way that the existence of each could be demonstrated, in the light of causal laws, to be a necessary and sufficient condition of the existence of the other? One objection, foreshadowed in previous discussion, is that the analysandum does, but the analysans does not, entail the existence of a and b. Suppose we add, in remedy, the condition that either a or b as described, exists. Then on the proposed analysis one can show that the causal relation holds between any two events. To apply the point in the direction of sufficiency, imagine some description '$(\imath x)Fx$' under which the existence of an event a may be shown sufficient for the existence of b. Then the existence of an arbitrary event c may equally be shown sufficient for the existence of b: just take as the description of c the following: '$(\imath y)(y = c \, \& \, (\exists!x) \, Fx)$'.[5] It seems unlikely that any simple and natural restrictions on the form of allowable descriptions would meet this difficulty, but since I have abjured the analysis of the causal relation, I shall not pursue the matter here.

There remains a legitimate question concerning the relation between causal laws and singular causal statements that may be raised independently. Setting aside the abbreviations successful analysis might authorize, what form are causal laws apt to have if from them, and a premiss to the effect that an event of a certain (acceptable) description exists, we are to infer a singular causal statement saying that the event caused, or was caused by, another? A possibility I find attractive is that a full-fledged causal law has the form of a conjunction:

$$(L) \begin{cases} (S) \quad (e)(n)((Fe \, \& \, t(e) = n) \rightarrow (\exists!f)(Gf \, \& \, t(f) = n + \epsilon \, \& \, C(e,f))) \, and \\ (N) \quad (e)(n)((Ge \, \& \, t(e) = n + \epsilon) \rightarrow (\exists!f)(Ff \, \& \, t(f) = n \, \& \, C(f,e))). \end{cases}$$

Here the variables 'e' and 'f' range over events, 'n' ranges over numbers, F and G are properties of events, '$C(e,f)$' is read 'e causes f', and 't' is a function that assigns a number to an event to mark the time the event occurs. Now, given the premiss:

(P) $\quad (\exists!e)(Fe \, \& \, t(e) = 3)$

(C) $\quad (\imath e)(Fe \, \& \, t(e) = 3)$ caused $(\imath e)(Ge \, \& \, t(e) = 3 + \epsilon)$.

It is worth remarking that part (N) of (L) is as necessary to the proof of (C) from (P) as it is to the proof of (C) from the premiss '$(\exists!e)(Ge \, \& \, t(e) = 3 + \epsilon))$'. This is perhaps more reason for holding that causes are, in the sense discussed above, necessary as well as sufficient conditions.

Explaining 'why an event occurred', on this account of laws, may take an instructively large number of forms, even if we limit explanation to the resources of deduction. Suppose, for example, we want to explain the fact that there was a fire in the house at 3.01 p.m. Armed with appropriate premises in the form of (P) and (L), we may deduce: that there was a fire in the house at 3.01 p.m.; that it was caused by a short-circuit at 3.00 p.m.;

---

[5] Here I am indebted to Professor Carl Hempel, and in the next sentence to John Wallace.

that there was only one fire in the house at 3.01 p.m.; that this fire was caused by the one and only short-circuit that occurred at 3.00 p.m. Some of these explanations fall short of using all that is given by the premises; and this is lucky, since we often know less. Given only (S) and (P), for example, we cannot prove there was only one fire in the house at 3.01 p.m., though we can prove there was exactly one fire in the house at 3.01 p.m. that was caused by the short-circuit. An interesting case is where we know a law in the form of (N), but not the corresponding (S). Then we may show that, given that an event of a particular sort occurred, there must have been a cause answering to a certain description, but, given the same description of the cause, we could not have predicted the effect. An example might be where the effect is getting pregnant.

If we explain why it is that a particular event occurred by deducing a statement that there is such an event (under a particular description) from a premiss known to be true, then a simple way of explaining an event, for example the fire in the house at 3.01 p.m., consists in producing a statement of the form of (C); and this explanation makes no use of laws. The explanation will be greatly enhanced by whatever we can say in favour of the truth of (C); needless to say, producing the likes of (L) and (P), if they are known true, clinches the matter. In most cases, however, the request for explanation will describe the event in terms that fall under no full-fledged law. The device to which we will then resort, if we can, is apt to be redescription of the event. For we can explain the occurrence of any event a if we know (L), (P), and the further fact that $a = (\iota e)(Ge \;\&\; t(e) = 3 + \in)$. Analogous remarks apply to the redescription of the cause, and to cases where all we want to, or can, explain is the fact that there was *an* event of a certain sort.

The great majority of singular causal statements are not backed, we may be sure, by laws in the way (C) is backed by (L). The relation in general is rather this: if 'a caused b' is true, then there are descriptions of a and b such that the result of substituting them for 'a' and 'b' in 'a caused b' is entailed by true premises of the form of (L) and (P); and the converse holds if suitable restrictions are put on the descriptions.[6] If this is correct, it does not follow that we must be able to dredge up a law if we know a singular causal statement to be true; all that follows is that we know there must be a covering law. And very often, I think, our justification for accepting a singular causal statement is that we have reason to believe an appropriate causal law exists, though we do not know what it is. Generalizations like 'If you strike a well-made match hard enough against a properly prepared surface, then,

---

[6] Clearly this account cannot be taken as a definition of the causal relation. Not only is there the inherently vague quantification over expressions (of what language?), but there is also the problem of spelling out the 'suitable restrictions'.

other conditions being favourable, it will light' owe their importance not to the fact that we can hope eventually to render them untendentious and exceptionless, but rather to the fact that they summarize much of our evidence for believing that full-fledged causal laws exist covering events we wish to explain.[7]

If the story I have told is true, it is possible to reconcile, within limits, two accounts thought by their champions to be opposed. One account agrees with Hume and Mill to this extent: it says that a singular causal statement '*a* caused *b*' entails that there is a law to the effect that 'all the objects similar to *a* are followed by objects similar to *b*' and that we have reason to believe the singular statement only in so far as we have reason to believe there is such a law. The second account (persuasively argued by C. J. Ducasse)[8] maintains that singular causal statements entail no law and that we can know them to be true without knowing any relevant law. Both of these accounts are entailed, I think, by the account I have given, and they are consistent (I therefore hope) with each other. The reconciliation depends, of course, on the distinction between knowing there is a law 'covering' two events and knowing what the law is: in my view, Ducasse is right that singular causal statements entail no law; Hume is right that they entail there is a law.

4

Much of what philosophers have said of causes and causal relations is intelligible only on the assumption (often enough explicit) that causes are individual events, and causal relations hold between events. Yet, through failure to connect this basic *aperçu* with the grammar of singular causal judgements, these same philosophers have found themselves pressed, especially when trying to put causal statements into quantificational form, into trying to express the relation of cause to effect by a sentential connective. Hence the popularity of the utterly misleading question: can causal relations be expressed by the purely extensional material conditional, or is some stronger (non-Humean) connection involved? The question is misleading because it

[7] The thought in these paragraphs, like much more that appears here, was first adumbrated in my 'Actions, Reasons, and Causes', *Journal of Philosophy*, 60 (1963), 685–700, esp. 696–9; repr. in Bernard Berofsky (ed.), *Free Will and Determinism* (New York, 1966). This conception of causality was subsequently discussed and, with various modifications, employed by Samuel Gorovitz, 'Causal Judgments and Causal Explanations', *Journal of Philosophy*, 62 (1965), 695–711, and by Bernard Berofsky, 'Causality and General Laws', ibid. 63 (1966), 148–57.

[8] See his 'Critique of Hume's Conception of Causality', *Journal of Philosophy*, 63 (1966), 141–8; *Causation and the Types of Necessity* (Seattle, 1924); *Nature, Mind, and Death* (La Salle, Ill., 1951), pt. 2. I have omitted from my 'second account' much that Ducasse says that is not consistent with Hume.

confuses two separate matters: the logical form of causal statements and the analysis of causality. So far as form is concerned, the issue of non-extensionality does not arise, since the relation of causality between events can be expressed (no matter how 'strong' or 'weak' it is) by an ordinary two-place predicate in an ordinary, extensional first-order language. These plain resources will perhaps be outrun by an adequate account of the form of causal laws, subjunctives, and counterfactual conditionals, to which most attempts to analyse the causal relation turn. But this is, I have urged, another question.

This is not to say there are no causal idioms that directly raise the issue of apparently non-truth-functional connectives. On the contrary, a host of statement forms, many of them strikingly similar, at least at first view, to those we have considered, challenge the account just given. Here are samples: 'The failure of the sprinkling system caused the fire,' 'The slowness with which controls were applied caused the rapidity with which the inflation developed,' 'The collapse was caused, not by the fact that the bolt gave way, but by the fact that it gave way so suddenly and unexpectedly,' 'The fact that the dam did not hold caused the flood.' Some of these sentences may yield to the methods I have prescribed, especially if failures are counted among events, but others remain recalcitrant. What we must say in such cases is that in addition to, or in place of, giving what Mill calls the 'producing cause', such sentences tell, or suggest, a causal story. They are, in other words, rudimentary causal explanations. Explanations typically relate statements, not events. I suggest therefore that the 'caused' of the sample sentences in this paragraph is not the 'caused' of straightforward singular causal statements, but is best expressed by the words 'causally explains'.[9]

A final remark. It is often said that events can be explained and predicted only in so far as they have repeatable characteristics, but not in so far as they are particulars. No doubt there is a clear and trivial sense in which this is true, but we ought not to lose sight of the less obvious point that there is an important difference between explaining the fact that there was *an* explosion

---

[9] Zeno Vendler has ingeniously marshalled the linguistic evidence for a deep distinction, in our use of 'cause', 'effect', and related words, between occurrences of verb-nominalizations that are fact-like or propositional, and occurrences that are event-like. See Zeno Vendler, 'Effects, Results and Consequences', in R. J. Butler (ed.), *Analytic Philosophy* (New York, 1962), 1–15. Vendler concludes that the 'caused' of 'John's action caused the disturbance' is always flanked by expressions used in the propositional or fact-like sense, whereas 'was an effect of' or 'was due to' in 'The shaking of the earth was an effect of (was due to) the explosion' is flanked by expressions in the event-like sense. My distinction between essentially sentential expressions and the expressions that refer to events is much the same as Vendler's and owes much to him, though I have used more traditional semantic tools and have interpreted the evidence differently. My suggestion that 'caused' is sometimes a relation, sometimes a connective, with corresponding changes in the interpretation of the expressions flanking it, has much in common with the thesis of J. M. Shorter's 'Causality, and a Method of Analysis', in *Analytic Philosophy*, 2 (1965), 145–57.

in the broom closet and explaining the occurrence of *the* explosion in the broom closet. Explanation of the second sort touches the particular event as closely as language can ever touch any particular. Of course this claim is persuasive only if there are such things as events to which singular terms, especially definite descriptions, may refer. But the assumption, ontological and metaphysical, that there are events, is one without which we cannot make sense of much of our most common talk; or so, at any rate, I have been arguing. I do not know any better, or further, way of showing what there is.

V

CAUSALITY AND DETERMINATION

G. E. M. ANSCOMBE

1

It is often declared or evidently assumed that causality is some kind of necessary connection, or alternatively, that being caused is—non-trivially—instancing some exceptionless generalization saying that such an event always follows such antecedents. Or the two conceptions are combined.

Obviously there can be, and are, a lot of divergent views covered by this account. Any view that it covers nevertheless manifests one particular doctrine or assumption. Namely:

> If an effect occurs in one case and a similar effect does not occur in an apparently similar case, there must be a relevant further difference.

Any radically different account of causation, then, by contrast with which all those diverse views will be as one, will deny this assumption. Such a radically opposing view can grant that often—though it is difficult to say generally when—the assumption of relevant difference is a sound principle of investigation. It may grant that there are necessitating causes, but will refuse to identify causation as such with necessitation. It can grant that there are situations in which, given the initial conditions and no interference, only one result will accord with the laws of nature; but it will not see general reason, in advance of discovery, to suppose that any given course of things has been so determined. So it may grant that in many cases difference of issue can rightly convince us of a relevant difference of circumstances; but it will deny that, quite generally, this *must* be so.

The first view is common to many philosophers of the past. It is also, usually but not always in a neo-Humean form, the prevailing received opinion throughout the currently busy and productive philosophical schools of the English-speaking world, and also in some of the European and Latin-American schools where philosophy is pursued in at all the same sort of way; nor is it confined to these schools. So firmly rooted is it that for many even outside pure philosophy, it routinely determines the meaning of 'cause', when consciously used as a theoretical term: witness the terminology of the contrast between "causal" and "statistical" laws, which is drawn by writers on physics—writers, note, who would not conceive themselves to be addicts of any philosophic school when they use this language to express that contrast.

The truth of this conception is hardly debated. It is, indeed, a bit of *Weltanschauung*: it helps to form a cast of mind which is characteristic of our whole culture.

The association between causation and necessity is old; it occurs for example in Aristotle's *Metaphysics*: 'When the agent and patient meet suitably to their powers, the one acts and the other is acted on OF NECESSITY.' Only with "rational powers" an extra feature is needed to determine the result: 'What has a rational power [e.g. medical knowledge, which can kill *or* cure] OF NECESSITY does what it has the power to do and as it has the power, when it has the desire.'[1]

Overleaping the centuries, we find it an axiom in Spinoza, 'Given a determinate cause, the effect follows OF NECESSITY, and without its cause, no effect follows.'[2] And in the English philosopher Hobbes: 'A cause simply, or an entire cause, is the aggregate of all the accidents both of the agents how many soever they be, and of the patients, put together; which when they are supposed to be present, IT CANNOT BE UNDERSTOOD BUT THAT THE EFFECT IS PRODUCED at the same instant; and if any of them be wanting, IT CANNOT BE UNDERSTOOD BUT THAT THE EFFECT IS NOT PRODUCED.'[3]

It was this last view, where the connection between cause and effect is evidently seen as *logical* connection of some sort, that was overthrown by Hume, the most influential of all philosophers on this subject in the English-speaking and allied schools. For he made us see that, given any particular cause—or "total causal situation" for that matter—and its effect, there is not in general any contradiction in supposing the one to occur and the other not to occur. That is to say, we'd know what was being described—what it would be like for it to be true—if it were reported, for example, that a kettle of water was put, and kept, directly on a hot fire, but the water did not heat up.

Were it not for the preceding philosophers who had made causality out as some species of logical connection, one would wonder at this being called a discovery on Hume's part: for vulgar humanity has always been over-willing to believe in miracles and marvels and *lusus naturae*. Mankind at large saw no contradiction, where Hume worked so hard to show the philosophic world—the Republic of Letters—that there was none.

The discovery was thought to be great. But as touching the equation of causality with necessitation, Hume's thinking did nothing against this but

---

[1] *Metaphysics*, bk. ix, ch. 5.   [2] *Ethics*, i. 3.
[3] *Elements of Philosophy Concerning Body*, ch. 9.

curiously reinforced it. For he himself assumed that NECESSARY CONNEC-
TION is an essential part of the idea of the relation of cause and effect,[4] and
he sought for its nature. He thought this could not be found in the situations,
objects, or events called 'causes' and 'effects', but was to be found in the
human mind's being determined, by experience of CONSTANT CONJUNC-
TION, to pass from the sensible impression or memory of one term of the
relation to the convinced idea of the other. Thus to say that an event was
caused was to say that its occurrence was an instance of some exceptionless
generalization connecting such an event with such antecedents as it occurred
in. The twist that Hume gave to the topic thus suggested a connection of the
notion of causality with that of deterministic laws—i.e. laws such that always, given initial conditions and the laws, a unique result is determined.

The well-known philosophers who have lived after Hume may have aimed
at following him and developing at least some of his ideas, or they may have
put up a resistance; but in no case, so far as I know,[5] has the resistance called
in question the equation of causality with necessitation.

Kant, roused by learning of Hume's discovery, laboured to establish causality as an a priori conception and argued that the objective time order
consists 'in that order of the manifold of appearance according to which, IN
CONFORMITY WITH A RULE, the apprehension of that which happens follows upon the apprehension of that which precedes . . . In conformity with
such a rule there must be in that which precedes an event the condition of a
rule according to which this event INVARIABLY and NECESSARILY follows.'[6] Thus Kant tried to give back to causality the character of a *justified*
concept which Hume's considerations had taken away from it. Once again
the connection between causation and necessity was reinforced. And this has
been the general characteristic of those who have sought to oppose Hume's
conception of causality. They have always tried to establish the necessitation
that they saw in causality: either a priori, or somehow out of experience.

Since Mill it has been fairly common to explain causation one way or
another in terms of 'necessary' and 'sufficient' conditions. Now 'sufficient
condition' is a term of art whose users may therefore lay down its meaning
as they please. So they are in their rights to rule out the query: 'May not the
sufficient conditions of an event be present, and the event yet not take place?'
For 'sufficient condition' is so used that if the sufficient conditions for *X* are
there, *X* occurs. But at the same time, the phrase cozens the understanding
into not noticing an assumption. For 'sufficient condition' sounds like:

[4] *Treatise of Human Nature*, i. 3, sects. 2 and 6.
[5] My colleague Ian Hacking has pointed out C. S. Peirce to me as an exception to this generalization.
[6] *Critique of Pure Reason*, bk. ii, ch. 2, sect. 3, second analogy.

'enough'. And one certainly *can* ask: 'May there not be *enough* to have made something happen—and yet it not have happened?'

Russell wrote of the notion of cause, or at any rate of the "law of causation" (and he seemed to feel the same way about "cause" itself), that, like the British monarchy, it had been allowed to survive because it had been erroneously thought to do no harm. In a destructive essay of great brilliance he cast doubt on the notion of necessity involved, unless it is explained in terms of universality, and he argued that upon examination the concepts of determination and of invariable succession of like objects upon like turn out to be empty: they do not differentiate between any conceivable course of things and any other. Thus Russell too assumes that necessity or universality is what is in question, and it never occurs to him that there may be any other conception of causality.[7]

Now it's not difficult to show it prima-facie wrong to associate the notion of cause with necessity or universality in this way. For, it being much easier to trace effects back to causes with certainty than to predict effects from causes, we often know a cause without knowing whether there is an exceptionless generalization of the kind envisaged, or whether there is a necessity.

For example, we have found certain diseases to be contagious. If, then, I have had one and only one contact with someone suffering from such a disease, and I get it myself, we suppose I got it from him. But what if, having had the contact, I ask a doctor whether I will get the disease? He will usually only be able to say, 'I don't know—maybe you will, maybe not.'

But, it is said, knowledge of causes here is partial; doctors seldom even know any of the conditions under which one invariably gets a disease, let alone all the sets of conditions. This comment betrays the assumption that there is such a thing to know. Suppose there is: still, the question whether there is does not have to be settled before we can know what we mean by speaking of the contact as cause of my getting the disease.

All the same, might it not be like this: knowledge of causes is possible without any satisfactory grasp of what is involved in causation? Compare the possibility of wanting clarification of "valency" or "long-run frequency", which yet have been handled by chemists and statisticians without such clarification; and valencies and long-run frequencies, whatever the right way of explaining them, have been known. Thus one of the familiar philosophic analyses of causality, or a new one in the same line, may be correct, though knowledge of it is not necessary for knowledge of causes.

There is something to observe here, that lies under our noses. It is little attended to, and yet still so obvious as to seem trite. It is this: causality

---

[7] 'The Notion of Cause', in *Mysticism and Logic*.

consists in the derivativeness of an effect from its causes. This is the core, the common feature, of causality in its various kinds. Effects derive from, arise out of, come of, their causes. For example, everyone will grant that physical parenthood is a causal relation. Here the derivation is material, by fission. Now analysis in terms of necessity or universality does not tell us of this derivedness of the effect; rather it forgets about that. For the necessity will be that of laws of nature; through it *we* shall be able to derive knowledge of the effect from knowledge of the cause, or vice versa, but that does not show us the cause as source of the effect. Causation, then, is not to be identified with necessitation.

If *A* comes from *B*, this does not imply that every *A*-like thing comes from some *B*-like thing or set-up or that every *B*-like thing or set-up has an *A*-like thing coming from it; or that given *B*, *A* had to come from it, or that given *A*, there had to be *B* for it to come from. Any of these may be true, but if any is, that will be an additional fact, not comprised in *A*'s coming from *B*. If we take 'coming from' in the sense of travel, this is perfectly evident.

'But that's because we can observe travel!' The influential Humean argument at this point is that we can't similarly observe causality in the individual case.[8] So the reason why we connect what we call the cause and what we call the effect as we do must lie elsewhere. It must lie in the fact that the succession of the latter upon the former is of a kind regularly observed.

There are two things for me to say about this. *First*, as to the statement that we can never observe causality in the individual case. Someone who says this is just not going to count anything as "observation of causality". This often happens in philosophy; it is argued that "all we find" is such-and-such, and it turns out that the arguer has excluded from his idea of "finding" the sort of thing he says we don't "find". And when we consider what we are allowed to say we do "find", we have the right to turn the tables on Hume, and say that neither do we perceive bodies, such as billiard balls, approaching one another. When we "consider the matter with the utmost attention", we find only an impression of travel made by the successive positions of a round white patch in our visual fields . . . , etc. Now a "Humean" account of causality has to be given in terms of constant conjunction of physical things, events, etc., not of experiences of them. If, then, it must be allowed that we "find" bodies in motion, for example, then what theory of perception can justly disallow the perception of a lot of causality? The truthful—though unhelpful—answer to the question: How did we come by our primary knowledge of causality? is that in learning to speak we learned the linguistic representation and application of a host of causal concepts. Very many of

---

[8] *Treatise of Human Nature*, i. 3, sect. 2.

them were represented by transitive and other verbs of action used in reporting what is observed. Others—a good example is 'infect'—form, not observation statements, but rather expressions of causal hypotheses. The word 'cause' itself is highly general. How does someone show that he has the concept *cause*? We may wish to say: only by having such a word in his vocabulary. If so, then the manifest possession of the concept presupposes the mastery of much else in language. I mean: the word 'cause' can be *added* to a language in which are already represented many causal concepts. A small selection: *scrape*, *push*, *wet*, *carry*, *eat*, *burn*, *knock over*, *keep off*, *squash*, *make* (e.g. noises, paper boats), *hurt*. But if we care to imagine languages in which no special causal concepts are represented, then no description of the use of a word in such languages will be able to present it as meaning *cause*. Nor will it even contain words for natural kinds of stuff, nor yet words equivalent to 'body', 'wind', or 'fire'. For learning to use special causal verbs is part and parcel of learning to apply the concepts answering to these, and many other, substantives. As surely as we learned to call people by name or to report from seeing it that the cat was on the table, we also learned to report from having observed it that someone drank up the milk or that the dog made a funny noise or that things were cut or broken by whatever we saw cut or break them.

(I will mention, only to set on one side, one of the roots of Hume's argument, the implicit appeal to Cartesian scepticism. He confidently challenges us to 'produce some instance, wherein the efficacy is plainly discoverable to the mind, and its operations obvious to our consciousness or sensation'.[9] Nothing easier: is cutting, is drinking, is purring not "efficacy"? But it is true that the apparent perception of such things may be only apparent: we may be deceived by false appearances. Hume presumably wants us to "produce an instance" in which *efficacy* is related to sensation as *red* is. It is true that we can't do that; it is not *so* related to sensation. He is also helped, in making his argument that we don't perceive "efficacy", by his curious belief that 'efficacy' means much the same thing as 'necessary connection'! But as to the Cartesian-sceptical root of the argument, I will not delay upon it, as my present topic is not the philosophy of perception.)

Second, as to that instancing of a universal generalization, which was supposed to supply what could not be observed in the individual case, the causal relation, the needed examples are none too common. 'Motion in one body in all past instances that have fallen under our observation, is follow'd upon impulse by motion in another':[10] so Hume. But, as is always a danger in making large generalizations, he was thinking only of the cases where we

[9] Ibid. i. 3, sect. 14.   [10] Ibid. ii. 3, sect. 1.

do observe this—billiard balls against free-standing billiard balls in an ordinary situation; not billiard balls against stone walls. Neo-Humeans are more cautious. They realize that if you take a case of cause and effect, and relevantly describe the cause *A* and the effect *B*, and then construct a universal proposition, 'Always, given an *A*, a *B* follows', you usually won't get anything true. You have got to describe the absence of circumstances in which an *A* would not cause a *B*. But the task of excluding all such circumstances can't be carried out. There is, I suppose, a vague association in people's minds between the universal propositions which would be examples of the required type of generalizations, and scientific laws. But there is no similarity.

Suppose we were to call propositions giving the properties of substances "laws of nature". Then there will be a law of nature running 'The flash-point of such a substance is . . .', and this will be important in explaining why striking matches usually causes them to light. This law of nature has not the form of generalization running 'Always, if a sample of such a substance is raised to such a temperature, it ignites'; nor is it equivalent to such a generalization, but rather to: 'If a sample of such a substance is raised to such a temperature and doesn't ignite, there must be a cause of its not doing so.' Leaving aside questions connected with the idea of a pure sample, the point here is that "normal conditions" is quite properly a vague notion. That fact makes generalizations running 'Always . . .' merely fraudulent in such cases; it will always be necessary for them to be hedged about with clauses referring to normal conditions; and we may not know in advance whether conditions are normal or not, or what to count as an abnormal condition. In exemplar analytical practice, I suspect, it will simply be a relevant condition in which the generalization, 'Always, if such and such, such and such happens . . .', supplemented with a few obvious conditions that have occurred to the author, turns out to be untrue. Thus the conditional 'If it doesn't ignite then there must be some cause' is the better gloss upon the original proposition, for it does not pretend to say specifically, or even disjunctively specifically, what *always* happens. It is probably these facts which make one hesitate to call propositions about the action of substances "laws of nature". The law of inertia, for example, would hardly be glossed: 'If a body accelerates without any force acting on it, there must be some cause of its doing so.' (Though I wonder what the author of *Principia* himself would have thought of that.) On the other hand just such "laws" as that about a substance's flash-point are connected with the match's igniting because struck.

Returning to the medical example, medicine is of course not interested in the hopeless task of constructing lists of all the sets of conditions under each of which people always get a certain disease. It is interested in finding what that is special, if anything, is always the case when people get a particular disease; and, given such a cause or condition (or in any case), in finding circumstances in which people don't get the disease, or tend not to. This is connected with medicine's concern first, and last, with things as they happen in the messy and mixed up conditions of life: only between its first and its last concern can it look for what happens unaffected by uncontrolled and inconstant conditions.

2

Yet my argument lies always open to the charge of appealing to ignorance. I must therefore take a different sort of example.

Here is a ball lying on top of some others in a transparent vertical pipe. I know how it got there: it was forcibly ejected with many others out of a certain aperture into the enclosed space above a row of adjacent pipes. The point of the whole construction is to show how a totality of balls so ejected always build up in rough conformity to the same curve. But I am interested in this one ball. Between its ejection and its getting into this pipe, it kept hitting sides, edges, other balls. If I made a film of it I could run it off in slow motion and tell the impact which produced each stage of the journey. Now was the result necessary? We would probably all have said it was in the time when Newton's mechanics was undisputed for truth. It was the impression made on Hume and later philosophers by that mechanics, that gave them so strong a conviction of the iron necessity with which everything happens, the 'absolute fate' by which 'Every object is determin'd to a certain degree and direction of its motion'.[11]

Yet no one could have deduced the resting place of the ball—because of the indeterminateness that you get even in the Newtonian mechanics, arising from the finite accuracy of measurements. From exact figures for positions, velocities, directions, spins, and masses you might be able to calculate the result as accurately as you chose. But the minutest inexactitudes will multiply up factor by factor, so that in a short time your information is gone. Assuming a given margin of error in your initial figure, you could assign an associated probability to that ball's falling into each of the pipes. If you want the highest probability you assign to be really high, so that you can take it as practical certainty, it will be a problem to reckon how tiny the permitted margins of inaccuracy must be—analogous to the problem: how small a fraction of a grain of millet must I demand is put on the first square of the chess board,

<hr>

[11] Ibid. ii. 3, sect. 1.

if after doubling up at every square I end up having to pay out only a pound of millet? It would be a figure of such smallness as to have no meaning as a figure for a margin of error.

However, so long as you believed the classical mechanics you might also think there could be no such thing as a figure for a difference that had no meaning. Then you would think that though it was not feasible for us to find the necessary path of the ball because our margins of error are too great, yet there *was* a necessary path, which could be assigned a sufficient probability for firm acceptance of it, by anyone (not one of us) capable of reducing his limits of accuracy in measurement to a sufficiently small compass. Admittedly, so small a compass that he'd be down among the submicroscopic particles and no longer concerned with the measurements, say, of the ball. And now we can say: with certain degrees of smallness we get to a region where Newton's mechanics is no longer believed.

If the classical mechanics can be used to calculate a certain real result, we may give a sense to, and grant, the "necessity" of the result, given the antecedents. Here, however, you can't use the mechanics to calculate the result, but at most to give yourself a belief in its necessity. For this to be reasonable the system has got to be acknowledged as true. Not, indeed, that that would be enough; but if so much were secured, then it would be worth while to discuss the metaphysics of absolute measures of continuous quantities.

The point needs some labouring precisely because "the system does apply to such bodies"—that is, to moderately massive balls. After all, it's Newton we use to calculate Sputniks! 'The system applies to these bodies' is true only in the sense and to the extent that it yields sufficient results of calculations about these bodies. It does not mean: in respect of these bodies the system is the truth, so that it just doesn't matter that we can't use it to calculate such a result in such a case. I am not saying that a deterministic system involves individual predictability: it evidently does not. But in default of predictability the determinedness declared by the deterministic system has got to be believed because the system itself is believed.

I conclude that we have no ground for calling the path of the ball determined—at least, until it has taken its path—but, it may be objected, is not each state of its path determined, even though we cannot determine it? My argument has partly relied on loss of information through multiplicity of impacts. But from one impact to the next the path is surely determined, and so the whole path is so after all.

It sounds plausible to say: each stage is determined and so the whole is. But what does 'determined' mean? The word is a curious one (with a curious history); in this sort of context it is often used as if it *meant* 'caused'. Or perhaps 'caused' is used as if it meant 'determined'. But there is at any rate one important difference—a thing hasn't been caused until it has happened; but it may be determined before it happens.

(It is important here to distinguish between being *determined* and being *determinate*. In indeterministic physics there is an apparent failure of both. I am concerned only with the former.)

When we call a result determined we are implicitly relating it to an antecedent range of possibilities and saying that all but one of these is disallowed. What disallows them is not the result itself but something antecedent to the result. The antecedences may be logical or temporal or in the order of knowledge. Of the many—antecedent—possibilities, *now* only one is—antecedently—possible.

Mathematical formulae and human decisions are limiting cases; the former because of the obscurity of the notion of antecedent possibilities, and the latter because decisions can be retrieved.

In a chess-game, the antecedent possibilities are, say, the powers of the pieces. By the rules, a certain position excludes all but one of the various moves that were in that sense antecedently possible. This is logical antecedence. The next move is determined.

In the zygote, sex and eye-colour are already determined. Here the antecedent possibilities are the possibilities for sex and eye-colour for a child; or more narrowly: for a child of these parents. *Now*, given the combination of this ovum and this spermatozoon, all but one of these antecedent possibilities is excluded.

It might be said that anything was determined once it had happened. There is now no possibility open: it *has* taken place! It was in this sense that Aristotle said that past and present were necessary. But this does not concern us: what interests us is *pre*-determination.

Then 'each stage of the ball's path is determined' must mean 'Upon any impact, there is only one path possible for the ball up to the next impact (and assuming no air currents, etc.).' But what ground could one have for believing this, if one does not believe in some system of which it is a consequence? Consider a steel ball dropping between two pins on a Galton board to hit the pin centred under the gap between them. That it should balance on this pin is not to be expected. It has two possibilities; to go to the right or to the left. If you have a system which forces this on you, you can say: 'There has to be a determining factor; otherwise, like Buridan's ass, the ball must balance.' But if you have not, then you should say that the ball may be undetermined until it does move to the right or the left. Here the ball had only two significant possibilities and was perhaps unpredetermined between them. This was because it cannot be called determined—no reasonable account can be given of insisting that it is so—within a small range of possibility, actualization within which will lead on to its falling either to the right or to the left. With our flying ball there will also be such a small range of possibility. The further consequences of the path it may take are not tied down to just two significant possibilities, as with one step down the Galton board: the range of further possibility gets wider as we consider the paths it may take. Otherwise, the two cases are similar.

We see that to give content to the idea of something's being determined, we have to have a set of possibilities, which something narrows down to one—before the event.

This accords well with our understanding of part of the dissatisfaction of some physicists with the quantum theory. They did not like the undeterminedness of individual quantum phenomena. Such a physicist might express himself by saying 'I believe in causality!' He meant: I believe that the real physical laws and the initial conditions must entail uniqueness of result. Of course, within a range of co-ordinate and mutually exclusive identifiable possible results, only one happens: he means that the result that happens ought to be understood as the only one that was possible before it happened.

Must such a physicist be a "determinist"? That is, must he believe that the whole universe is a system such that, if its total states at t and t' are thus and so, the laws of nature are such as then to allow only one possibility for its total state at any other time? No. He may not think that the idea of a total state of the universe at a time is one he can do anything with. He may even have no views on the uniqueness of possible results for whatever may be going on in any arbitrary volume of space. For 'Our theory should be such that only the actual result was possible for that experiment' doesn't mean 'Our theory should have excluded the experiment's being muffed or someone's throwing a boot, so that we didn't get the result', but rather: 'Our theory should be such that only this result was possible as *the result of the experiment*.' He hates a theory, even if he has to put up with it for the time being, that essentially assigns only probability to a result, essentially allows of a range of possible results, never narrowed down to one until the event itself.

It must be admitted that such dissatisfied physicists very often have been determinists. Witness Schrödinger's account of the "principle of causality": 'The exact physical situation at *any* point P at a given moment t is unambiguously determined by the exact physical situation within a certain surrounding of P at any previous time, say $t - \tau$. If τ is large, that is if that previous time lies far back, it may be necessary to know the previous situation for a wide domain around P.'[12] Or Einstein's more modest version of a notorious earlier claim: if you knew all about the contents of a sphere of

---

[12] Erwin Schrödinger, *Science and Humanism* (Cambridge, 1951).

radius 186,000 miles, and knew the laws, you would be able to know for sure what would happen at the centre for the next second. Schrödinger says: *any* point *P*; and *a* means *any* sphere of that radius. So their view of causality was not that of my hypothetical physicist, who I said may not have views on the uniqueness of possible results for whatever may be going on in any arbitrary volume of space. My physicist restricts his demand for uniqueness of result to situations in which he has got certain processes going in isolation from inconstant external influences, or where they do not matter, as the weather on a planet does not matter for predicting its course round the sun.

The high success of Newton's astronomy was in one way an intellectual disaster: it produced an illusion from which we tend still to suffer. This illusion was created by the circumstance that Newton's mechanics *had a good model in the solar system*. For this gave the impression that we had here an ideal of scientific explanation; whereas the truth was, it was mere obligingness on the part of the solar system, by having had so peaceful a history in recorded time, to provide such a model. For suppose that some planet had at some time erupted with such violence that its shell was propelled rocket-like out of the solar system. Such an event would not have violated Newton's laws; on the contrary, it would have illustrated them. But also it would not have been calculable as the past and future motions of the planets are presently calculated on the assumption that they can be treated as the simple "bodies" of his mechanics, with no relevant properties but mass, position, and velocity and no forces mattering except gravity.

Let us pretend that Newton's laws were still to be accepted without qualification: no reserve in applying them in electrodynamics; no restriction to bodies travelling a good deal slower than light; and no quantum phenomena. Newton's mechanics is a deterministic system; but this does not mean that believing them commits us to determinism. We could say: of course nothing violates those axioms or the laws of the force of gravity. But animals, for example, run about the world in all sorts of paths and no path is dictated for them by those laws, as it is for planets. Thus in relation to the solar system (apart from questions like whether in the past some planet has blown up), the laws are like the rules of an infantile card game: once the cards are dealt we turn them up in turn, and make two piles each, one red, one black; the winner has the biggest pile of red ones. So once the cards are dealt the game is determined, and from any position in it you can derive all others back to the deal and forward to win or draw. But in relation to what happens on and inside a planet the laws are, rather, like the rules of chess; the play is seldom determined, though nobody breaks the rules.[13]

[13] I should have made acknowledgements to Gilbert Ryle (*The Concept of Mind* (London, 1949), 77) for this comparison. But his use of the openness of chess is somewhat ambiguous

Why this difference? A natural answer is: the mechanics does not give the special laws of all the forces. Not, for example, for thermal, nuclear, electrical, chemical, muscular forces. And now the Newtonian model suggests the picture: given the laws of all the forces, then there is total coverage of what happens and then the whole game of motion is determined; for, by the first law, any acceleration implies a force of some kind, and must not forces have laws? My hypothetical physicist at least would think so; and would demand that they be deterministic. Nevertheless he still does not have to be a "determinist"; for many forces, unlike gravity, can be switched on and off, are generated, and also shields can be put up against them. It is one thing to hold that in a clear-cut situation—an astronomical or a well-contrived experimental one designed to discover laws—"the result" should be determined: and quite another to say that in the hurly-burly of many crossing contingencies whatever happens next must be determined; or to say that the generation of forces (by human experimental procedures, among other things) is always determined in advance of the generating procedure; or to say that there is always a law of composition, of such a kind that the combined effect of a set of forces is determined in every situation.

Someone who is inclined to say those things, or implicitly to assume them, has almost certainly been affected by the impressive relation between Newton's mechanics and the solar system.

We remember how it was in mechanics. By knowing the position and velocity of a particle at one single instant, by knowing the acting forces, the whole future path of the particle could be foreseen. In Maxwell's theory, if we know the field at one instant only, we can deduce from the equations of the theory how the whole field will change in space and time. Maxwell's equations enable us to follow the history of the field, just as the mechanical equations enabled us to follow the history of material particles . . . With the help of Newton's laws we can deduce the motion of the earth from the force acting between the sun and the earth.[14]

'By knowing the acting forces'—that must of course include the *future* acting forces, not merely the present ones. And similarly for the equations which enable us to follow the history of the field; a change may be produced by an external influence. In reading both Newton and later writers one is often led to ponder that word 'external'. Of course, to be given "the acting forces" is to be given the external forces too and any new forces that may later be introduced into the situation. Thus those first sentences are true, if true, without the special favour of fate, being general truths of mechanics and

and is not the same as mine. For the contrast with a closed card game I was indebted to A. J. P. Kenny.

[14] Albert Einstein and Leopold Infeld, *The Evolution of Physics* (New York, 1938; paperback edn. 1967), 146.

physics, but the last one is true by favour, by the brute fact that only the force acting between earth and sun matters for the desired deductions.

The concept of necessity, as it is connected with causation, can be explained as follows: a cause C is a necessitating cause of an effect E *when* (I mean: on the occasions when) if C occurs it is certain to cause E unless something prevents it. C and E are to be understood as general expressions, not singular terms. If "certainty" should seem too epistemological a notion: a necessitating cause C of a given kind of effect E is such that it *is* not possible (on the occasion) that C should occur and should not cause an E, nor should there be anything that prevents an E from occurring. A non-necessitating cause is then one that can fail of its effect without the intervention of anything to frustrate it. We may discover *types* of necessitating and non-necessitating cause; e.g. rabies is a necessitating cause of death, because it is not possible for one who has rabies to survive without treatment. We don't have to tie it to the occasion. An example of a non-necessitating cause is mentioned by Feynman: a bomb is connected with a Geiger counter, so that it will go off if the Geiger counter registers a certain reading; whether it will or not is not determined, for it is so placed near some radioactive material that it may or may not register that reading.

There would be no doubt of the cause of the reading or of the explosion if the bomb did go off. Max Born is one of the people who has been willing to dissociate causality from determinism: he explicates cause and effect in terms of dependence of the effect on the cause. It is not quite clear what "dependence" is supposed to be, but at least it seems to imply that you would not get the effect without the cause. The trouble about this is that you might—from some other cause. That this effect was produced by this cause does not at all show that it could not, or would not, have been produced by something else in the absence of this cause.

Indeterminism is not a possibility unconsidered by philosophers. C. D. Broad, in his inaugural lecture, given in 1934, described it as a possibility; but added that whatever happened without being determined was accidental. He did not explain what he meant by being accidental; he must have meant more than not being necessary. He may have meant being uncaused; but, if I am right, not being determined does not imply not being caused. Indeed, I should explain indeterminism as the thesis that not all physical effects are necessitated by their causes. But if we think of Feynman's bomb, we get some idea of what is meant by "accidental". It was random: it "merely happened" that the radio-active material emitted particles in such a way as to activate the Geiger counter enough to set off the bomb. Certainly the motion of the Geiger counter's needle is caused; and the actual emission is caused too; it occurs because there is this mass of radioactive material here. (I have already indicated that, contrary to the opinion of Hume, there are many different sorts of causality.) But all the same the *causation* itself is, one could say, *mere hap*. It is difficult to explain this idea any further.

Broad used the idea to argue that indeterminism, if applied to human action, meant that human actions are "accidental". Now he had a picture of choices as being determining causes, analogous to determining physical causes, and of choices in their turn being either determined or accidental. To regard a choice as such—i.e. any case of choice—as a predetermining causal event now appears as a naïve mistake in the philosophy of mind, though that is a story I cannot tell here.

It was natural that when physics went indeterministic, some thinkers should have seized on this indeterminism as being just what was wanted for defending the freedom of the will. They received severe criticism on two counts: one, that this "mere hap" is the very last thing to be invoked as the physical correlate of "man's ethical behaviour"; the other, that quantum laws predict statistics of events when situations are repeated; interference with these, by the *will*'s determining individual events which the laws of nature leave undetermined, would be as much a violation of natural law as would have been interference which falsified a deterministic mechanical law.

Ever since Kant it has been a familiar claim among philosophers that one can believe in both physical determinism and "ethical" freedom. The reconciliations have always seemed to me to be either so much gobbledegook, or to make the alleged freedom of action quite unreal. My actions are mostly physical movements; if these physical movements are physically predetermined by processes which I do not control, then my freedom is perfectly illusory. The truth of physical indeterminism is thus indispensable if we are to make anything of the claim to freedom. But certainly it is insufficient. The physically undetermined is not thereby "free". For freedom at least involves the power of acting according to an idea, and no such thing is ascribed to whatever is the subject (what would be the relevant subject?) of unpredetermination in indeterministic physics. Nevertheless, there is nothing unacceptable about the idea that that "physical haphazard" should be the only physical correlate of human freedom of action; and perhaps also of the voluntariness and intentionalness in the conduct of other animals which we do not call "free". The freedom, intentionalness, and voluntariness are not to be analysed as the same thing as, or as produced by, the physical haphazard. Different sorts of pattern altogether are being spoken of when we mention them, from those involved in describing elementary processes of physical causality.

The other objection is, I think, more to the point. Certainly if we have a statistical law, but undetermined individual events, and then enough of these are supposed to be pushed by will in one direction to falsify the statistical law, we have again a supposition that puts will into conflict with natural laws. But it is not at all clear that the same train of minute physical events should have to be the regular correlate of the same action; in fact, that suggestion looks immensely implausible. It is, however, required by the objection.

Let me construct an analogy to illustrate this point. Suppose that we have a large glass box full of millions of extremely minute coloured particles, and the box is constantly shaken. Study of the box and particles leads to statistical laws, including laws for the random generation of small unit patches of uniform colour. Now the box is remarkable for also presenting the following phenomenon: the word 'Coca-Cola', formed like a mosaic, can always be read when one looks at one of the sides. It is not always the same shape in the formation of its letters, not always the same size or in the same position, it varies in its colours; but there it always is. It is not at all clear that those statistical laws concerning the random motion of the particles and their formation of small unit patches of colour would have to be supposed violated by the operation of a cause for this phenomenon which did not derive it from the statistical laws.

It has taken the inventions of indeterministic physics to shake the rather common dogmatic conviction that determinism is a presupposition, or perhaps a conclusion, of scientific knowledge. Not that that conviction has been very much shaken even so. Of course, the belief that the laws of nature are deterministic has been shaken. But I believe it has often been supposed that this makes little difference to the assumption of macroscopic determinism: as if undeterminedness were always encapsulated in systems whose internal workings could be described only by statistical laws, but where the total upshot, and in particular the outward effect, was as near as makes no difference always the same. What difference does it make, after all, that the scintillations, whereby my watch dial is luminous, follow only a statistical law—so long as the gross manifest effect is sufficiently guaranteed by the statistical law? Feynman's example of the bomb and Geiger counter smashes this conception; but as far as I can judge it takes time for the lesson to be learned. I find deterministic assumptions more common now among people at large, and among philosophers, than when I was an undergraduate.

The lesson is welcome, but indeterministic physics (if it succeeds in giving the lesson) is only culturally, not logically, required to make the deterministic picture doubtful. For it was always a mere extravagant fancy, encouraged in the "age of science" by the happy relation of Newtonian mechanics to the solar system. It ought not to have mattered whether the laws of nature were or were not deterministic. For them to be deterministic is for them, together with the description of the situation, to entail unique results in situations defined by certain relevant objects and measures, and where no part is played by inconstant factors external to such definition. If that is right, the laws' being deterministic does not tell us whether "determinism" is true. It is the total coverage of every motion that happens that is a fanciful claim. But I do not mean that any motions lie outside the scope of physical laws, or that one cannot say, in any given context, that certain motions would be violations of physical law. Remember the contrast between chess and the infantile card game.

Meanwhile in non-experimental philosophy it is clear enough what are the dogmatic slumbers of the day. It is over and over again assumed that any singular causal proposition implies a universal statement running 'Always when this, then that'; often assumed that true singular causal statements are derived from such "inductively believed" universalities. Examples indeed are recalcitrant, but that does not seem to disturb. Even a philosopher acute enough to be conscious of this, such as Davidson, will say, without offering any reason at all for saying it, that a singular causal statement implies *that there is* such a true universal proposition[15]—though perhaps we can never have knowledge of it. Such a thesis needs some reason for believing it! "Regularities in nature": that is not a reason. The most neglected of the key topics in this subject are: interference and prevention.

[15] Donald Davidson, 'Causal Relations', *Journal of Philosophy*, 64 (Nov. 1967) (Ch. IV above).

VI

ON THE LOGIC AND EPISTEMOLOGY OF THE CAUSAL RELATION

G. H. VON WRIGHT

1

The aim of my paper is threefold. First, I shall discuss some uses of formal logic to clarify the nature of causal relationships. Second, I shall examine the epistemological foundations of the concepts used in this formal analysis. Third, in the light of these formal and epistemological considerations, I shall discuss the place of causation and of causal categories in the philosophy of science.

It goes without saying that the discussion of such vast topics within the scope of a relatively brief paper must be very sketchy indeed. It can do little more than outline a conceptual framework and try to place some of the traditional problems of causation in the new frame. It is my hope that this approach may stimulate further discussion within this frame or challenge criticism of the framework itself. If it had the one or the other effect, or both, some light might be thrown on what is notoriously one of the most entangled problem-bundles in the whole of philosophy.

2

It has been thought that the notion of causality ought to be expurgated from the philosophy of science on the ground either that it is too heavily loaded metaphysically or that it is too imprecise logically to have a place in exact thinking. People who have thought thus have sometimes supported their view by alleging that the role of causation has grown progressively smaller as science has advanced. So, for example, Bertrand Russell in a famous and influential essay written at the beginning of the century.[1] Thinking in terms of cause and effect, it is said, is being replaced by thinking in terms of functional relationships and probabilistic correlations or in terms of

---

[1] 'On the Notion of Cause', *Proceedings of the Aristotelian Society*, 13 (1912–13), 1–26.

conditionship relations between events or states of affairs. This may be a true description of current trends. But their significance to the philosophic problems of causality is not that they make these problems obsolete, but rather that they enable us to present them with an increased degree of clarity and precision.

There can be little doubt about the usefulness, not least for purposes of logic, of analysing causal relationships in terms of conditions. By means of these analytic tools one can make a number of distinctions which, as long as one speaks loosely about 'causes' and 'effects' only, remain blurred or cannot be made at all. Thus, for example, causal factors which are necessary conditions of given effects behave logically rather differently from causal factors which are sufficient conditions. Failure to observe these differences has been responsible for disastrous confusions in traditional inductive logic. For this branch of logical study, the theory of conditions has therefore opened new prospects which are only beginning to be explored.

Condition concepts, however, cannot be regarded as logical primitives. They must be analysed in the terms of some other concepts and their theory thus incorporated into more 'standard' branches of logic. What are these other concepts? Here, two answers seem possible.

One analysis is in terms of quantifiers. If p and q are two (generic) states of affairs, then that (the obtaining of) p is a sufficient condition of (the obtaining of) q might mean that *whenever* p is the case, then q is the case too. The notion of 'whenever' is a temporal or tense-logical quantifier.

The other analysis is in terms of modal concepts. That p is a sufficient condition of q would then mean something like this: it is *necessary* that q obtains, if p obtains.

I shall call the first analysis of condition concepts extensional, the second intensional. In the extensional view, the 'ground-form' of a conditionship and therewith also of a causal relation is that of a universal implication. In the intensional view, the ground-form is that of a strict (necessary) implication.

That an extensional analysis may appear inadequate, and an intensional analysis needful, is perhaps best shown by the following observation: Let p be a (causally) sufficient condition of q. This, it would normally be thought, entitles us to maintain that had p obtained on any given occasion when in fact it did *not* obtain, then q too would have obtained on that occasion. A causal relation should provide a valid basis for so-called contrary-to-fact conditional assertions. The accidental uniformity that q is always there with p cannot by itself provide this basis. Must we not therefore assume a 'nomic necessity' connecting p and q, if counterfactual conditionals are to be extracted from their connection? Some, but by no means all philosophical logicians think that the correct answer to this question will commit us to what I have called here an intensional analysis of causal relationships.

Both an extensional and an intensional analysis of conditions leave unsolved the following problem:

To say that whenever p is the case q is the case too is equivalent to saying that whenever q is not the case p is not the case either. And to say that necessarily, if p then q, is equivalent to saying that necessarily, if not-q then not-p. It would then, on either analysis of the notion of a sufficient condition, follow that p is a sufficient condition of q if and only if not-q is a sufficient condition of not-p. This, as such, need not be thought objectionable. But if a relation of sufficient conditionship is thought of as a causal relation, the fact just mentioned is bound to worry us. For to say that p is a cause of q and to say that not-q causes not-p can hardly mean the same. Heavy rainfall may be the cause of flooding, but we should not normally regard the fact that no flooding occurs as a *cause* of the absence of rain. Causal relations have an *asymmetry* which their analysis in terms of condition concepts seems incapable, by itself, of capturing. I shall refer to the puzzle here as the Problem of Asymmetry of Cause and Effect.

It may be thought that the problem is solved if we add to the definition of causal relations in terms of conditionship a temporal qualification separating the conditioning from the conditioned terms of the relations. For example, we could stipulate that, on an instantiation of the causal relation, the conditioning or cause-factor must materialize before, or at least not later than, the conditioned or effect-factor.

I am not sure, however, that the attempts to distinguish between cause and effect on the basis of temporality and condition concepts alone will be successful. I incline to think that they will not, and shall later give reasons for this opinion.

3

The tools which I am going to use in the formal analysis are exceedingly simple. They consist of 'ordinary' propositional logic, a propositional modal logic, and a propositional tense-logic.

As modal primitive I shall use the notion of possibility. Its symbol will be M. As a symbol for necessity I shall use N, which is an abbreviation for the complex sign $\sim M \sim$.

The tense-logic concerned has two primitives. One is a binary connective. Its symbol will be T and can be read 'and next'. The other is a temporal quantifier. Its symbol $\vee$ is read 'sometime (in the future)'. As an abbreviation for the complex $\sim \vee \sim$ we shall use $\wedge$; it means 'always (in the future)'.

The logic of the connective T may be characterized as the logic of changes among states of affairs over a finite succession of discrete temporal occasions. It can easily be axiomatized and shown to be semantically complete with regard to a criterion of logical truth which is substantially that of a truth-functional tautology.

The logic of the quantifiers is structurally isomorphic with a weakened version of the modal system S4.3. When the logic of $\vee$ is combined with that of T, some additional principles of an axiomatic character are needed to cater for the peculiarities of quantification in a *discrete* time-medium.

I need not here discuss further the problems of tense-logic. The tense-logic involved in our analysis of causality does not embody anything over and above things already known from the literature.[2] As to the modal logic involved, some comments will be made on this later.

4

Let us entertain here the following picture of the logical build of the world:

We assume that the total state of the world at any given point in time (I shall also call it 'occasion') can be completely described by telling, for any one of the members of a set of states of affairs $p, q, \ldots$, whether this state obtains or not on that occasion. If the set is finite and has n logically independent members, the number of possible total states of the world is 2^n and the number of possible successions of total states on m occasions is 2^{mn}. We shall call any such succession a possible *history* of the world of length m.

If the world at a given stage of its history is in a certain state, it can, as far as logic is concerned, at the next stage be in any one of the (2^n) logically possible different states. But this 'logical freedom' of development can, for non-logical reasons, be restricted. I shall call these non-logical reasons (restrictions) 'causal'. Thus the number of causally possible histories of length m of the world, starting from a given initial world state, may be less than the number 2^{mn} of logically possible histories. We can picture these possibilities of world developments in a topological figure ('tree'). (See picture below.)

In this picture circles represent total states of the world. The circle to the extreme left is the state on the first occasion. A progression of circles from

[2] Cf. von Wright, 'And Next', *Acta Philosophica Fennica*, 18 (1965), 293–304; 'And Then', *Commentationes Physico-Mathematicae, Societas Scientiarum Fennica*, 32 (1966), 1–11; 'Always', *Theoria*, 34 (1968), 208–21; H. Kamp, review of 'And Next' and 'And Then', *Journal of Symbolic Logic*, 35 (1970), 459–60.

the left to the right represents a possible history of the world. The bifurcations after any given circle indicate the various alternative developments which are immediately open to the world represented by that circle.

Looking towards the future from any given circle in the figure, there are so many possible histories ahead of us. We do not know in advance which of the possible histories would be the actual history of the world if the circle in question happened to represent the actual total state of the world at that stage in its development. But we know that *one* of the possible histories would come true. I shall call this singular history the *natural* development of the world after the state in question. (An important addition will shortly be made to our definition of this notion of a 'natural' development or history of the world. See Section 7 below.) We shall adopt the convention that the natural development after any given circle is always represented by the topmost layer of circles in the branch of the tree which has the given circle as its apex. Thus, in our figure, the horizontal strings of circles represent the various possible natural developments.

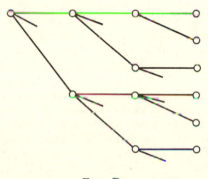

FIG. D

Let there be k alternative developments immediately after a given circle. The fraction $(k-1)/(2^n - 1)$ can then be said to measure the degree of freedom (or of determinism) which the world, at that given point of its history, enjoys as far as its immediate development is concerned. If $k = 1$ and the fraction = 0, this freedom is nil. The course of the world from that given state to the next is completely determined. If k equals the maximum 2^n, the fraction has the value 1, which means that the course of world development at this point is completely undetermined. (The various alternatives may also be correlated with probabilities, adding up to 1, but this case will not be considered by us here.)

The picture which we have been entertaining concerning the logical build of the world is a version of the position called *logical atomism*. All of its basic assumptions may be questioned. Is the total state of the world a truth-functional compound of logically independent atomic states of affairs? Is its history a succession of logically independent total states? Is time a discrete flow of successive occasions? Is the number of atomic states a finite constant? Has the world a beginning in time?

Some of these questions may have an affirmative and others a negative answer. I shall not attempt to answer any of them here. (But this does not mean that I regard them as unimportant in themselves or irrelevant to the problems of causality.) I shall regard the logico-atomistic structure, which we have just characterized, as being a 'fiction' or 'model' of what a world might be like, logically speaking. My primary interest is to define and study causal relations in this model. This will give us a *sharp* picture of causality. With it may be compared the more or less *blurred* pictures of causality which are employed in scientific practice and underlie the causal talk of natural and social scientists and historians. As a consequence of this comparison, we may come to a better appreciation also of the claims philosophers have made regarding the limitations and scope of causal explanations and regarding the operations of causality in the web of facts constituting reality.

One can relax in various ways the model of an atomistic world which we are building. One could, for example, give up the assumption that the members of the set of atomic states are invariably the same and/or that their number is finite, but retain the assumption that they are logically independent. One could also replace the assumption that time is discrete with the assumption that it is dense or continuous, and replace the assumption that the world has a beginning in time with the assumption that neither the past nor the future of the world has an end. It would be of interest to inquire how these modifications would influence the causal notions as defined for the stricter model. As the core of the notion of an atomistic world model, I should regard the logical independence of the atomic components of the world states on the one hand, and of the temporally separated total states of the world on the other hand. But these requirements of independence too could be 'relaxed' and the consequences of this relaxation for the causal notions studied.

5

What does it mean that on a certain occasion a certain state p is (causally) possible? Which is the modal logic of our topological tree?

These questions have no univocal answer. I shall here mention two ways of answering them. They are not the only ones, but they are of particular relevance to our problems.

That 'Mp' is true of a given world (circle in our figure) can mean that the generic state p, e.g. that it is raining, obtains in at least one of the worlds which are possible immediately after the given world. But it can also mean that p obtains in at least one of the worlds which are possible either immediately after the given world, or at some later time.

On both interpretations, possibility is, so to speak, a forward-looking idea. It is a 'potency' inherent in a world to develop into a world of which a certain feature is true. On the first interpretation this potency has to manifest itself immediately, if at all. This feature of the interpretation can be modified by replacing the word 'immediately' with the phrase 'on one of the next n occasions'.

The two interpretations yield different systems of modal logic. In neither system does the *ab esse ad posse* principle, or $p \to Mp$, hold true. But in both the principle holds that if p is true of the world on the next occasion, then p is a possibility in the world now. In symbols: $tTp \to Mp$, where t stands for an arbitrary tautology of propositional logic.

This failure of the *ab esse ad posse* principle, incidentally, should not be regarded as an oddity. It is in fact not very natural to say of that which is true that it is also possible. It is in better accord with ordinary usage to say that the obtaining of a state of affairs in the world proves that this was a possible world development. What *is* true *was* possible—but whether it still is a potency of the world is not certain.

On both interpretations the usual distribution principles for the modal operators hold true. Possibility distributes disjunctively, according to the equivalence $M(p \lor q) \leftrightarrow Mp \lor Mq$; necessity conjunctively according to the dual formula $N(p \,\&\, q) \leftrightarrow Np \,\&\, Nq$.

On the first interpretation, the second-order possibility MMp means the following thing: At least one world immediately after the world of which MMp is true has the potency Mp of becoming a world of which p is true. In other words: p is true of some world which may come true two steps from now. The truth of this statement obviously does not entail the truth of Mp or that p is true of some world which may come true at the very next moment.

On the second interpretation, MMp means that p obtains in some world which is possible after some world which is possible after the world of which MMp is true. This clearly entails the truth of Mp or that p is true of some world which is possible after the world of which Mp is true. $MMp \to Mp$ thus holds under this interpretation. On this ground I shall call it S4-like.

It is easy to convince oneself that none of the modal principles $MNp \rightarrow$ NMp or $MNp \rightarrow p$ or $MNp \rightarrow Np$ holds on either interpretation.

Consider the interpretation of $M(tTp)$ or the formula which says that a given world may develop into a world which a moment later will be a p-world. On the first interpretation this entails that p is true in some world which it is possible to reach in two steps from the given world, i.e. it entails MMp. On the second interpretation, it entails that p is true in some world after the given world, i.e. it entails Mp. Thus, under the first interpretation, the formula $M(tTp) \rightarrow MMp$ holds; and under the second, the formula $M(tTp) \rightarrow Mp$.

It should be observed that neither one of these last implications can be reversed. Assume that $M(tTp)$ is true. Then there is some world— either immediately after the given world or somewhere later in the tree of possible histories—such that p obtains in the world which *will* come true immediately after this world. And this is a stronger statement than to say merely that p obtains in some world which *may* come true immediately after the world in question, i.e. it is a stronger statement than either MMp or Mp.

Consider finally the formula $\bigvee p$. It says that on some later occasion p will obtain in the world. If this is true, then, on our second interpretation of possibility, Mp will be true too, i.e. p will be true of some possible future world. Thus we have $\bigvee p \rightarrow Mp$. By contraposition, and substituting $\sim p$ for p we can also write this entailment in the form $Np \rightarrow \bigwedge p$, which says that if p is necessary, in the sense of the second interpretation, then it is true for all the future. The causally necessary is also universally true, one could say. But universal truth is weaker than causally necessary truth.

Together with the axioms of propositional logic and of the quantified tense-logic for discrete time, the principles which we have been elucidating constitute, as far as I can see, a sufficient axiomatic basis for the modal logic of causally possible world segments under the two alternative interpretations of possibility. We can write down the axioms in a table:

Interpretation I

A1	$(tTp) \rightarrow Mp$	$(Np \rightarrow (tTp))$
A2	$M(tTp) \rightarrow MMp$	$(NNp \rightarrow N(tTp))$
A3	$M(p \vee q) \rightarrow Mp \vee Mq$	$(N(p \& q) \leftrightarrow Np \& Nq)$

Interpretation II

B1	$M(tTp) \rightarrow Mp$	$(Np \rightarrow N(tTp))$
B2	$MMp \rightarrow Mp$	$(Np \rightarrow NNp)$
B3	$M(p \vee q) \rightarrow Mp \vee Mq$	$(N(p \& q) \leftrightarrow Np \& Nq)$
B4	$\bigvee p \rightarrow Mp$	$(Np \rightarrow \bigwedge p)$

We shall not here prove theorems. Be it only noted that from B4 immediately get the formula $(tTp) \to Mp$, which we said was valid also for the second interpretation.

Since we have given two interpretations, someone may raise the question as to which of them yields an *adequate* logic of the causal modalities. The answer is that both the interpretations which we have mentioned, and some others which we have not mentioned here, are relevant to the logical study of causal relationships—but also that it is the second, S4-like interpretation that is of prime importance to our topic.

6

The proposition that p is a cause of q is often equated with the proposition that p, by itself, is a sufficient condition of q. This is a great, but nevertheless useful, oversimplification.

As regards the proposition that p is a sufficient condition of q we can, moreover, distinguish several cases, depending upon how p and q are thought to be related in time. The two factors and the relationship between them may obtain on one and the same occasion, or the conditioning factor p may obtain on a given occasion and the conditioned factor q on the next, or p may obtain on a given occasion and q on *some* occasion after that. (I shall here omit altogether from consideration the possibility that p may obtain after q and yet be said to condition it causally.)

In 'formalizing' the relation, we begin with the second case. Since we have found that in the S4-like interpretation of the causal modalities Np entails $\bigwedge p$, we can conveniently read the formula $N(p \to tTq)$ as saying that necessarily, whenever p is the case, q immediately follows. And this we may, for present purposes, equate with a statement to the effect that p is a causally sufficient condition of q.

When p and q are simultaneous and the conditionship relation holds between them, the above formula becomes $N(p \to q)$. When p is supposed to be followed by q on *some* later occasion, the formula will be $N(p \to \bigvee q)$. We may regard as standard the case when the effect follows immediately in time upon the cause.

As regards the proposition that p is a necessary condition of q one can similarly distinguish several cases. We may regard as standard the case, when q cannot obtain unless p was there on the immediately preceding occasion, or in symbols: $N(tTq \to p)$. The implication can of course be contraposited to $N(\sim p \to (tT \sim q))$. From this it is seen that the proposition that p is a necessary condition of q is equivalent to the proposition that not-p is a sufficient condition of not-q. In *this* way the two types of condition are, incontestably, interdefinable.

$N(p \rightarrow (tTq))$ is not equivalent to $N(\sim q \rightarrow (tT \sim p))$. That p is a sufficient condition of q is thus not (generally) equivalent to the proposition that q is a necessary condition of p. The two types of condition are not interdefinable by means of such an equivalence.

7

I now turn to the epistemological aspect of our problem. How, if at all, can we come to know that p is the sufficient cause of q? Let us confine ourselves here to the case when q is supposed to be there immediately after p.

$N(p \rightarrow tTq)$ entails the generalization $\bigwedge (p \rightarrow tTq)$. The truth of contingent generalizations, it is universally agreed, we cannot, in a strict sense, come to *know* at all. But we may have observed numerous instances when p was followed by q, and no counter-instances, and then generalized the observed regular sequence. We may feel very confident of the truth of the generalization, so confident of it that we are willing to stake that on any occasion when p was *not* there, q would have followed had p been there. Then our confidence is that the generalization reflects ('flows from') a natural necessity ($N(p \rightarrow tTq)$) and that p is a *cause* of q and not merely an accidental, though regular, antecedent.

Our question now is: what can give us this eminent degree of confidence here? Continued observation may induce us to advance a *hypothesis* that the regularity reflects a causal connection. What we are in search of is something that would confirm us in *this* belief *as distinct from* the belief in the universal nature of the regularity.

Continued observation will never satisfy this craving. It is tied to the 'surface of reality' so to speak. What is required is a peep under this surface, somehow; a dive into the depths of unactualized possibilities for the sake of making sure that even if the actual course of events had been different from what it was, whenever p might have obtained, q would have followed.

There is also another way of expressing what I take to be substantially the same craving or requirement: we want to 'substitute' for a given world in which p is *not* the case another world in which p is the case, so as to be able to show that had p been true of the given world, q would be true of the following one.

But is it not obvious that we are asking for the moon here? In some sense this is certainly so. There is no substituting for a world which is or was, another world where different states obtain. Nor can one step back in our topological tree and make a fresh start along a different branch. With the future, however, the case is different.

Is it then not so that *che sarà, sarà* as the saying goes? I shall maintain that in a logically interesting and philosophically important sense this is *not* so.

At any given point in our topological tree there are alternative histories ahead of us. We do not know *which* one will come true—only that *some* one will be true. And we decided that the branches should be so drawn that the topmost progression of circles after any given circle pictures that history which would be the true one, if the given circle were to picture the true world. The phrase 'would be true' I shall now qualify by the following addition 'unless interference with the course of nature takes place'. What the topmost branches picture is thus the course of future developments if nature is left 'alone', 'untouched', 'to itself', to continue its course from any given point. It may have come to this point either 'of itself', from some previous point in the same 'natural' history, or thanks to some act of interference. This last means that the development from some point in another history was 'deflected' so as to become the starting-point of a new history. Such deflections can happen, in principle, at any point in any of the natural histories. They could also be called 'shifts of reality'. They are by no means impossible, nor even uncommon happenings. They occur whenever agents act.

In order to see clearly what all this amounts to, we must inspect somewhat more closely the logic of action. Assume that a certain world obtains and in it a state of affairs $\sim p$. We feel confident—presumably on the basis of past experience, or for some other reason—that p will continue to be absent from the world on the next occasion unless we produce it, i.e. change the world into one that contains the state p. We feel confident, moreover, that we can do this, say, because we have *learnt* (been taught) how to do it.

But, you will ask, what is this confidence worth? Can we not be mistaken in thinking that p will not come about 'of itself', but only if we produce it? And may we not be mistaken in thinking that we *can* make p come about? Certainly! Unexpected changes sometimes occur in nature 'of themselves' and unexpected disabilities sometimes befall a man. But, by and large, the type of confidence to which I am here referring is trustworthy. Were it not so, *action* would not be possible. It is a conceptual feature of the utmost importance of that which we call action that certain changes in nature would not have occurred had we not produced them—or would have happened had we not prevented them. (One can refer to this as the *counterfactual element* involved in every action.)

Now imagine that we do interfere in the above situation and make a p-world out of a world which would otherwise have remained in the state not-*p*. We let this newly created world continue without touching it and find that it immediately changes to a *q*-world. This operation will, usually, 'impress' us strongly and confirm the surmise, if we had made it, that the regular sequence of *p* and *q* in the past was no mere accident but signified a causal tie between the two factors.

But perhaps *q* would have come into being even if we had refrained from interference and let the initial world continue as a ~ *p*-world. This we cannot check *post hoc*. But we can wait for, or perhaps ourselves produce, a new situation in which *p* is not there and will remain absent unless we interfere and *then* abstain from interfering. If now *q* is *not* there immediately after—or at least is not always there on such-like occasions—this further strengthens our belief in the causal connection.

Of these two operations, viz. that of producing *p* and always finding *q* on the next occasion and that of letting *p* remain absent and not always finding *q* on the next occasion, I shall say that they come 'as near as is logically conceivable' to the verification of the counterfactual statement that on the past occasions when *p* was not there, *q* would have immediately followed had *p* been there. It is no proof, of course, that the counterfactual is true. But it is what makes us believe this. It confirms our belief that an observed regularity amounts to a causal or nomic connection.

Granted that these operations have this influence on our causal beliefs and hypotheses, we may raise the question of *why* they should have it. This is, at least partly, a question pertaining to the *logic* of the case. There seem to be two reasons why the observations which I described should have the effect which I attributed to them.

As long as we restrict ourselves to observing the regular sequence of *q* upon *p*, two possibilities will forever remain open which, if true, would make us withdraw the statement that *p* is the cause of *q*. One is that *p* and *q* have a *common cause*, i.e. that there is some factor which causes the succession *pTq* invariably to take place. If such a common cause were found one would not say that there is a causal tie *between p* and *q*. The other possibility is that *q* has some more remote cause, so that *q* would have been there in any case, whether or not *p* happened to 'pop up' immediately before it. If this turned out to be the case, we should again not say that it was *p* which caused *q*.

Now, the first of these possibilities, viz. that of a common cause, is eliminated by the experiment in which we shifted to a new succession of natural developments. For, at the point where the shift took place, the world would, we feel confident, have continued to be in the state not-*p* had we not 'steered' it to the state *p*, and this possibility of 'steering' the world rules out the existence of an antecedent cause which would have taken the world to *p*, i.e.

produced p, and thereby also rules out the possibility of a cause responsible for the succession of q upon p.

Again the second possibility, viz. that the effect-factor would have occurred in any case and that the alleged cause-factor had no share in bringing it about, is excluded by the simple observation that when we refrain from producing the cause we also, on the whole, lose the effect. It is essential to say here 'on the whole' or 'generally' and not to insist on 'always'. For we do not, of course, wish to rule out the possibility that there may exist other causes of q beside p and that some of them happen to operate when p is not there. We must only make sure that such a cause is not constantly operating when p can be experimentally introduced. For otherwise, we should have no indication of the independent causal efficacy of p.

I have tried to argue that what confers on observed regularities the character of causal or nomic connections is the possibility of subjecting cause-factors to experimental test by interfering with the 'natural' course of events. In an important sense, therefore, the causal relation can be said to be dependent upon the concept of (human) *action*. This dependence is *epistemological*, rather than ontological, because it has to do with the way causal relations are established and distinguished from accidental regularities. But this dependence is also, in a sense which I have tried to make as precise as possible, *logical*, because it is connected with features which are peculiar to the *concept* of action.

The conceptual relationships in this region are complex and intricate and I am afraid that the view of causality which I have put forward can easily be misunderstood. I shall here give warning of two of the many possible misunderstandings:

The characteristic procedures whereby causal ties are tested do not by any means amount to a verification of nomic connections. Calling causal connections natural necessities may be convenient, but it does not mean that causal laws are *a priori* any more than ordinary inductive generalizations are. Their truth is a matter of future experience which can never be exhausted, and they share with inductive generalizations the characteristic asymmetry with regard to verifiability and falsifiability.

The second misunderstanding is a confusion between the epistemic and the ontic aspect. By no means have I wanted to maintain that the operation of a cause always results from action. Causation, needless to say, operates throughout nature independently of agency, also in regions of the world forever inaccessible to human interference. But the test-procedures characteristic of causal laws, including those whose operation is far removed from us in space or time, belong to the scientists' laboratories—and they belong there *essentially*, because of their conceptual connection with the mode of action we call experiment.

8

We have now a clue to answering what I called the *asymmetry problem*. This was the question of what distinguishes cause from effect, the conditioning from the conditioned factor in a nomic relationship. What makes *p* a cause-factor relative to the effect-factor *q* is, I shall maintain, the fact that by *manipulating p*, i.e. by producing changes in it 'at will' as we say, we could bring about changes in *q*. This applies both to cause-factors which are sufficient and those which are necessary conditions of the corresponding effect-factor.

In the normal cases, the effect brought about by the operation of the cause occurs later. In such cases time has already provided the distinction. More problematic is the case when cause and effect are supposed to be simultaneous. Those who think of the cause–effect distinction in terms of temporality alone will be at a loss here. But when the distinction is made in terms of manipulability, the difficulty can be solved.

Consider the following example. There is a container with two valves. On a given occasion, one valve is open: this state of affairs I shall call not-*p*, the other valve is shut: this I shall symbolize by *q*. If the first valve is being closed, the second will at the very same time open. If, again, the second valve is being opened, the first will at the very same time close. In the first case we should say that (the coming into being of) *p* causes not-*q*, i.e. causes *q* to cease to be. In the second case we would say that not-*q* caused *p* (to come about). If the states which obtain are *p* and not-*q* and we do not know how this situation came to be, we could not tell whether the first valve is shut because the second is open, or whether the second is open because the first is shut. But whether or not one of the two states, when they obtain, can be singled out as cause and the other as effect, the two states can quite correctly be said to be *causally connected*. That they are causally connected means that we can influence the one by manipulating the other. (We must not say that *because* they are causally connected we can influence the one by manipulating the other.)

This observation is relevant to the question of the relation of causal laws to functional laws. Functional laws such as the Gas Law or Ohm's Law can quite appropriately be said to express *causal relationships*. But this does not mean that functional laws relate factors as causes and effects. Therefore there is good reason for not calling them 'causal laws'. What is causal about the relationship is that by manipulating one term one can induce changes in other terms. And when such manipulation takes place, one can distinguish cause from effect—even in cases when the changes occur simultaneously. The cause–effect distinction refers to the history of an individual occasion, one could say, and does not reside in the relation between the generic factors themselves.

Sometimes not all the factors in a functional relationship are manipulable. Then the non-manipulable factors can only assume the role of effects, never that of causes. Assume, for example, that there is no other way of changing the volume of a gas than by changing either pressure or temperature. Then changes in volume are always effects and never causes. And it is for a similar reason that the absence of flooding is not a *cause* of the absence of rain, although rain may cause flooding and therefore from the non-occurrence of flooding we can conclude to the non-occurrence of rain by virtue of that causal relation. We can, given our present knowledge of the laws of nature, imagine ways of controlling floods by controlling rainfall, but not the other way round. That it should be so, however, is contingent.

9

The idea of causation which I have been discussing could be termed *manipulative* or *experimentalist* causation. It is an idea which sees an essential connection between causation and (human) action.

A logical presupposition of manipulative causation is (familiarity with) recurrent situations of generically identical states, fragments of world states, with which we (know we) can interfere. Such (knowledge of) ability entails, i.e. presupposes also, knowledge of how the world will develop if we do *not* interfere with it.

Another logical basis for this kind of causation is (the existence of some degree of) logical atomism, i.e. the conceptual and verificational separability of states of affairs between which a causal connection is either asserted or denied. In particular, it must be possible to come to know the occurrence of the alleged cause-factor independently of (coming to know) the occurrence of the alleged effect-factor, and conversely.

A third presupposition is (familiarity with) regularities, for example that q regularly follows upon p in our experience. This presupposition entails familiarity with recurrent situations but not necessarily situations with which we have learnt to interfere.

In a world where these suppositions are not fulfilled there is no room for manipulative causation either. If we were placed in such a world our notion of *action* (interference with nature) and this notion of causation would have no application.

The presuppositions, however, can be satisfied to a greater or lesser extent and the notion of manipulative causation can accordingly have a more or less restricted applicability. If we identify 'causation' with 'manipulative causation' these restrictions could be said to set limits to the reign of causation. If we refrain from this identification, we should have to reckon with different 'types' of causation.

It will be agreed offhand, I think, that manipulative causation is at home *primarily* in the natural sciences, including both the physical sciences and the life sciences. But is *all* causation in the natural sciences of the kind I here call manipulative? And is causation of this type applicable to the human sciences at all?

The answer to the first question will partly depend upon what one is willing to call 'causation' in the contexts of natural science—and also upon where we wish to draw the border between natural and 'not-natural' science. There is no need to insist upon any sharp border at all—and there is good reason not to be over-strict with the meaning of 'causation'. But this being granted, it seems to me that one can make a strong case for the thesis that causation in the natural sciences (better: causation in nature) is primarily and on the whole of the manipulative type. I shall advance a few arguments in support of this view.

When a regularity is recorded between phenomena which are not subject to direct interference by manipulation—for example, because they take place in remote parts of the universe—we are, I think, on the whole hesitant to speak of them as 'causally related' or of the regularity as a 'causal law'. The regularity is rather what Mill[3] called an 'empirical law'. We may e.g. doubt whether there is not a cause for the regularity itself so that when, say, *r* regularly follows upon *q* this is because of the previous occurrence of *p*. Now it often happens that observed regularities are raised to the rank of laws because of their being explained, i.e. deduced from laws. And thereby they in fact often assume a 'causal' appearance as well. Why is this?

The answer, I think, is that the laws themselves from which the observed uniformity has been deduced are established by laboratory procedures—and not just by passive observations. Our knowledge of causes and effects in remote regions in space, or, as in geological or palaeontological research, in time, is based on and 'mediated' by our knowledge of natural laws for which we have sufficient experimental evidence from our laboratories.

In speaking of 'laws of nature' I have here in the first place been thinking of such laws as those of falling bodies, or the Gas Law, or Ohm's Law, or

---

[3] J. S. Mill, *A System of Logic* (London, 1843), bk. iii, ch. 16.

Snell's Law. They are typically 'experimentalist laws'. But not all laws have this character, to be sure. Some laws of a very general nature are more like conceptual principles, constitutive of the frame of reference within which experiments are conducted and results interpreted. The discovery of the law of inertia, for instance, is a fascinating chapter of experimental science. But the law itself is not a causal law, nor was it discovered through experiments. It is rather a conceptual frame for distinguishing a 'causeless' state of affairs from states for the existence or origination of which we have to look for causes. And something similar is true of such laws as the principle of the conservation of energy or the law of entropy, etc. It is not very natural to think of them as *causal*.

10

It is a traditional matter of debate whether, or to what extent, causal categories are applicable to the human sciences. The question raised and the answers given in these debates are often all too sweeping and vague. A useful way of clarifying things is, I think, to try to relate ideas concerning manipulative causation to questions of explanation and prediction in the realm of human action.

Explanation of action is often and typically, even if not exclusively, given in terms of intentions, motives, and reasons. We also say that in acting an agent is aiming at something, an end of action, and we explain his conduct in terms of his aims and ends. Such explanations are called teleological.

It can hardly be called in question that teleological explanations are 'legitimate' within their appropriate orbit. But it is very much an open question what their logical status is, and in particular, how they are related to causal explanations.

Many recent authors have stressed what they take to be a basic difference between causal explanations on the one hand and intentionalist, motivational, or teleological explanations on the other hand. The supposed difference is this: in a causal relation cause and effect are logically independent. But the relation of actions to their motivating reasons, it is said, is not one between logically independent terms.

I think those philosophers are right, who point to this difference between the two types of explanation. But the way in which they have presented the Logical Connection Argument, as it is called, has often been faulty or else unconvincing. Let q be the result of a certain agent's action, i.e. the state of affairs which is there when this agent has done a certain thing. And let p be the reason which prompted his action, e.g. the fact that he wanted something for which this action was instrumental or intended to achieve something for which the action was necessary. I shall here lump all such action-prompting factors, be they intentions, motives, aims, or ends, under one label 'reasons'.

Now let p, the reason, be there on an occasion prior to the one when the action is supposed to follow. We must then think of p as remaining present until the action is effected. For otherwise it would cease to be a reason for the agent to act upon. (We shall refer to a change in p as a 'change of mind'.) q, on the other hand, must be absent on the occasion when the action is initiated. For, otherwise, there would be no opportunity for performing the action. This occasion, moreover, must be such that not only the agent himself but also the person who describes the case or explains the action feels confident that q will not come about unless the agent acts. So we have to reckon with at least two causally possible world-segments here, one leading to q and another one leading to not-q. This alone excludes that q could, of causal necessity, follow upon p. If it did, the agent would not have acted.

We could, of course, have predicted the action, once p was known to be there. And we might have been very confident indeed of the truth of the prediction, thinking that once the agent has this reason, he will certainly act accordingly. This would be a comparable confidence to the one which we have in an action situation of our own, the confidence that the world will not change in a certain respect unless we interfere. This 'practical certainty', however, is not derived from belief in causal laws.

But here someone may say that we are begging the question. Once p is there and remains, q *must* follow and not-q is no longer a causal possibility in the action-situation—even though the agent may think it is. If reasons operate like causes, then, when the reasons are there, the agents are no longer free to *let* the world take the course which it would have taken independently of their action. To think otherwise is to be under an illusion. In this argument there is some truth and some error.

When viewing the action from before it has taken place, but when the reason for its performance is already there, there is no such 'must' at all. The reason may 'drop out' before the action has taken place, i.e. the agent may change his mind. Or the reason may continue to be there for him to act—and the agent may try but fail to accomplish the action. Or something may happen which prevents him.

Assume, however, that the agent has performed the action. This rules out the possibility that he tried but was not successful, or that he was prevented. Assume also that his reason for acting was continuously present. Then, to say that he acted *because* of that reason is indeed to make a statement of necessity. But not, I think, a causal one. For the omission of the action would now be a criterion or standard whereby we judge that the agent has changed his mind. When both the action and the reason *for it*, i.e. the reason why he acted, are there, then their connection is conceptual, logical, and not causal. This, on my understanding of this complex problem, is the gist of truth contained in the so-called Logical Connection Argument.

It is indeed a 'logical illusion' to think that an agent could, without changing his mind, act contrary to the reasons for his action—in our example, *let* the world stay at not-*q* instead of taking it to *q*. Having had a reason can, after the action, be said to have necessitated the action. Having a reason, however, can never be said to necessitate an agent not to change his mind before he acts. The existence of reasons therefore does not obliterate the bifurcation of possibilities which is characteristic of an action situation. This is why it is no 'causal illusion' to think of an agent as free even when his actions flow from so-called 'compelling reasons'.

Yet someone may still protest against this conceptual separation between causal explanations and explanations of action. Reasons too can be manipulated, first of all. There are numberless ways in which we can produce reasons for a man to act upon and then watch his behaviour—like any other event in nature. Starve a man and he will seize the first opportunity of getting food, threaten him at gunpoint and he will raise his arms, put requests or orders to him and under normal circumstances you can count upon his reaction. Why think that this is all that unique and different from causal relationships of stimuli and responses?

The answer is that we need not think of this as different from causation at all. We can ignore the bifurcations in the acting-situations as pictured in our topological tree; we can think that there is essentially only one continuation from *p* to *q*, and attribute a failure of the effect to materialize to the intervention of some unforeseen 'counteracting cause' which explains the failure. This is exactly analogous to procedures familiar from the methodology and practice of the natural sciences.

Such a view of human behaviour is indeed possible and may also be fruitful. It is a view largely accepted, I should think, in 'scientific' social and psychological studies. It can be called a *reified* view of man as an agent, using for it a term well known from Hegelian and Marxist philosophy.

To discuss the scope and limits of this reified view of man would be to enter a jungle of controversy in the philosophy of the social sciences. This we cannot do here. Let it only be said in conclusion that what I have done in this paper has been to argue for *one* essential limitation to the reification and thus also 'causalization' of action. This limitation is set by the implicit dependence of the very notion of cause on an (unreified) concept of agency and action. To regard things as being causally related is the intellectual privilege of agents who think they are free to interfere with the world. This thought is the basis of man's technology and mastery of nature. But only through a misunderstanding of its conceptual foundations can man snare himself in the deterministic connections which his scientific intelligence unravels in nature.

VII

ON THE NATURE
AND THE OBSERVABILITY
OF THE CAUSAL RELATION

C. J. DUCASSE

The aim of this paper is to set forth two related theses. The first is that the correct definition of the causal relation is to be framed in terms of one single case of sequence, and that constancy of conjunction is therefore no part of it, but merely, under certain conditions, a corollary of the presence of the causal relation. The second thesis is that the causal relation, when correctly defined, is as directly observable as many other facts, and that the alleged mysteriousness of the causal tie is therefore a myth due only to a mistaken notion of what a tie is.

1. MEANING OF 'A CORRECT DEFINITION'

The problem of giving a 'correct' definition of the causal relation is that of making analytically explicit the meaning which the term 'cause' has in actual concrete phrases that our language intuition acknowledges as proper and typical cases of its use. For obviously it is one thing to 'know what cause means' in the cheap sense of being able to understand intuitively such an assertion as that the Santa Barbara earthquake caused the collapse of numberless chimneys; and it is another and a much more difficult and rarer thing to 'know what cause means' in the sense of being able to give a correct definition of it. To say that a definition of it is correct means that that definition can be substituted for the word 'cause' in any such assertion as the above, in which the word occurs, *without in the least changing the meaning which the assertion is felt to have.* Any ventured definition of such a philosophical term as cause is thus capable of being correct or incorrect in strictly the same sense as that in which a scientific hypothesis is so, viz. either it fits the facts or it does not. The only difference is that in the case of scientific hypotheses the facts are perceptual objects and their relations, while in the case of philosophical hypotheses the facts are the intuited meanings of actual phrases in which the word to be defined occurs. The great inductive method of hypothesis–deduction–verification is thus no less that of philosophy than that of science.

2. TWO PRELIMINARY REMARKS

Before attempting to formulate a definition of the term 'cause', attention must briefly be called to two essential preliminary points.[1]

1. The first is that nothing can, in strict propriety, ever be spoken of as a cause or an effect, except an *event*. And by an event is to be understood either a change or an absence of change (whether qualitative or relational) of an object.[2] On the other hand, objects themselves (in the sense of substances, e.g. gold; or things, e.g. a tree) never can properly be spoken of as causes or effects,[3] but only as agents or patients, as components or compounds, as parts or wholes. These relations, although closely allied to the causal relation, are nevertheless distinct from it, and cannot be discussed here.

2. The second point to be borne in mind is that when the term 'causal connection' is used, any one of four distinct objective relations may actually be meant, namely, objectively sufficient to, necessary to, necessitated by, contingent upon. And to these four relations correspond respectively the four functional terms, cause, condition, effect, resultant. So that, more explicitly, if a given particular event is regarded as having been *sufficient to* the occurrence of another, it is said to have been its *cause*; if regarded as having been *necessary to* the occurrence of another, it is said to have been a *condition of* it; if regarded as having been *necessitated by* the occurrence of another, it is said to have been its *effect*; and if regarded as having been *contingent upon* the occurrence of another, it is said to have been a *resultant* of that other. Much confusion has resulted in discussions of causality from the failure to keep these four relations at all times clearly distinguished, Mill, indeed, pushing perversity to the point of convincing himself and some of his readers that there was no sound basis for a distinction between cause and condition. But it is, on the contrary, essential to remember that to be sufficient is one thing, to be necessary another thing, and to be *both* sufficient and necessary (which is what Mill's definition would make cause mean) yet a third thing.

[1] In a monograph on causation by the writer, these two points are argued at some length. See *Causation and the Types of Necessity* (Seattle, 1924), 52 ff.

[2] More technically, an event can be defined as either a change or an absence of change in the relation of an object to either an intensive or an extensive standard of reference, during a specified time interval.

[3] Cf. Arthur Schopenhauer, *The Fourfold Root of the Principle of Sufficient Reason*, trans. K.Hillebrand (London, 1903), 38 ff.; and Wilhelm Wundt, *Logik*, 3rd edn. (Stuttgart, 1906–8), 1. 586.

Of the four relations, cause, condition, effect, resultant, which a given particular event may have to another with which it is connected, we shall have space here to discuss only the first, namely, cause. And we shall, moreover, confine ourselves to cases—much the more frequent—where the events contemplated are changes, rather than absences of change.

3. DEFINITION OF CAUSE

Taking it as an admitted fact of the language that if the occurrence of a particular change suffices to the occurrence of a given other it is then said to have caused that other, the all-important question now arises how such sufficing is to be defined. I suggest that the correct definition of it, framed in terms of a hypothetical situation, is as follows:

Considering two changes, C and K (which may be either of the same or of different objects), the change C is said to have been sufficient to, i.e. to have caused, the change K, if:

1. The change C occurred during a time and through a space terminating at the instant I at the surface S.[4]

2. The change K occurred during a time and through a space beginning at the instant I at the surface S.

3. No change other than C occurred during the time and through the space of C, and no change other than K during the time and through the space of K.

More roughly, but in briefer and more easily intuited terms, we may say that *the cause of the particular change K was such particular change C as alone occurred in the immediate environment of K immediately before.*

4. SOME BEARINGS OF THE DEFINITION

A number of important points may be noted in connection with the above definition of cause.

1. The first is that it presents the causal relation as involving not two terms only, but essentially three terms, namely, (*a*) the environment of an object, (*b*) some change in that environment, (*c*) the resulting change in the object. As soon as it is clearly realized that the expression 'the cause of an event' thus has any meaning at all only in terms of some definite environment, either

---

[4] The limit of a change of a solid is obviously a surface, not a point.

concretely given or abstractly specified, Mill's contention that the distinction between cause and conditions is arbitrary and capricious is seen to be absurd. To take up the environment into the 'cause', as Mill's definition of cause[5] tries to do, is impossible because the cause consists of a change in that environment. No event can be spoken of as the cause of anything, except relatively to certain conditions; and vice versa, as regards conditions.

2. The second remark for which the definition of cause above gives occasion concerns the immediate spatial and temporal contiguity of cause and effect. The alleged impossibility of such immediate contiguity is the chief ground upon which Russell has advocated the extrusion of the term 'cause' from the philosophical vocabulary.[6] The difficulties raised by him, however, are easily disposed of if two things are kept in mind. The first is that the terms 'a time' and 'a place' are ambiguous. It is essential to distinguish clearly 'a time' in the sense of an instant, i.e. a *cut* of the time series, from 'a time' in the sense of a *segment* of the time series, limited by two cuts. And similarly with regard to the space order, the cuts of it (viz. point, lines, or surfaces according as one-, two-, or three-dimensional space is considered) are to be carefully distinguished from the *parts* of space, which have such cuts as limits. The second thing to bear in mind is that an event (whether a change or an 'un-change')[7] cannot be said to occur *at* a time (cut), but only *during* a time (segment); nor *at* a point (or other cut of space), but only *through* a space (between cuts). Thus, a change is essentially a process which has extent both in time and in space, and is therefore divisible; any division yielding segments of the process that are themselves extended in time and space and therefore further divisible, *ad infinitum*.[8] The immediate contiguity of cause and effect in space and time, specified in our definition, then means only that one identical space–time *cut* marks both the end of the cause process and the beginning of the effect process; the one extending up to, and the other from, that cut; the cut itself, however (by the very nature of a cut

---

[5] 'The cause . . . is the sum total of the conditions, positive and negative taken together . . . which being realized, the consequent invariably follows' (*System of Logic*, 3.5.3). This definition is obviously in flagrant contradiction with Mill's characterization of the cause as the single difference in the circumstances, in the canon of the 'Method of Difference'.

[6] 'On the Notion of Cause', *Proceedings of the Aristotelian Society*, 13 (1912–13), 1–26.

[7] The apt term 'unchange' is borrowed from Dr Charles Mercier's book, *On Causation: with a Chapter on Belief* (London, 1916).

[8] A stage might, however, conceivably be reached, at which the parts obtained by the division of a change would, *in terms of the particular test of changing used at the previous stages of division*, be themselves not changes, but unchanges (though, of course, none the less extended in time and space and therefore divisible). That is, the assertion that something changes, or, equally, does not change, remains ambiguous so long as some definite test of such change has not been specified as standard. Thus the assertion might be true in terms of one test and false in terms of another. Cf. my 'A Liberalistic View of Truth', in the *Philosophical Review* for Nov. 1925.

as distinguished from a segment), having no space–time dimension at all.[9]
With cause and effect and their space–time relation[10] so conceived, there is
no possibility that, as Russell contended, some other event should creep in
between the cause and the effect and thwart the production of the effect. Nor
are we compelled, as he also contended, to trim down indefinitely the beginning part of the cause (and, *mutatis mutandis*, the end part of the effect) on
the ground that the early part of the cause is not necessary to the effect so
long as the end part of the cause occurs. For, once more, the cause means
something which was sufficient, and not as the objection assumes, something
which was both sufficient and necessary to the effect. Thus the space–time
limit of the cause process at the outer end is as elastic as we please, and varies
with the space–time scope of the particular description of the cause that we
give in each concrete case. And the same is true of the outer end of the effect
process.[11]

3. The third observation to be made on the definition of cause proposed is
that it defines the cause of a particular event in terms of but a single occurrence of it, and thus in no way involves the supposition that it, or one like
it, ever has occurred before or ever will again. The supposition of recurrence
is thus wholly irrelevant to the meaning of cause; that supposition is relevant
only to the meaning of law. And recurrence becomes related at all to causation only when a law is considered which happens to be a generalization of
facts themselves individually causal to begin with. A general proposition
concerning such facts is, indeed, a causal law, but it is not causal because
general. It is general, i.e. a law, only because it is about a class of resembling
facts; and it is causal only because each of them already happens to be a
causal fact individually and in its own right (instead of, as Hume would have
it, by right of its co-membership with others in a class of pairs of successive
events). The causal relation is essentially a relation between concrete individual events; and it is only so far as these events exhibit likeness to others,
and can therefore be grouped with them into kinds, that it is possible to pass

[9] In practice, no space–time dimension of a relevant order of magnitude. Clock ticks and
graduation lines as used are never perfectly dimensionless.
[10] This view of the space–time relation of cause and effect, I was gratified to find, is also that set
forth by William Ernest Johnson in vol. iii of his *Logic* ((Cambridge, 1924), 74), which appeared
at virtually the same time as the monograph on causation referred to above.
[11] It is interesting to note that the analysis of the space–time relation of cause and effect given
above reveals an essential connection between the two notions of Change and of Causation. For,
taking any given change process, by specifying a space–time cut of it, one splits it into a cause and
an effect; and, on the other hand, taking any given cause and its effect, by abstracting from the
particular space–time cut in terms of which as common limit the cause process is distinguished from
the effect process, one obtains a process describable as one change. This calls to mind Kant's very
inadequately argued contention in the Second Analogy, that (objective) change involves the category
of causation.

from individual causal facts to causal laws. On the other hand, in the case of laws obtained, not by experimentation and generalization of the result of it by abstraction, but in a purely statistical manner (the only manner directly relevant to Hume's notion of cause), it is only quite accidentally that the terms of such 'constant conjunctions' as these laws describe stand one to the other as cause and effect. Much more frequently they are not such and are not regarded as such; and uniformity of succession thus constitutes not at all the meaning of the cause–effect relation, but at the most only evidence of the existence of some causal connection, perhaps very remote and indirect, *and yet to be discovered*, between the terms of the succession. A causal connection explains the regularity of the succession, but is not constituted by such regularity, which is but a corollary of the causal connection whenever the cause or the chain of causes happens to occur again. Hume himself, indeed, on the very page of the *Enquiry* where he gives his definition of cause (in terms of regularity of succession), says that that definition is 'drawn from circumstances foreign to the cause'; 'from something extraneous and foreign to it'. And it was to avoid having to say, as Hume's definition would require, that day was the cause of night and night the cause of day, that Mill added, in his own definition, the requirement of 'unconditionality' to that of invariability of sequence—without perceiving, however, that as soon as 'unconditionality' was introduced, invariability became superfluous. For if the effect 'unconditionally' follows from the cause, i.e. is *necessitated by* the cause, then, obviously, as often as the cause recurs the effect *must* recur also. But this so-called unconditionality of an effect upon a cause, i.e. the necessitation of the effect by the cause, was the very thing which Mill had declared was not revealed by mere observed regularity of sequence. It must then be ascertained by the experimental 'method of difference', i.e. by the analytical observation of an individual case. But Mill never sees that this amounts to *defining* cause in terms of single difference in one experiment. Hume refers to single difference as a 'Rule' by which to judge of causes and effects,[12] and Mill, borrowing the blunder, throughout persists in regarding single difference as a 'method' for the roundabout ascertainment of something other than itself, viz. of invariable sequence; instead of, and properly, regarding it as the very definition of cause. This is perhaps in part explicable by the fact that Mill never clearly perceived the difference between experimentation and generalization[13] by abstraction; he never was adequately conscious that it is one thing to introduce a single difference, i.e. make a single change, in a given concrete set of circumstances, and note what happens; and a very

---

[12] *Treatise*, 1.3.15.

[13] This has been noted by William Stanley Jevons, *Pure Logic and Other Minor Works*, ed. R. Adamson and H. A. Jevons (London, 1890), 251.

different thing to compare two such experiments, one of which yielded a certain effect and the other failed to, and note what single difference there was between the single antecedent changes introduced in the two cases into the (same) set of circumstances.

4. As a last remark upon the definition of cause in terms of a single case given above, it may be noted that it is the only one which is faithful to the manner in which the word 'cause' is actually used by every person whose English has not been contaminated by Hume. As Russell himself notes, we cannot without 'intolerable circumlocution'[14] avoid speaking of one particular event as causing another particular event. And, I ask, why seek to avoid it, when just that is so plainly what we do mean? When any philosophically pure-minded person sees a brick strike a window and the window break, he judges that the impact of the brick was the cause of the breaking, *because* he believes that impact to have been the only change which took place then in the immediate environment of the window. He may, indeed, have been mistaken, and acknowledge that he was mistaken, in believing that impact to have been the only change in the environment. But if so he will nevertheless maintain that *if* it had been the only change, it would have been the cause. That is, he will stand by the definition of cause, and admit merely that what he perceived was not a true case of what he meant and still means by cause.

5. THE OBSERVABILITY OF THE CAUSAL RELATION

This now brings us to the second of the two theses mentioned at the beginning of this paper, namely, that concerning the observability of the causal relation. Hume's view that no connection between a cause and its effect is objectively observable would be correct only under the assumption that a 'connection' is an entity of the same sort as the terms themselves between which it holds, that is, for Hume and his followers, a sense impression. For it is true that neither a colour, nor an odour, nor a sound, nor a taste, nor any other sense impression, 'connecting' the cause and the effect, is observable between them. Indeed, we must even add that if a sense impression were present between those said to constitute the cause and the effect, it would, from its very nature as a sense impression, be quite incapable of doing any connecting and would itself but constitute one more of the entities to be connected. This is true in particular of the feeling of expectation which Hume would have us believe is what the words 'necessary connection' ultimately denote.

[14] *Scientific Method in Philosophy* (Oxford, 1914), 220.

But there is fortunately no need for us to attempt to persuade ourselves that whenever people during the past centuries have talked of objective connection they thus have not really meant it at all. For the fact is that causal connection is not a sensation at all, but a relation. The nature of that relation has already been minutely described above. It is, as we have seen, a relation which has individual concrete events for its terms; and, as analysed by us, its presence among such events is to be observed every day. We observe it whenever we perceive that a certain change is the *only* one to have taken place immediately before, in the immediate environment of another.

But at this point it becomes necessary for us to consider two apparently weighty objections which can be urged against the observability of what we have defined as constituting the causal relation. One of them is that we are never theoretically certain that we have observed as much as the definition demands; and the other is that, on the other hand, we are often certain that the cause is less than the definition would permit us so to call. Each of these difficulties in turn must be carefully examined.

1. The first of them, more explicitly stated, is this: we never can be certain that the change which we have observed in any given case was, as the definition requires, the *only* change that occurred then and there, and therefore it is always possible that a part of the cause has escaped us. In considering this objection, it is, of course, well to bear in mind that our definition specifies contiguity in space as well as in time of the cause to the effect, and in addition permits us to set the *outer* space–time limit of the environment to be observed as near to the effect as we find convenient; so that the definition relieves us of the sometimes alleged obligation to observe the antecedent change of the entire universe. But even confining our observation to as externally limited a region of the contiguous space–time as we please, the possibility still always remains that we have not in a given case observed the whole of the change in that environment.

This predicament, it must frankly be admitted, is inescapable. But we must state also, and with all possible emphasis, that it is not peculiar to the definition of causation proposed.[15] Nor, indeed, is it, in its essence, peculiar even to definitions of cause. Rather it is a predicament involved *in every attempt to observe a universal negative*. Thus, even such an assertion as that 'this man is Mr So-and-so' is theoretically always precarious in exactly the same manner, for there is no theoretically absolute guarantee that the man before us is not someone else, who merely happens to be exactly like Mr

---

[15] The corresponding difficulty with the Humean definition of cause as regular sequence is that experience never can guarantee that exceptions to the regularity of the sequence have not escaped our observation; or, more generally, that the sample of the character of the sequence, which we have observed, is a 'fair sample'.

So-and-so in the particular respects to which our observation has turned.[16] The predicament mentioned, thus, does not constitute the least evidence against the correctness of our definition of cause, for the very same difficulty would arise no matter what other definition were proposed.

All that we are then called upon to do in connection with that predicament is, first, to call attention to its existence and nature, and sagely class it as a fact illustrating the platitude that life is a precarious business in many ways; and, second, to state explicitly the proviso subject to which cases of causation as defined are observable. This proviso is obviously that *the change which we observed in the antecedently contiguous space–time was really the only change which occurred in it.* That is not something which we know to be true, but only something which we hope is true, and which for *practical* purposes we must suppose true; i.e. it is a *postulate*—the first of those underlying the present theory of causation. There is, however, no doubt that when, as in the laboratory, we have a high degree of control over the environment, and good opportunity to observe what occurs in it at a given moment, we do make the assumption just stated.

2. The second of the difficulties which we have to examine is of a logical rather than of a practical nature. It arises from the fact that in the face of the definition of cause given, we cannot without a contradiction refuse to take into the cause *any part* of the total change observed in the contiguous space–time environment of the effect; while, on the contrary, we very frequently in fact seem so to use the word 'cause' as to do just that. Thus, at the instant a brick strikes a window pane, the pane is struck, perhaps, by the air waves due to the song of a canary near by. Yet we usually would say that the cause of the breakage was the impact of the brick, and that the impact of the air waves, although it was part of the prior total change in the contiguous space–time, was no part of the cause. This being the way in which the word 'cause' actually is used, how, then, can a definition which forbids us to call the cause anything less than *the whole* of the prior change in the contiguous space–time be regarded as a correct analysis of the meaning which the term 'cause' actually possesses?

The contradiction, however, is only apparent, and depends upon a confusion between two different questions, due in turn to a certain ambiguity in the expression 'the cause of an event'. The first of the two questions is, *what did cause, i.e. what did then and there suffice to, the occurrence of that concrete individual event?* The second question, on the other hand, is really a double question, for it assumes the answer to the first as already possessed,

---

[16] This difficulty becomes particularly acute when the opportunity for observation is limited, as e.g. in establishing one's identity over the telephone; or, again, in the endeavour of psychical researchers to check up the alleged identity of the 'controls' of their mediums.

and goes on to ask, *which part of what did suffice would be left if we subtracted from what did suffice such portions of it as were unnecessary to such an effect?* This is a perfectly significant question, for to say 'sufficient to' is one thing; and to say 'no more than sufficient to' is another thing: a 100-pound rock may well have been that which sufficed to the crushing of a worm, but it cannot be said to have been no more than what would have sufficed, since the tenth part of it would also have been enough. The second and double question, moreover, is usually that which we mean to ask when we enquire concerning the cause of an event; but, as will appear directly, it is not, like the first, really an enquiry after the cause of one individual concrete event strictly as such. It is, on the contrary, an enquiry concerning *what is common to it and to the causes of certain other events of the same kind.* This much of a generalization, indeed, is indissolubly involved in the mere assigning of *a name* to the cause and to the effect perceived; although *it is not involved in the merely perceiving them.* This is an extremely important point, which constitutes the very key to the whole matter. That this is so will become fully evident if the significance of the second of the two questions above is more explicitly analysed.

If we enquire what exactly is required to define the meaning of that (double) question, we find that at least *two* hypothetical cases are needed. For to say that in a given case a certain change *sufficed* to the occurrence of a given event, means, as we have seen, that no other change than it did occur in the prior contiguous space–time; and to say that a certain portion of that change was *unnecessary* means that in a case where that portion of the change did *not* occur—*which case therefore cannot be the very identical case, but only a case that is otherwise similar*—an(other) event of the same sort as the effect considered nevertheless did result. But now the fact that at least two hypothetical cases are thus necessary to define the meaning of our second question above implies that that question is wholly meaningless with regard to one single concrete event. It is a question not, like the first, concerning the cause of one single concrete event, but concerning what was, or would be, *common to the causes* of at least two such.

The apparent contradiction which we faced is therefore now disposed of, for if, by 'the cause of an event', we really mean the cause of one individual concrete event, and not merely of some case of a sort of event, then we must include in our answer *the whole* of the antecedent change in the contiguous space–time. And if, on the other hand, our answer leaves out any part of that change (as it often does), then the only question to which it can be a correct answer is one as to *what was common to the individual causes* of two or more individual events of a given sort. Thus, if we say that the impact of a brick was the cause of the breaking of the window, and that the song of the canary had no part in it, then the words 'the breaking of the window' do not refer to an individual event considered in its full concreteness, but only to a _case-of-a-kind_, uniquely placed and dated indeed, but not qualitatively specified otherwise than by the characters that define its kind, viz. 'breaking of window'. And it is solely owing to this that we can truly say that the song of the canary had nothing to do with it, for that means, then, nothing to do with what occurred _in so far as what occurred is viewed merely as a case of breakage of a window_. As already explained, to say that the song of the canary was unnecessary is not to say that it was not part of what did then and there suffice; it _is_ to say only that in _another_ case, otherwise similar, where the song did not occur, an effect of the _same sort_, viz. breaking, nevertheless did occur.

The whole of our answer to the objection we have been discussing may, after all this detail, be summarized by saying that the expression 'the cause of the breaking of this window' has two senses, one strict, and the other elliptical. In the strict sense, it means 'the fully concrete individual event which caused all the concrete detail of this breaking of this window'. In the elliptical (and indeed more practically interesting) sense, it means 'that which the cause of this breaking of this window has in common with the individual causes of certain other individual events of the same sort'.

6. THE GENERALIZATION OF OBSERVED CAUSAL FACTS

It is, of course, to be acknowledged that, as the parenthesis in the last sentence suggests, we are interested in causes and effects primarily for practical purposes, and that for such purposes causal knowledge is of direct value only so far as it has been generalized. This means that the interest of strictly concrete individual facts of causation to us is chiefly the indirect one of constituting raw material for generalization. And this explains why we so naturally and so persistently confuse the question, what did cause one given concrete event, with the very different question, in what respects does that cause resemble the causes of certain other events of the same sort previously observed in similar environments. For it is from the answer to this second question that we learn what in such environments is the most we must do to cause the occurrence of another event of the given sort. And evidently just that is the very practically valuable information that we desire ultimately to obtain. But although it is true that, as practical beings, we are not directly interested in concrete individual facts of causation, it is not true that there are no such facts; nor, as we have seen, is it true that generality or recurrence is any part of the meaning of cause.

To round out the outline of the theory of the causal relation which this paper sets forth, there remains only to state the two postulates which condition, respectively, the validity of the descriptions by names which we formulate to fit sets of individual causal facts, and the validity of the applications we make of such generalizing descriptions to new cases.

The postulate which conditions the correctness of any answer we venture to give to the problem of description, viz. the problem in what respects the cause of a given concrete event resembles the causes of certain others of the same sort previously observed in similar environments,[17] is that *the respects of resemblance which we include in our answer* (through the name by which we describe the cause) *are really the only ones that there were*. This postulate, which may be called that of the *descriptibility* of our causal observations, is then the second postulate of our theory. The first, which it will be recalled was that no change that was not observed occurred in the prior contiguous space–time environment, may be called that of the *observability* of causal facts. And the third postulate, which we may term that of the *applicability* of our descriptions of our observations of causal facts to new cases, is that *the new case* (*or cases*) *differs from those on the basis of which the description was formulated not otherwise nor more widely than they differed among themselves.*

---

[17] Mill correctly states that 'It is inherent in a description to be the statement of a resemblance, or resemblances,' *A System of Logic* (London, 1843), 452.

VIII

PROBABILISTIC CAUSALITY*

WESLEY C. SALMON

Although many philosophers would be likely to brand the phrase 'probabilistic causality' as a blatant solecism, embodying serious conceptual confusion, it seems to me that probabilistic causal concepts are used in innumerable contexts of everyday life and science. We hear that various substances are known to cause cancer in laboratory animals—see the label on your favourite diet soft-drink can—even though there is no presumption that every laboratory animal exposed to the substance developed any malignancy. We say that a skid on a patch of ice was the cause of an automobile accident, though many cars passed over the slick spot, some of them skidding upon it, without mishap. We have strong evidence that exposure to even low levels of radiation can cause leukaemia, though only a small percentage of those who are so exposed actually develop leukaemia. I sometimes complain of gastric distress as a result of eating very spicy food, but such discomfort is by no means a universal sequel to well-seasoned Mexican cuisine. It may be maintained, of course, that in all such cases a fully detailed account would furnish invariable cause–effect relations, but this claim would amount to no more than a declaration of faith. As Patrick Suppes has ably argued, it is as pointless as it is unjustified.[1]

There are, in the philosophical literature, three attempts to provide theories of probabilistic causality: Hans Reichenbach, I. J. Good, and Patrick Suppes have offered reasonably systematic treatments.[2] In the vast philosophical literature on causality they are largely ignored. Moreover, Suppes makes no mention of Reichenbach's, later discussion and Good gives it only the

* This material is based upon work supported by the National Science Foundation under Grant No. SOC-7809146. The author wishes to express his gratitude for this support, and to thank I. J. Good, Paul Humphreys, Merrilee H. Salmon, Patrick Suppes, and Philip von Bretzel for valuable comments on an earlier version of this paper.

[1] *A Probabilistic Theory of Causality* (Amsterdam, 1970), 7–8.

[2] Hans Reichenbach, *The Direction of Time* (Berkeley, Calif. and Los Angeles, 1956); I. J. Good, 'A Causal Calculus I', *British Journal for the Philosophy of Science*, 11/44 (1961), 305–18, 'A Causal Calculus II', ibid. 12/45 (1962), 43–51, and 'Errata and Corrigenda', ibid. 13/41 (1963), 88; Suppes, *A Probabilistic Theory*. Both Good and Reichenbach published earlier discussions of probabilistic causality, but both authors regard them as superseded by the works cited here.

slightest note,[3] though both offer brief critical remarks on some of his earlier work. Suppes makes the following passing reference to Good's theory: 'After working out most of the details of the definitions given here in lectures at Stanford, I discovered that a closely related analysis of causality had been given in an interesting series of articles by I. J. Good (1961, 1962), and the reader is urged to look at Good's articles for a development similar to the one given here, although worked out in rather different fashion formally and from a different viewpoint.'[4] Even amongst those who have done constructive work on probabilistic causality, there is no sustained discussion of the three important extant theories.

The aim of the present article is to take a close critical look at the proposals of Good, Reichenbach, and Suppes. Each of the three is, for reasons which I shall attempt to spell out in detail, seriously flawed. We shall find, I believe, that the difficulties arise from certain rather plausible assumptions about probabilistic causality, and that the objections lead to some rather surprising general results. In the concluding section, I shall briefly sketch what seem to me the appropriate ways of circumventing the problems associated with these three theories of probabilistic causality. . . .

2. REICHENBACH'S MACROSTATISTICAL THEORY

Unlike Good and Suppes, who attempt to provide analyses of probabilistic causality for their own sake, Reichenbach develops his analysis as a part of his programme of implementing a causal theory of time. Thus, in contrast to the other two authors, he does not build into his definitions the stipulation that causes are temporally prior to effects. Instead, he attempts to construct a theory of causal relations which will yield a causal asymmetry which can then be used to define a relation of temporal priority. Two of the key causal concepts introduced in this construction are the relation of *causal betweenness* and the structure known as a *conjunctive fork*. The main use of the betweenness relation is to establish a linear time order; the conjunctive fork is employed to impose a direction or asymmetry upon the linear time order. In the present discussion, I shall not attempt to evaluate the temporal ramifications of Reichenbach's theory; instead, I shall confine my attention to the adequacy of the causal concepts as such.

Reichenbach's formal definition of causal betweenness, translated from his notation into a standard notation, reads as follows:[5]

An event B is *causally between* the events A and C if the relations hold:

---

    [3] 'A Causal Calculus II', 45.   [4] *A Probabilistic Theory*, 11.   [5] *Direction of Time*, 190.

$$1 > P(C|B) > P(C|A) > P(C) > 0^6 \qquad (8)$$

$$1 > P(A|B) > P(A|C) > P(A) > 0 \qquad (9)$$

$$P(C|A.B) = P(C|B) \qquad (10)$$

Together with the principle of *local comparability of time order*, the relation of causal betweenness can, according to Reichenbach, be used to construct causal nets and chains similar to those mentioned by Good in his causal calculus. Unlike Good, however, Reichenbach does not attempt a quantitative characterization of the strengths of such chains and nets. It is worth noting that formulas (8) and (9) embody several statistical relevance relations: A is relevant to the occurrence of C, but B is more highly relevant to C; conversely, C is relevant to the occurrence of A, but B is more highly relevant to A. Moreover, according to (10), B screens A off from C and C off from A—that is, B renders A and C statistically irrelevant to one another. A chain of events $A \rightarrow B \rightarrow C$ thus has the Markov property which Good demanded of his causal chains.

The inadequacy of Reichenbach's definition of causal betweenness was pointed out by Clark Glymour, in conversation, a number of years ago, when he was a graduate student at Indiana University. The cases we discussed at that time were similar in principle to an excellent example, due to Deborah Rosen, reported by Suppes:[7]

> ... suppose a golfer makes a shot that hits a limb of a tree close to the green and is thereby deflected directly into the hole, for a spectacular birdie. ... If we know something about Mr. [sic] Jones' golf we can estimate the probability of his making a birdie on this particular hole. The probability will be low, but the seemingly disturbing thing is that if we estimate the conditional probability of his making a birdie, given that the ball hit the branch, ... we would ordinarily estimate the probability as being still lower. Yet when we see the event happen, we recognize immediately that hitting the branch in exactly the way it did was essential to the ball's going into the cup.

If we let A be the event of Jones teeing off, B the event of the ball striking the tree limb, and C the event of the ball dropping into the cup at one under par for the hole, we have a violation of Reichenbach's condition (8), for

---

[6] [Ed. note] Throughout this article, Salmon uses 'P' to stand for physical probability, and other italic capital letters to designate classes of individuals or events. Thus '$P(C)$' stands for the physical probability of an occurrence of an event which is a member of class C, while '$P(C|B)$' stands for the physical probability of an occurrence of an event which is a member of class C, given the occurrence of an event which is a member of class B. Salmon construes physical probabilities as relative frequencies, but he points out that those who prefer other concepts of physical probability can easily make any adjustments that seem appropriate. Finally, Salmon also points out that he sometimes speaks of the occurrence of an event A, instead of using the more cumbrous expression, 'occurrence of an event which is a member of the class A'.

[7] *A Probabilistic Theory*, 41.

$P(C|B) < P(C|A)$. The event B is, nevertheless, causally between events A and C.[8] Various retorts can be made to this purported counter-example. One could maintain[9] that sufficiently detailed information about the physical interaction between the ball and the branch might enable us to raise the conditional probability of the ball going into the hole, given these precisely specified physical circumstances, above the conditional probability of Jones making a birdie given only that he [*sic*] tees off. As von Bretzel himself notes, this kind of response seems *ad hoc* and artificial, and there is no good reason to suppose that it would take care of all such counter-examples even if it were adequate for this particular one. Indeed, it seems to me that many examples can be found which are immune to dismissal on these grounds.

Rosen's colourful example involves a near-miraculous occurrence, but we do not need to resort to such unusual happenings in order to find counter-examples to Reichenbach's definition of causal betweenness. The crucial feature of Rosen's example is that Jones makes her birdie 'the hard way'. Since much which goes on in life happens 'the hard way', we should be able to find an abundance of every-day sorts of counter-examples; in fact, we have already considered one. When the game of tetrahedron tossing and card drawing was used in the previous section to raise the second objection to Good's causal calculus, we looked at the case in which the player drew the red card and won the prize 'the hard way'. In that case the tetrahedron came to rest on side 4, forcing the player to draw from the deck with a smaller proportion of red cards. As the original game was set up, the player's initial probability of drawing a red card is 10/16, but if he is required, as a result of his toss, to draw from the less favourable deck, his probability of drawing a red card is only 1/4. Nevertheless, when the player who tosses the tetrahedron fails to show side 4, but succeeds in drawing a red card from the unfavourable deck, the draw from the unfavourable deck is causally between the toss of the tetrahedron and the winning of the prize. Drawing a red card from a deck which contains four red and twelve black cards can hardly be considered a near-miracle.

Once we see the basic feature of such examples, we can find others in profusion. The expression, 'the hard way', is used in the game of craps, and this game provides another obvious example.[10] The shooter wins if he throws

<hr/>

[8] In most cases, of course, the shot from the tee is not the one which strikes the branch, for there are few, if any, par 2 holes. However, the fact that there are other strokes does not alter the import of the example with respect to Reichenbach's definition of causal betweenness.

[9] See Philip von Bretzel, 'Concerning a Probabilistic Theory of Causation Adequate for the Causal Theory of Time', *Synthese*, 35/2 (1977), 173–90, at 182. (This article is repr. in Wesley C. Salmon (ed.), *Hans Reichenbach: Logical Empiricist* (Dordrecht and Boston, 1979), 385–402.)

[10] The basic features of this game are given clearly and succinctly by Irving Copi (*Introduction to Logic*, 4th edn. (New York, 1972), 481–2). A shooter whose point is 4, for example, is

7 or 11 on the first toss; he loses if he throws 2, 3, or 12 on the first toss. If the first toss results in any other number, that is his 'point', and he wins if in subsequent tosses he makes his point before he throws a 7. The probability of the shooter winning in one or another of these ways is just slightly less than 1/2. A player who throws 4 on his initial toss clearly reduces his chances of winning (this conditional probability is 1/3), but nevertheless he can win by making his point. Throwing 4 is, however, causally between the initial toss and the winning of the bet on that play.

A pool player has an easy direct shot to sink the 9-ball, but he chooses, for the sake of his subsequent position, the much more difficult play of shooting at the 2-ball and using it to put the 9-ball in the pocket. The initial probability of his sinking the 9-ball is much greater than the probability of getting the 9-ball in the pocket if his cue-ball strikes the 2-ball, but the collision with the 2-ball is causally between the initiation of the play and the dropping of the 9-ball into the pocket. Similar examples can obviously be found in an enormous variety of circumstances in which a given result can occur in more than one way, and in which the probabilities of the result differ widely given the various alternative ways of reaching it. The attempt to save Reichenbach's definition of causal betweenness by *ad hoc* devices appears to be a hopeless undertaking. We shall see, however, that Good suggests a method for handling such examples, and that Rosen offers a somewhat different defence on behalf of Suppes.

Reichenbach's definition of *conjunctive fork* does not fare much better. The basic motivation for introducing this concept is to characterize the situation in which an otherwise improbable coincidence is explained by appeal to a common cause. There are many familiar examples—e.g. the explanation of the simultaneous illness of many residents of a particular dormitory in terms of tainted food in a meal they all shared. Reichenbach defines the conjunctive fork in terms of the following formulas[11] which I have renumbered and translated into standard notation:

$$P(A.B|C) = P(A|C) \times P(B|C) \tag{11}$$

$$P(A.B|\bar{C}) = P(A|\bar{C}) \times P(B|\bar{C}) \tag{12}$$

$$P(A|C) > P(A|\bar{C}) \tag{13}$$

$$P(B|C) > P(B|\bar{C}) \tag{14}$$

In order to apply these formulas to the foregoing example, we may let A stand for the illness of Smith on the night in question, B the illness of Jones on the

said to make it 'the hard way' if he does so by getting a double 2, which is less probable than a 3 and a 1.

[11] *Direction of Time*, 159.

same night, and C the presence of spoiled food in the dinner served at their dormitory that evening.

The following example, due to Ellis Crasnow, shows the inadequacy of Reichenbach's formulation. Brown usually arrives at his office about 9.00 a.m., fixes himself a cup of coffee, and settles down to read the morning paper for half an hour before beginning any serious business. Upon occasion, however, he arrives at 8.00, and his secretary has already brewed a fresh pot of coffee, which she serves him immediately. On precisely the same occasions, some other person meets him at his office and they begin work quite promptly. This coincidence—the coffee being ready and the other person being at his office—demands explanation in terms of a common cause. As it happens, Brown usually takes the 8.30 bus to work in the morning, but on those mornings when the coffee is prepared for his arrival and the other person shows up, he takes the 7.30 bus. It can plausibly be argued that the three events, A (the coffee being ready), B (the other person showing up), and C (Brown taking the 7.30 bus), satisfy Reichenbach's requirements for a conjunctive fork. Clearly, however, Brown's bus ride is not a cause of either the coffee being made or the other person's arrival. The coincidence does, indeed, require a common cause, but that event is a telephone appointment made by the secretary on the preceding day.

The crucial feature of Crasnow's counter-example is easy to see. Brown arises early and catches the 7.30 bus if and only if he has an early appointment which was previously arranged by his secretary. The conjunctive fork is constructed out of the two associated effects and another effect which is strictly correlated with the bona fide common cause. When we see how this example has been devised, it is easy to find many others of the same general sort. Suppose it is realized before anyone actually becomes ill that spoiled food has been served in the dormitory. The head resident may place a call to the university health service requesting that a stomach pump be dispatched to the scene; however, neither the call to the health service nor the arrival of the stomach pump constitutes a genuine common cause, though either could be used to form a conjunctive fork.[12]

Inasmuch as two of Reichenbach's key concepts—causal betweenness and conjunctive fork—are unacceptably explicated, we must regard his attempt to provide an account of probabilistic causality as unsuccessful.

---

[12] The day after I wrote this paragraph, an announcement was broadcast on local radio stations informing parents that students who ate lunch at several elementary schools may have been infected with salmonella, which probabilistically causes severe gastric illness. Clearly the consumption of unwholesome food, not the radio announcement, is the common cause of the unusually high incidence of sickness within this particular group of children.

3. SUPPES'S PROBABILISTIC THEORY

In spite of his passing remark about Good's causal calculus, Suppes's theory bears much more striking resemblance to Reichenbach's theory than to Good's. As mentioned earlier, Suppes and Good agree in stipulating that causes must, by definition, precede their effects in time, and in this they oppose Reichenbach's approach. But here the similarities between Good and Suppes end. Like Reichenbach, and unlike Good, Suppes does not attempt to introduce any quantitative measures of causal strength. Like Reichenbach, and unlike Good, Suppes frames his definitions in terms of measures of probability, without introducing any explicit measure of statistical relevance. It is evident, of course, that considerations of statistical relevance play absolutely fundamental roles in all three theories, but as I commented regarding Good's approach, the use of statistical relevance measures instead of probability measures involves a crucial sacrifice of information. In addition, Suppes introduces a number of causal concepts, and in the course of defining them, he deploys the relations of positive statistical relevance and screening off in ways which bear strong resemblance to Reichenbach. A look at several of his most important definitions will exhibit this fact.

In definition 1[13] an event B is said to be a *prima-facie cause* of an event A if B occurs before A and B is positively relevant, statistically, to A.[14] Suppes offers two definitions of spurious causes, the second of which is the stronger and is probably preferable.[15] According to this definition (3), an event B is a *spurious cause* of an event A if it is a prima-facie cause of A and it is screened off from A by a partition of events C_i which occur earlier than B. We are told,[16] though not in a numbered definition, that a *genuine cause* is a prima-facie cause which is not spurious. These concepts can easily be applied to *the* most familiar example. The falling barometer is a prima-facie cause of a subsequent storm, but it is also a spurious cause, for it is screened-off from the storm by atmospheric conditions which precede both the storm and the drop in barometric reading.

---

[13] *A Probabilistic Theory*, 12.

[14] In defining many of his causal concepts, Suppes uses conditional probabilities of the form $P(B|A)$. Since, according to the standard definition of conditional probability $P(B|A) = P(A.B)/P(A)$, this probability would not be well defined if $P(A) = 0$, Suppes explicitly includes in his definitions stipulations that the appropriate probabilities are non-zero. In my discussion I shall, without further explicit statement, assume that all conditional probabilities introduced into the discussion are well defined.

[15] *A Probabilistic Theory*, 23, 25. Suppes refers to these as 'spurious in sense one' and 'spurious in sense two'. Since I shall adopt sense two uniformly in this discussion, I shall not explicitly say 'in sense two' in the text.

[16] Ibid. 24.

There is a close similarity between Suppes's definition of spurious cause and Reichenbach's definition of conjunctive fork. It is to be noted first, as Reichenbach demonstrates,[17] that

$$P(A.B) > P(A) \times P(B) \qquad (15)$$

follows from relations (11)–(14) above. Therefore, A and B are positively relevant to one another. If A and B are not simultaneous, then one is a prima-facie cause of the other. Second, Reichenbach's relations (11) and (12) are equivalent to screening-off relations. According to the multiplication axiom,

$$P(A.B|C) = P(A|C) \times P(B|A.C); \qquad (16)$$

therefore, it follows from (11) that

$$P(A|C) \times P(B|C) = P(A|C) \times P(B|A.C). \qquad (17)$$

Assuming $P(A|C) > 0$, we divide through by that quantity, with the result

$$P(B|C) = P(B|A.C), \qquad (18)$$

which says that C screens off A from B. In precisely parallel fashion, it can be shown that (12) says that $\bar{C}$ screens off A from B. But, $\{C, \bar{C}\}$ constitutes a partition, so B is a spurious cause of A or vice versa.[18] Suppes does not define the concept of conjunctive fork. Since he assumes temporal priority relations already given, he does not need conjunctive forks to establish temporal direction, and since he is not concerned with scientific explanation, he does not need them to provide explanations in terms of common causes. Nevertheless, there is a considerable degree of overlap between Reichenbach's conjunctive forks and Suppes's spurious causes.

Although Reichenbach defines conjunctive forks entirely in terms of the relations (11)–(14) above, without imposing any temporal constraints, his informal accompanying remarks[19] strongly suggest that the events A and B occur simultaneously, or nearly so. One might be tempted to suppose that Reichenbach wished to regard A and B as simultaneous to a sufficiently precise degree that a direct causal connection between them would be relativistically precluded. Such a restriction would, however, make no real sense in the kinds of examples he offers. Since the velocity of light is approximately 1 foot per nano-second (1 nsec = 10^{-9} sec), the onsets of vomiting in the case of two room-mates in the tainted food example (above) would presumably have to occur within perhaps a dozen nano-seconds of one another.

[17] *Direction of Time*, 158, 160.

[18] In an easily overlooked remark (ibid. 159), Reichenbach says, 'If there is more than one possible kind of common cause, C may represent the disjunction of these causes.' Hence, Reichenbach recognizes the need for partitions finer than $\{C, \bar{C}\}$, which makes for an even closer parallel between his notion of a conjunctive fork and Suppes's notion of a spurious cause.

[19] Ibid. 158–9.

Reichenbach's basic intent can be more reasonably characterized in the following manner. Suppose events of the types A and B occur on some sort of clearly specified association more frequently than they would if they were statistically independent of one another. Then, if we can rule out a direct causal connection from A to B or from B to A, we look for a common cause C which, along with A and B, constitutes a conjunctive fork. Thus, if Smith and Jones turn in identical term papers for the same class—even if the submissions are far from simultaneous—and if careful investigation assures us that Smith did not copy directly from Jones and also that Jones did not copy directly from Smith, then we look for the common cause C (e.g. the paper in the fraternity file from which both of them plagiarized their papers). It is the absence of a direct causal connection between A and B, not simultaneous occurrence, which is crucial in this context. Thus, in Reichenbach's conjunctive forks A may precede B or vice versa, and hence, one may be a prima-facie cause of the other.

Suppes does not introduce the relation of causal betweenness, but he does define the related notions of direct and indirect causes. According to definition 5[20] an event B is a *direct cause* of an event A if it is a prima-facie cause of B and there is no partition C_i temporally between A and B which screens B off from A. A prima-facie cause which is not direct is *indirect*. Use of such terms as 'direct' and 'indirect' strongly suggests betweenness relations. Suppes's definition of indirect cause clearly embodies a condition closely analogous to formula (10) of Reichenbach's definition of causal betweenness, but Suppes does not invoke the troublesome relations (8) and (9) which brought Reichenbach's explication to grief. It appears, however, that Suppes's theory faces similar difficulties.

Let us take another look at Rosen's example of the spectacular birdie. As above, let A stand for Jones teeing off, B for the ball striking the tree limb, and C for the ball going into the cup. If this example is to be at all relevant to the discussion, we must suppose that A is a prima-facie cause of C, which requires that $P(C|A) > P(C)$. We must, therefore, select some general reference class or probability space with respect to which $P(A)$ can be evaluated. The natural choice, I should think, would be to take the class of all cases of teeing off at that particular hole as the universe.[21] We may then suppose that Jones is a better-than-average golfer; when she tees off there is a higher probability of a birdie than there is for golfers in general who play that particular course. We may further assume that A is a genuine cause of C, since there is no plausible partition of earlier events which would screen A

off from C. Certainly B cannot render A as a spurious cause of C, for B does not even happen at the right time (prior to A).

There is a more delicate question of whether A is a direct or indirect cause of C. We may reasonably assume that B screens A off from C, for presumably it makes no difference which player's shot from the rough strikes the tree limb. It is less clear, however, that B belongs to a partition, each member of which screens A from C. In other cases, birdies will occur as a result of a splendid shot out of a sand trap, or sinking a long putt, or a fine chip shot from the fairway. In these cases, it seems to me, it would not be irrelevant that Jones, rather than some much less accomplished player, was the person who teed off (A). It might be possible to construct a partition B_i which would accomplish the required screening off by specifying the manner in which the ball approaches the cup, rather than referring merely to where the ball came from on the final shot. But this ploy seems artificial. Just as we rejected the attempt to save Reichenbach's definition of causal betweenness by specifying the physical parameters of the ball and the branch at the moment of collision, so also, I think, must we resist the temptation to resort to similar physical parameters to find a partition which achieves screening off. We are, after all, discussing a golf game, not Newtonian particle physics, as Suppes is eager to insist. The most plausible construal of this example, from the standpoint of Suppes's theory, is to take A to be a direct cause of C, and to deny that the sequence A, B, C has the Markov property. In contrast to Good and Reichenbach. Suppes does not require causal sequences to be Markovian.

The crucial problem about B, it seems to me, is that it appears not to qualify even as a prima-facie cause of C. It seems reasonable to suppose that even the ordinary duffer has a better chance of making a birdie $P(C)$ than Jones has of getting the ball in the hole by bouncing it off the tree limb $P(C|B)$. In Suppes's definitions, however, being a prima-facie cause is a necessary condition of being any kind of cause (other than a negative cause). Surely, as Suppes himself remarks, we must recognize B as a link in the causal chain. The same point applies to the other examples introduced above to show the inadequacy of Reichenbach's definition of causal betweenness. Since the crap-shooter has a better chance of winning at the outset $P(C)$, than he does of winning if he gets 4 on the first toss $P(C|B)$, shooting 4 is not even a prima-facie cause of his winning. Even though Suppes desists from defining causal betweenness, the kinds of examples which lead to difficulty for Reichenbach on that score result in closely related troubles in Suppes's theory.

The fundamental problem at issue here is what Rosen[22] calls 'Suppes' thesis that a cause will always raise the probability of the effect'. Although

---

[22] Deborah A. Rosen, 'In Defense of a Probabilistic Theory of Causality', *Philosophy of Science*, 45 (1978), 604–13.

both Suppes and Rosen[23] sometimes refer to it as the problem of unlikely or improbable consequences, this latter manner of speaking can be confusing, for it is *not* the small degree of probability of the effect, given the cause, which matters; it is the *negative statistical relevance* of the cause to the occurrence of the effect which gives rise to the basic problem. While there is general agreement that positive statistical relevance is not a sufficient condition of direct causal relevance—we all recognize that the falling barometric reading does not cause a storm—the question is whether it is a necessary condition. Our immediate intuitive response is, I believe, that positive statistical relevance is, indeed, a necessary ingredient in causation, and all three of the theories we are discussing make stipulations to that effect. Reichenbach assumes 'that causal relevance is a special form of positive [statistical] relevance'.[24] Suppes makes positive statistical relevance a defining condition of prima-facie causes, and every genuine cause is a prima-facie cause.[25] Good incorporates the condition of positive statistical relevance into his definition of causal chains.[26]

In a critical note on Suppes's theory, Germund Hesslow challenges this fundamental principle:

> The basic idea in Suppes' theory is of course that a cause raises the probability of its effect, and it is difficult to see how the theory could be modified without upholding this thesis. It is possible however that examples could be found of causes that lower the probability of their effects. Such a situation could come about if a cause could lower the probability of other more efficient causes. It has been claimed, e.g., that contraceptive pills (C) can cause thrombosis (T), and that consequently there are cases where C_t caused $T_{t'}$. [The subscripts t and t' are Suppes's temporal indices.] But pregnancy can also cause thrombosis, and C lowers the probability of pregnancy. I do not know the values of $P(T)$ and $P(T|C)$ but it seems possible that $P(T|C) < P(T)$, and in a population which lacked other contraceptives this would appear a likely situation. Be that as it may, the point remains: *it is entirely possible that a cause should lower the probability of its effect.*[27]

Rosen defends Suppes against this challenge by arguing,

> ... based on the available information represented by the above probability estimates, we would be hesitant, where a person suffers a thrombosis, to blame the person's taking of contraceptive pills. But it does not follow from these epistemic observations that a particular person's use of contraceptive pills lowers the probability that she may suffer

---

[23] Suppes, *A Probabilistic Theory*, 41, and Rosen, 'In Defense', 607.

[24] *Direction of Time*, 201.

[25] *A Probabilistic Theory*, 12 and 24 respectively.

[26] 'A Causal Calculus II', 45.

[27] 'Two Notes on the Probabilistic Approach to Causality', *Philosophy of Science*, 43 (1976), 290–2, at 291 (Hesslow's italics).

a thrombosis, for, unknown to us, her neurophysiological constitution (N) may be such that the taking of the pills definitely contributes to a thrombosis. Formally,

$$P(T|C.N) > P(T)$$

represents our more complete and accurate causal picture. We wrongly believe that taking the pills always lowers a person's probability of thrombosis because we base our belief on an inadequate and superficial knowledge of the causal structures in this medical domain where unanticipated and unappreciated neurophysiological features are not given sufficient attention or adequate weighting.[28]

Rosen comments upon her own example of the spectacular birdie in a similar spirit: 'Suppes' first observation in untangling the problems of improbable consequences is that it is important not to let the curious event be rendered causally spurious by settling for a superficial or narrow view.'[29] As I have indicated above, I do not believe that this is a correct assessment of the problem. If the causal event in question—e.g. the ball striking the branch—is negatively relevant to the final outcome, it is not even a prima-facie cause. *A fortiori*, it cannot achieve the status of a spurious cause, let alone a genuine cause. She continues:

. . . it is the angle and the force of the approach shot together with the deflection that forms our revised causal picture. Thus we begin to see that the results are unlikely only from a narrow standpoint. A broader picture is the more instructive one.[30]

As a result of her examination of Hesslow's example, as well as her own, she concludes that it is a virtue of Suppes's probabilistic theory to be able to accommodate 'unanticipated consequences'.[31]

Rosen's manner of dealing with the problem of causes which appear to bear negative statistical relevance relations to their effects (which is similar to that mentioned by von Bretzel) might be called *the method of more detailed specification of events*. If some event C, which is clearly recognized as a cause of E, is nevertheless negatively relevant to the occurrence of E, it is claimed that a more detailed specification of C (or the circumstances in which C occurs) will render it positively relevant to E. I remain sceptical that this approach—though admittedly successful in a vast number of instances—is adequate in general to deal with all challenges to the principle of positive statistical relevance.

Good was clearly aware of the problem of negative statistical relevance, and he provided an explicit way of dealing with it. His approach, which differs from Rosen's, might be called *the method of interpolated causal links*. In an appendix[32] . . . he offers an example along with a brief indication of his manner of dealing with it:

[28] 'In Defense', 606.   [29] Ibid. 608.   [30] Ibid.   [31] Ibid.
[32] 'A Causal Calculus I', 318.

Sherlock Holmes is at the foot of a cliff. At the top of the cliff, directly overhead, are Dr Watson, Professor Moriarty, and a loose boulder. Watson, knowing Moriarty's intentions, realizes that the best chance of saving Holmes's life is to push the boulder over the edge of the cliff, doing his best to give it enough horizontal momentum to miss Holmes. If he does not push the boulder, Moriarty will do so in such a way that it will be nearly certain to kill Holmes. Watson then makes the decision (event F) to push the boulder, but his skill fails him and the boulder falls on Holmes and kills him (event E).

This example shows that $Q(E|F)$ [the tendency of F to cause E] and $\chi(E:F)$ [the degree to which F caused E] cannot be identified, since F had a tendency to prevent E and yet caused it. We say that F was a cause of E because there was a chain of events connecting F to E, each of which was strongly caused by the preceding one.

This example seems closely related to the remark, later appended to theorem T2, to the effect that a cut chain can be uncut by filling in more of the details. Good could obviously take exception to any of the examples discussed above on the ground that the spatio-temporal gaps between the successive events in these chains are too great. He could, with complete propriety, insist that these gaps be filled with intermediate events, each of which is spatio-temporally small, and each of which is contiguous with its immediate neighbours.[33] I am not convinced, however, that every 'cut chain' which needs to be welded back together can be repaired by this device;[34] on the contrary, it seems to me that size is not an essential feature of the kinds of examples which raise problems for Suppes's and Reichenbach's theories. We can find examples, I believe, which have the same basic features, but which do not appear to be amenable to Good's treatment.

Consider the following fictitious case, which has the same statistical structure as the first tetrahedron-cum-card example. We have an atom in an excited state which we shall refer to as the 4th energy level. It may decay to the ground state (zeroeth level) in several different ways, some of which involve intermediate occupation of the 1st energy level. Let $P(m \rightarrow n)$ stand

[33] Ibid. 307–8; 'A Causal Calculus II', 45.

[34] Paul Humphreys has provided a theorem which has an important bearing upon the question of the mending of cut chains. In any two-state Markov chain, the statistical relevance of the first to the last member is zero if and only if at least one link in the chain exhibits zero relevance, and the statistical relevance of the first to the last member is negative only if an odd number of links exhibit negative relevance. The first member of a two-state Markov chain is positively relevant to the last if and only if no link has zero relevance and an even number (including none) of the links exhibit negative relevance. In other words, the signs of the relevance measures of the links multiply exactly like the signs of real numbers. Thus, it is impossible for a two-state Markov chain whose first member is negatively relevant to its last, or whose first member is irrelevant to its last, to be constructed out of links all of which exhibit positive relevance—just as it is impossible for the product of positive real numbers to be zero or negative. It may, however, be possible to achieve this goal if, in the process of interpolating additional events, the two-state character is destroyed by including new alternatives at one or more stages.

for the probability that an atom in the mth level will drop directly to the nth level. Suppose we have the following probability values:[35]

$$P(4 \rightarrow 3) = 3/4 \qquad P(3 \rightarrow 1) = 3/4 \qquad (19)$$
$$P(4 \rightarrow 2) = 1/4 \qquad P(2 \rightarrow 1) = 1/4$$

It follows that the probability that the atom will occupy the 1st energy level in the process of decaying to the ground state is 10/16; if, however, it occupies the 2nd level on its way down, then the probability of its occupying the 1st level is 1/4. Therefore, occupying the 2nd level is negatively relevant to occupation of the 1st level. Nevertheless, if the atom goes from the 4th to the 2nd to the 1st level, that sequence constitutes a causal chain, in spite of the negative statistical relevance of the intermediate stage. Moreover, in view of the fact that we cannot, so to speak, 'track' the atom in its transitions from one energy level to another, it appears that there is no way, even in principle, of filling in intermediate 'links' so as to 'uncut the chain'. Furthermore, it seems unlikely that the Rosen method of more detailed specification of events will help with this example, for when we have specified the type of atom and its energy levels, there are no further facts which are relevant to the events in question. Although this example is admittedly fictitious, one finds cases of this general sort in examining the term schemes of actual atoms.[36]

There is another type of example which seems to me to cause trouble for both Reichenbach and Suppes. In a previous discussion of the principle of the common cause[37] I suggested the need to take account of *interactive forks* as well as conjunctive forks. Consider the following example. Pool balls lie on the table in such a way that the player can put the 8-ball into one corner pocket at the far end of the table if and almost only if his cue-ball goes into the other far corner pocket. Being a relative novice, the player does not realize that fact; moreover, his skill is such that he has only a 50–50 chance of sinking the 8-ball even if he tries. Let us make the further plausible assumption that, if the two balls drop into the respective pockets, the 8-ball will fall before the cue-ball does. Let event A be the player attempting that shot, B the dropping of the 8-ball into the corner pocket, and C the dropping of the cue-ball into the other corner pocket. Among all of the various shots the player may attempt, a small proportion will result in the cue-ball landing in that pocket. Thus, $P(C|B) > P(C)$; consequently, the 8-ball falling into one

---

[35] We assume that the transition from the 3rd to the 2nd level is prohibited by the selection rules.

[36] See e.g. the cover design on the well-known elementary text, Eyvind H. Wichmann, *Quantum Physics* (Berkeley Physics Course, 4; New York, 1967), which is taken from the term scheme for neutral thallium. This term scheme is given in fig. 34A, p. 199.

[37] Wesley C. Salmon, 'Why Ask "Why?"'?—An Inquiry Concerning Scientific Explanation', *Proceedings and Addresses of the American Philosophical Association*, 51/6 (Aug. 1978), 683–705.

corner pocket is a prima-facie cause of the cue-ball falling into the other pocket. This is as it should be, but we must also be able to classify B as a spurious cause of C. It is not quite clear how this is to be accomplished. The event A, which must surely qualify as a direct cause of both B and C, does not screen B off from C, for $P(C|A) = 1/2$ while $P(C|A.B) = 1$.

It may be objected, of course, that we are not entitled to infer, from the fact that A fails to screen off B from C, that there is no event prior to B which does the screening. In fact, there is such an event—namely, the compound event which consists of the state of motion of the 8-ball and the state of motion of the cue-ball shortly after they collide. The need to resort to such artificial compound events does suggest a weakness in the theory, however, for the causal relations among A, B, and C seem to embody the salient features of the situation. An adequate theory of probabilistic causality should, it seems to me, be able to handle the situation in terms of the relations among these events, without having to appeal to such *ad hoc* constructions.

4. A MODEST SUGGESTION

. . . It seems to me that the fundamental source of difficulty in all three of the theories discussed above is that they attempt to carry out the construction of causal relations on the basis of probabilistic relations among discrete events, without taking account of the physical connections among them. This difficulty, I believe, infects many non-probabilistic theories as well. When discrete events bear genuine cause–effect relations to one another—except, perhaps, in some instances in quantum mechanics—there are spatio-temporally continuous causal processes joining them.[38] It is my view that these processes transmit causal influence (which may be probabilistic) from one region of space–time to another. . . .

There is a strong tendency on the part of philosophers to regard causal connections as being composed of chains of intermediate events, as Good brings out explicitly in his theory, rather than spatio-temporally continuous entities which enjoy fundamental physical status, and which do *not* need to be constructed out of anything else. Such a viewpoint can lead to severe frustration, for we are always driven to ask about the connections among *these* events, and interpolating additional events does not seem to mitigate

---

[38] I do not believe quantum indeterminacy poses any particular problems for a probabilistic theory of causality, or for the notion of continuous causal processes. This quantum indeterminacy is, in fact, the most compelling reason for insisting upon the need for probabilistic causation. The really devastating problems arise in connection with what Reichenbach called 'causal anomalies'—such as the Einstein–Podolsky–Rosen problem—which seem to involve some form of action-at-a-distance. I make no pretence of having an adequate analysis of such cases.

the problem. In his discussion of Locke's concept of power, Hume[39] seems to have perceived this difficulty quite clearly. I am strongly inclined to reverse the position, and to suggest that we accord fundamental status to processes. . . .

It is beyond the scope of this paper to attempt a rigorous construction of a probabilistic theory of causality, but the general strategy should be readily apparent. To begin, we can easily see how to deal with the three basic sorts of counter-examples discussed above. First, regarding Rosen's example, we shall say that the striking of the limb by the golf ball is causally between the teeing-off and the dropping into the hole because there is a spatio-temporally continuous causal process—the history of the golf ball—which connects the teeing-off with the striking of the limb, and connects the striking of the limb with the dropping into the hole. Second, we can handle the pool-ball example by noting that the dropping of the 8-ball into the pocket is not a genuine cause of the cue-ball falling into the other pocket, because there is no causal process leading directly from the one event to the other. Third, we can deal with the Crasnow example by pointing out that the telephone appointment made by Brown's secretary constitutes a common cause for the coffee being ready and for the arrival of the business associate, because there is a causal process which leads from the appointment to the making of the coffee and another causal process which leads from the appointment to the arrival of the other person. However, there are no causal processes leading from Brown's boarding of the early bus to the making of the coffee or to the arrival of the other person. . . .

The most difficult problem, it seems to me, involves the dictum that cause–effect relations must always involve relations of positive statistical relevance. I believe that the examples already discussed show that this dictum cannot be accepted in any simple and unqualified way; at the same time, it seems intuitively compelling to argue that a cause which contributes probabilistically to bringing about a certain effect must at least raise the probability of that effect *vis-à-vis* some other state of affairs. For example, in the tetrahedron-cum-card game, once the tetrahedron has been tossed and has landed on side 4, the initial probability of drawing a red card in the game is irrelevant to the causal process (or sequence[40]) which leads to the draw of a red card from the deck which is poorer in red cards. What matters is that a causal process has been initiated which may eventuate in the drawing of a

[39] *An Enquiry Concerning Human Understanding* (1748), sect. 7. 1.

[40] Actually, in this example as in most others, we have a *sequence of events* joined to one another by a *sequence of causal processes*. The events, so to speak, mark the ends of the segments of processes; they are the points at which one process joins up with another. Events can, in most if not all cases, be regarded as intersections of processes.

red card; it makes no difference that an alternative process might have been initiated which would have held a higher probability of yielding a red card.

Once the tetrahedron has come to rest, one of two alternative processes is selected. There is an important sense in which it possesses an *internal* positive relevance with respect to the draw of a red card. When this example was introduced above, I made the convenient but unrealistic simplifying assumption that a draw would be made from the second deck if and only if the tetrahedron toss failed to show side 4. However, a player who has just made a toss on which the tetrahedron landed on side 4 might simply get up and walk away in disgust, without drawing any card at all. In this case, of course, he is certain not to draw a red card. When we look at the game in this way, we see that, given the result of the tetrahedron toss, the probability of getting a red card by drawing from the second deck is greater than it is by not drawing at all—thus, drawing from the second deck *is* positively relevant to getting a red card. . . .

The essential ingredients in a satisfactory qualitative theory of probabilistic causality are, it seems to me: (1) a fundamental distinction between causal processes and causal interactions, (2) an account of the propagation of causal influence via causal processes, (3) an account of causal interactions in terms of interactive forks, (4) an account of causal directionality in terms of conjunctive forks, and (5) an account of causal betweenness in terms of causal processes and causal directionality. The 'at-at' theory of causal influence[41] gives, at best, a symmetric relation of causal connection. Conjunctive forks are needed to impose the required asymmetry upon connecting processes.

If an adequate theory of probabilistic causality is to be developed, it will borrow heavily from the theories of Reichenbach and Suppes; these theories require supplementation rather than outright rejection. Once we are in possession of a satisfactory qualitative theory, we may be in a position to undertake Good's programme of quantification of probabilistic causal relations. These goals are, I believe, eminently worthy of pursuit.

[41] Wesley C. Salmon, 'An "At-At" Theory of Causal Influence', *Philosophy of Science*, 44/2 (June 1977), 215–24.

IX

CAUSALITY: PRODUCTION
AND PROPAGATION*

WESLEY C. SALMON

A standard picture of causality has been around at least since the time of Hume. The general idea is that we have two (or more) distinct events which bear some sort of cause–effect relation to one another. There has, of course, been considerable controversy regarding the nature of both the relation and the relata. It has sometimes been maintained, for instance, that facts or propositions (rather than events) are the sorts of entities which can constitute the relata. It has long been disputed whether individual events or only classes of events can sustain cause–effect relations. The relation itself has sometimes been taken to be that of sufficient condition, sometimes necessary condition, or perhaps a combination of the two.[1] Some authors have even proposed that certain sorts of statistical relations constitute causal relations.[2]

It is my conviction that this standard view, in all of its well-known variations, is profoundly mistaken, and that a radically different notion should be developed. I shall not attempt to mount arguments against the standard conception;[3] instead, I shall present a rather different approach for purposes of comparison. I hope that the alternative will stand on its own merits.

1. TWO BASIC CONCEPTS

There are, I believe, two fundamental causal concepts which need to be explicated, and if that can be achieved, we will be in a position to deal with the problems of causality in general. The two basic concepts are *production* and *propagation*, and both are familiar to common sense. When we say that the blow of a hammer drives a nail, we mean that the impact produces

* This material is based upon work supported by the National Science Foundation under Grant No. SES-7809146.
[1] See John L. Mackie, *The Cement of the Universe* (Oxford, 1974).
[2] See Wesley C. Salmon, 'Probabilistic Causality', *Pacific Philosophical Quarterly*, 61 (1980), 50–74.
[3] Some are given in 'Probabilistic Causality'.

penetration of the nail into the wood. When we say that a horse pulls a cart, we mean that the force exerted by the horse produces the motion of the cart. When we say that lightning starts a forest fire we mean that the electrical discharge produces ignition. When we say that a person's embarrassment was due to a thoughtless remark we mean that an inappropriate comment produced psychological discomfort. Such examples of causal production occur frequently in everyday contexts.

Causal propagation (or transmission) is equally familiar. Experiences which we had earlier in our lives affect our current behaviour. By means of memory, the influence of these past events is transmitted to the present. A sonic boom makes us aware of the passage of a jet airplane overhead; a disturbance in the air is propagated from the upper atmosphere to our location on the ground. Signals transmitted from a broadcasting station are received by the radio in our home. News or music reaches us because electromagnetic waves are propagated from the transmitter to the receiver. In 1775 some Massachusetts farmers 'fired the shot heard "round the world"'. As all of these examples show, what happens at one place and time can have significant influence upon what happens at other places and times. This is possible because causal influence can be propagated through time and space. Although causal production and causal propagation are intimately related to one another, we should, I believe, resist any temptation to try to reduce one to the other.

2. PROCESSES

One of the fundamental changes which I propose in approaching causality is to take processes rather than events as basic entities. I shall not attempt any rigorous definition of processes; rather, I shall cite examples and make some very informal remarks. The main difference between events and processes is that events are relatively localized in space and time, while processes have much greater temporal duration, and in many cases, much greater spatial extent. In space–time diagrams, events are represented by points, while processes are represented by lines. A baseball colliding with a window would count as an event; the baseball, travelling from the bat to the window, would constitute a process. The activation of a photocell by a pulse of light would be an event; the pulse of light, travelling, perhaps from a distant star, would be a process. A sneeze is an event. The shadow of a cloud moving across the landscape is a process. Although I shall deny that all processes qualify as causal processes, what I mean by a process is similar to what Bertrand Russell characterized as a *causal line*: 'A causal line may always

be regarded as the persistence of something—a person, a table, a photon, or
what not. Throughout a given causal line, there may be constancy of quality,
constancy of structure, or a gradual change of either, but not sudden changes
of any considerable magnitude'.[4] Among the physically important processes
are waves and material objects which persist through time. As I shall use
terms, even a material object at rest will qualify as a process. . . .

We need to make a distinction between what I shall call *causal processes*
and *pseudo-processes*: . . . causal processes are those which are capable of
transmitting signals; pseudo-processes are incapable of doing so.

Consider a simple example. Suppose that we have a very large circular
building—a sort of super-Astrodome, if you will—with a spotlight mounted
at its centre. When the light is turned on in the otherwise darkened building,
it casts a spot of light upon the wall. If we turn the light on for a brief
moment, and then off again, a light pulse travels from the light to the wall.
This pulse of light, travelling from the spotlight to the wall, is a paradigm of
what we mean by a causal process. Suppose, further, that the spotlight is
mounted on a mechanism which makes it rotate. If the light is turned on and
set into rotation, the spot of light which it casts upon the wall will move
around the outer wall in a highly regular fashion. This 'process'—the moving
spot of light—seems to fulfil the conditions Russell used to characterize
causal lines, but it is not a causal process. It is a paradigm of what we mean
by a pseudo-process.

The basic method for distinguishing causal processes from pseudo-
processes is the criterion of mark transmission. A causal process is capable
of transmitting a mark; a pseudo-process is not. Consider, first, a pulse of
light which travels from the spotlight to the wall. If we place a piece of
red glass in its path at any point between the spotlight and the wall, the
light pulse, which was white, becomes and remains red until it reaches
the wall. A single intervention at one point in the process transforms it
in a way which persists from that point on. If we had not intervened, the
light pulse would have remained white during its entire journey from
the spotlight to the wall. If we do intervene locally at a single place we
can produce a change which is transmitted from the point of intervention
onward. We shall say, therefore, that the light pulse constitutes a causal
process, whether it is modified or not, since in either case it is capable of
transmitting a mark. Clearly, light pulses can serve as signals and can transmit messages.

Now, let us consider the spot of light which moves around the wall as the
spotlight rotates. There are a number of ways in which we can intervene to

---

[4] *Human Knowledge: Its Scope and Limits* (New York, 1948), 459.

change the spot at some point; for example, we can place a red filter at the wall with the result that the spot of light becomes red at that point. But if we make such a modification in the travelling spot, it will not be transmitted beyond the point of interaction. As soon as the light spot moves beyond the point at which the red filter was placed, it will become white again. The mark can be made, but it will not be transmitted. We have a 'process' which, in the absence of any intervention, consists of a white spot moving regularly along the wall of the building. If we intervene at some point, the 'process' will be modified *at that point*, but it will continue on beyond that point just as if no intervention had occurred. We can, of course, make the spot red at other places if we wish. We can install a red lens in the spotlight, but that does not constitute a *local* intervention at an isolated point in the process itself. We can put red filters at many places along the wall, but that would involve *many* interventions rather than a single one. We could get someone to run around the wall holding a red filter in front of the spot continuously, but that would not constitute an intervention *at a single point* in the 'process'. . . .

A given process, whether it be causal or pseudo, has a certain degree of uniformity—we may say, somewhat loosely, that it exhibits a certain structure. The difference between a causal process and a pseudo-process, I am suggesting, is that the causal process transmits its own structure, while the pseudo-process does not. The distinction between processes which do and those which do not transmit their own structures is revealed by the mark criterion. If a process—a causal process—is transmitting its own structure, then it will be capable of transmitting modifications in that structure. Radio broadcasting presents a clear example. The transmitting station sends a carrier wave which has a certain structure—characterized by amplitude and frequency, among other things—and modifications of this wave, in the form of modulations of amplitude (AM) or frequency (FM), are imposed for the purpose of broadcasting. Processes which transmit their own structure are capable of transmitting marks, signals, information, energy, and causal influence. Such processes are the means by which causal influence is propagated in our world. Causal influences, transmitted by radio, may set your foot to tapping, or induce someone to purchase a different brand of soap, or point a television camera aboard a spacecraft toward the rings of Saturn. A causal influence transmitted by a flying arrow can pierce an apple on the head of William Tell's son. A causal influence transmitted by sound waves can make your dog come running. A causal influence transmitted by ink marks on a piece of paper can gladden one's day or break someone's heart. Pseudo-processes can do no such things.

It is evident, I think, that the propagation or transmission of causal influence from one place and time to another must play a fundamental role in the causal structure of the world. As I shall argue below, causal processes constitute precisely the causal connections which Hume sought, but was unable to find.[5]

3. CONJUNCTIVE FORKS

In order to approach the second basic causal concept, *production*, it will be necessary to consider the nature of causal forks. There are three types with which we must deal—namely, conjunctive, interactive, and perfect forks. All three types are concerned with situations in which a common cause gives rise to two or more effects which are somehow correlated with one another. The point of departure for this discussion is Reichenbach's *principle of the common cause*, and his statistical characterization of the conjuctive fork as a device to elaborate that fundamental causal principle.[6]

The principle of the common cause states, roughly, that when improbable coincidences recur too frequently to attribute them to chance, they can be explained by reference to a common causal antecedent. Consider some familiar examples. If two students in a class turn in identical term papers, and if we can rule out the possibility that either copied directly from the other, then we search for a common cause—for example, a paper in a fraternity file from which both of them copied independently of each other. If two friends, who have spent a pleasant day in the country together, both suffer acute gastro-intestinal distress in the evening, we may find that their illnesses can be traced to poisonous mushrooms they collected and consumed. Many such examples have been mentioned in the literature, and others come readily to mind. . . .

In an attempt to characterize the structure of such examples of common causes, Reichenbach introduced the notion of a *conjunctive fork*, defined in terms of the following four conditions:[7]

$$P(A.B|C) = P(A|C) \times P(B|C) \tag{1}$$

$$P(A.B|\bar{C}) = P(A|\bar{C}) \times P(B|\bar{C}) \tag{2}$$

---

[5] In Wesley C. Salmon, 'An "At-At" Theory of Causal Influence', *Philosophy of Science*, 44 (1977), 215–24, I have attempted to provide a detailed analysis of the notion of transmission or propagation of causal influence by causal processes, and a justification for the claim that they legitimately qualify as causal connections.

[6] Hans Reichenbach, *The Direction of Time* (Berkeley and Los Angeles, 1956), sect. 19.

[7] Ibid., sect. 19. The variables *A*, *B*, *C* which appear in the probability expressions are taken by Reichenbach to denote classes, and the probabilities themselves are understood as statistical frequencies.

$$P(A|C) > P(A|\bar{C}) \tag{3}$$

$$P(B|C) > P(B|\bar{C}) \tag{4}$$

For reasons which will be made clear below, we shall stipulate that none of the probabilities occurring in these relations is equal to zero or one. Although it is not immediately obvious, conditions (1)–(4) entail

$$P(A.B) > P(A) \times P(B)^8 \tag{5}$$

These relations apply quite straightforwardly in concrete situations. Given two effects A and B, which occur together more frequently than they would if they were statistically independent of one another, there is some prior event C which is a cause of A and is also a cause of B, and which explains the lack of independence between A and B. In the case of plagiarism, the cause C is the presence of the term paper in the file to which both students had access. In the case of simultaneous illness, the cause C is the common meal which included the poisonous mushrooms. . . .

To say of two events X and Y that they occurred independently of one another means that they occur together with a probability equal to the product of the probabilities of their separate occurrences; i.e.,

$$P(X.Y) = P(X) \times P(Y) \tag{6}$$

Thus, in the examples we have considered, as relation (5) states, the two effects A and B are not independent. However, given the occurrence of the common cause C, A and B do occur independently, as the relationship among the conditional probabilities in equation (1) shows. Thus, in the case of illness, the fact that the probability of both individuals being ill at the same time is greater than the product of the probabilities of their individual illnesses is explained by the common meal. In this example, we are assuming that the fact that one person is afflicted does not have any direct causal influence upon the illness of the other. Moreover, let us assume for the sake of simplicity that, in this situation, there are no other potential common causes of severe gastro-intestinal illness.[9] Then, in the absence of the common cause C—that is, when $\bar{C}$ obtains—A and B are also independent of one another, as the relationship among the conditional probabilities in equation (2) states. Relations (3) and (4) simply assert that C is a positive cause of A and B, since the probability of each is greater in the presence of C than in the absence of C.

There is another useful way to look at equations (1) and (2). Recalling that, according to the multiplication theorem,

---

[8] Reichenbach, ibid. 160–1.

[9] If other potential common causes exist we can form a partition $C_1, C_2, C_3 \ldots$ and the corresponding relations will obtain.

$$P(A.B|C) = P(A|C) \times P(B|A.C) \tag{7}$$

we see that, provided $P(A|C) \neq 0$, equation (1) entails

$$P(B|C) = P(B|A.C). \tag{8}$$

In Reichenbach's terminology, this says that C screens off A from B. A similar argument shows that C screens off B from A. To screen off *means* to make statistically irrelevant. Thus, according to equation (1), the common cause C makes each of the two effects A and B statistically irrelevant to one another. By applying the same argument to equation (2), we can easily see that it entails that the absence of the common cause also screens off A from B.

To make quite clear the nature of the conjunctive fork, I should like to use an example deliberately contrived to exhibit the relationships involved. Suppose we have a pair of dice which are rolled together. If the first die comes to rest with side 6 on top, that is an event of the type A; if the second die comes to rest with side 6 uppermost, that is an event of type B. These dice are like standard dice except for the fact that each one has a tiny magnet embedded in it. In addition, the table on which they are thrown has a powerful electromagnet embedded in its surface. This magnet can be turned on or off with a concealed switch. If the dice are rolled when the electromagnet is on, it is considered an instance of the common cause C; if the magnet is off when the dice are tossed, the event is designated as $\bar{C}$. Let us further assume that, when the electromagnet is turned off, these dice behave exactly as standard dice. The probability of getting 6 with either die is $1/6$, and the probability of getting double 6 is $1/36$.[10] If the electromagnet is turned on, let us assume, the chance of getting 6 with either die is $1/2$, and the probability of double 6 is $1/4$. It is easily seen that conditions (1)–(4) are fulfilled. Let us make a further stipulation, which will simplify the arithmetic, but which has no other bearing upon the essential features of the example— namely, that half of the tosses of this pair of dice are made with the electromagnet turned on, and half are made with it turned off. We might imagine some sort of random device which controls the switch, and which realizes this equi-probability condition. We can readily see that the overall probability of 6 on each die, regardless of whether the electromagnet is on or off, is $1/3$. In addition, the overall probability of double 6 is the arithmetical average of $1/4$ and $1/36$, which equals $5/36$. If the occurrence of 6 on one die were independent of 6 occurring on the other, the overall probability of double 6 would be $1/3 \times 1/3 = 1/9 \neq 5/36$. Thus, the example satisfies relation (5), as of course it must, in addition to relations (1)–(4).

---

[10] We are assuming that the magnet in one die does not affect the behaviour of the other die.

It may initially seem counterintuitive to say that the results on the two dice are statistically independent if the electromagnet is off, and they are statistically independent if it is on, but that overall they are not independent. Nevertheless, they are, indeed, non-independent, and this non-independence arises from a clustering of sixes which is due simply to the fact that in a subset of the class of all tosses the probability of 6 is enhanced for each die. The dependency arises, not because of any physical interaction between the dice, but because of special background conditions which obtain on certain of the tosses. The same consideration applies to the earlier, less contrived, cases. When the two students each copy from a paper in a fraternity file, there is no direct physical interaction between the process by which one of the papers is produced and that by which the other is produced—in fact, if either student had been aware that the other was using that source, the unhappy coincidence might have been avoided. Likewise, as explicitly mentioned in the mushroom poisoning example, the illness of one friend had no effect upon the illness of the other. The coincidence resulted from the fact that a common set of background conditions obtained, namely, a common food supply from which both ate. . . .

Reichenbach claimed—correctly, I believe—that conjunctive forks possess an important asymmetry. Just as we can have two effects which arise out of a given common cause, so also may we find a common effect resulting from two distinct causes. For example, by getting results on two dice which add up to seven, one may win a prize. Reichenbach distinguished three situations:

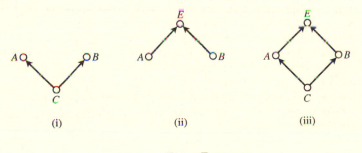

(i)   (ii)   (iii)

FIG. E

(i) a common cause C giving rise to two separate effects, A and B, without any common effect arising from A and B conjointly; (ii) two events A and B which, in the absence of a common cause C, jointly produce a common effect E; and (iii) a combination of (i) and (ii) in which the events A and B have both a common cause C and a common effect E. He characterized situations (i) and (ii) as 'open forks', while (iii) is closed on both ends. Reichenbach's asymmetry thesis was that situations of type (ii) never represent conjunctive forks; conjunctive forks which are open are always open to the future and never to the past. Since the statistical relations which are found in conjunctive forks are said to explain otherwise improbable coincidences, it follows that such coincidences are explained only in terms of common causes, never common effects. I believe that an even stronger claim is warranted—though I shall not try to argue it here—namely, that conjunctive forks, whether open or closed by a fourth event, always point in the same temporal direction. Reichenbach allowed that in situations of type (iii), the two events A and B along with their common effect E could form a conjunctive fork. Here, of course, there must also be a common cause C, and it is C rather than E which explains the coincidental occurrence of A and B. I doubt that, even in these circumstances, A, B, and E can form a conjunctive fork.[11]

It would be a mistake to suppose that the statistical relations given in conditions (1)–(4) are sufficient to characterize common causes in their role as explanations of correlated effects, as an example, due to Ellis Crasnow, clearly demonstrates.[12] Consider a man who usually arrives at his office at about 9.00 a.m., makes a cup of coffee, and settles down to read the morning paper. On some occasions, however, he arrives promptly at 8.00 a.m., and on these very same mornings his secretary has arrived somewhat earlier and prepared a fresh pot of coffee. Moreover, on just these mornings, he is met at his office by one of his associates who normally works at a different location. Now, if we consider the fact that the coffee is already made when he arrives (A) and the fact that his associate shows up on that morning (B) as the coincidence to be explained, then it might be noted that on such mornings he always catches the 7.00 a.m. bus (C), while on other mornings he usually takes the 8.00 a.m. bus ($\bar{C}$). In this example, it is plausible enough to suppose that A, B, and C form a conjunctive fork satisfying (1)–(4), but obviously C cannot be considered a cause either of A or of B. The actual common cause is an entirely different event C', namely, a telephone appointment made the day before by his secretary. C' is, in fact, the common cause of A, B, and C.

In order to distinguish the cases in which the event C in a conjunctive fork constitutes a bona fide common cause from those in which it does not, let us add the condition that there must be a suitable causal process connecting C with A and another connecting C with B. These causal processes constitute

---

[11] The reader is urged to compare the illuminating account of causal asymmetry offered by Paul W. Humphreys in 'Probabilistic Causality and Multiple Causation', in Peter D. Asquith and Ronald N. Giere (eds.), *PSA 1980* (East Lansing, Mich., 1981), 25–37.

[12] I had previously attributed this erroneous view to Reichenbach, but Paul Humphreys kindly pointed out that my attribution was incorrect.

the mechanisms by which causal influence is transmitted from the cause to each of the effects. These causal connections are an essential part of the causal fork, and without them, the event C at the vertex of a conjunctive fork cannot qualify as a common cause.

4. INTERACTIVE FORKS

There is another, basically different, type of common cause which violates the statistical conditions used to define the conjunctive fork. Consider a simple example. Two pool balls, the cue ball and the 8-ball, lie upon a pool table. A relative novice attempts a shot which is intended to put the 8-ball into one of the far corner pockets, but given the positions of the balls, if the 8-ball falls into one corner pocket, the cue ball is almost certain to go into the other far corner pocket, resulting in a 'scratch'. Let A stand for the 8-ball dropping into the one corner pocket, let B stand for the cue ball dropping into the other corner pocket, and let C stand for the collision between the cue ball and the 8-ball which occurs when the player executes the shot. We may reasonably assume that the probability of the 8-ball going into the pocket is 1/2 if the player tries the shot, and that the probability of the cue ball going into the pocket is also about 1/2. It is immediately evident that A, B, and C do not constitute a conjunctive fork, for C does not screen A and B from one another. Given that the shot is attempted the probability that the cue ball will fall into the pocket (approx. 1/2) is *not* equal to the probability that the cue ball will go into the pocket given that the shot has been attempted and that the 8-ball has dropped into the other far corner pocket (approx. 1).

In discussing the conjunctive fork, I took some pains to point out that forks of that sort occur in situations in which separate and distinct processes, which do not directly interact, arise out of special background conditions. In the example of the pool balls, however, there is a direct interaction—a collision—between the two causal processes which consist in portions of the histories of the two balls. For this reason, I have suggested that forks which are exemplified by such cases be called *interactive forks*.[13] Since the common cause C does not statistically screen the two effects A and B from one another, interactive forks violate condition (1) in the definition of conjunctive forks.

The best way to look at interactive forks, I believe, is in terms of spatio-temporal intersections of processes. In some cases, two processes may intersect without producing any lasting modification in either. This will happen,

---

[13] See Wesley C. Salmon, 'Why Ask "Why?"?—An Inquiry Concerning Scientific Explanation', *Proceedings and Addresses of the American Philosophical Association*, 51/6 (Aug. 1978), 683–705.

for example, when both processes are pseudo-processes. If the paths of two airplanes, flying in different directions at different altitudes on a clear day, cross one another, the shadows on the ground may coincide momentarily. But as soon as the shadows have passed the intersection, both move on as if no such intersection had ever occurred. In the case of the two pool balls, however, the intersection of their paths results in a change in the motion of each which would not have occurred if they had not collided. Energy and momentum are transferred from one to the other; their respective states of motion are altered. Such modifications occur, I shall maintain, only when two causal processes intersect. If either or both of the intersecting processes are pseudo-processes, no such mutual modification occurs. However, it is entirely possible for two causal processes to intersect without any subsequent modification in either. Barring the extremely improbable occurrence of a particle–particle type collision between two photons, light rays normally pass right through one another without any lasting effect upon either one of them. The fact that two intersecting processes are both causal is a necessary but not sufficient condition of the production of lasting changes in them.

When two causal processes intersect and suffer lasting modifications after the intersection, there is some correlation between the changes which occur in them. In many cases—and perhaps all—energy and/or momentum transfer occurs, and the correlations between the modifications are direct consequences of the respective conservation laws.[14] This is nicely illustrated by the Compton scattering of an energetic photon from an electron which can be considered, for practical purposes, initially at rest. The difference in energy between the incoming photon $h\nu$ and the scattered photon $h\nu'$ is equal to the kinetic energy of the recoiling electron. Similarly, the momentum change in the photon is exactly compensated by the momentum change in the electron.[15]

When two processes intersect, and they undergo correlated modifications which persist after the intersection, I shall say that the intersection constitutes a *causal interaction*. This is the basic idea behind what I want to take as a fundamental causal concept. Let C stand for the event consisting of the intersection of two processes. Let A stand for a modification in one and B for a modification in the other. Then, in many cases, we find a relation analogous to equation (1) in the definition of the conjunctive fork, except that the equality is replaced by an inequality:

---

[14] For a valuable discussion of the role of energy and momentum transfer in causality, see David Fair, 'Causation and the Flow of Energy', *Erkenntnis*, 14 (1979), 219–50.

[15] As explained in Salmon, 'Why Ask "Why?"?', the example of Compton scattering has the advantage of being irreducibly statistical, and thus, not analysable, even in principle, as a perfect fork (discussed below).

$$P(A.B|C) > P(A|C) \times P(B|C) \tag{9}$$

Moreover, given a causal interaction of the foregoing sort, I shall say that the change in each process is *produced* by the interaction with the other process.

I have now characterized, at least partially, the two fundamental causal concepts mentioned at the outset. Causal processes are the means by which causal influence is *propagated*, and changes in processes are *produced* by causal interactions. We are now in a position to see the close relationship between these basic notions. The distinction between causal processes and pseudo-processes was formulated in terms of the criterion of mark transmission. A mark is a modification in a process, and if that modification persists, the mark is transmitted. Modifications in processes occur when they intersect with other processes; if the modifications persist beyond the point of intersection, then the intersection constitutes a causal interaction and the interaction has produced marks which are transmitted. For example, a pulse of white light is a process, and a piece of red glass is another process. If these two processes intersect—i.e. if the light pulse goes through the red glass— then the light pulse becomes and remains red, while the filter undergoes an increase in energy as a result of absorbing some of the light which impinges upon it. Although the newly acquired energy may soon be dissipated into the surrounding environment, the glass retains some of the added energy for some time beyond the actual moment of interaction.

We may, therefore, turn the presentation around in the following way. We live in a world which is full of processes (causal or pseudo), and these processes undergo frequent intersections with one another. Some of these intersections constitute causal interactions; others do not. If an intersection occurs which does not qualify as an interaction, we can draw no conclusion as to whether the processes involved are causal or pseudo. If two processes intersect in a manner which does qualify as a causal interaction, then we may conclude that both processes are causal, for each has been marked (i.e. modified) in the intersection with the other, and each process transmits the mark beyond the point of intersection. Thus, each process shows itself capable of transmitting marks, since each one has transmitted a mark generated in the intersection. Indeed, the operation of marking a process is accomplished by means of a causal interaction with another process. Although we may often take an active role in producing a mark in order to ascertain whether a process is causal (or for some other purpose), it should be obvious that human agency plays no essential part in the characterization of causal processes or causal interactions. We have every reason to believe that the world abounded in causal processes and causal interactions long before there were any human agents to perform experiments.

5. RELATIONS BETWEEN CONJUNCTIVE AND INTERACTIVE FORKS

Suppose that we have a shooting-gallery with a number of targets. The famous sharpshooter, Annie Oakley, comes to this gallery, but it presents no challenge to her, for she can invariably hit the bull's-eye of any target at which she aims. So, to make the situation interesting, a hardened steel knife-edge is installed in such a position that a *direct* hit on the knife-edge will sever the bullet in a way which makes one fragment hit the bull's-eye of target A while the other fragment hits the bull's-eye of target B. If we let A stand for a fragment striking the bull's-eye of target A, B for a fragment striking the bull's-eye of target B, and C for the severing of the bullet by the knife-edge, we have an interactive fork quite analogous to the example of the pool balls. Indeed, we may use the same probability values, setting $P(A|C) = P(B|C) = 1/2$, while $P(A|C.B) = P(B|C.A) \simeq 1$. Statistical screening-off obviously fails.

We might, however, consider another event C^*. To make the situation concrete, imagine that we have installed between the knife-edge and the targets a steel plate with two holes in it. If the shot at the knife-edge is good, then the two fragments of the bullet will go through the two holes, and each fragment will strike its respective bull's-eye with probability virtually equal to 1. Let C^* be the event of the two fragments going through their respective holes. Then, we may say, A, B, and C^* will form a conjunctive fork. That happens because C^* refers to a situation which is subsequent to the physical interaction between the parts of the bullet. By the time we get to C^*, the bullet has been cut into two separate pieces, and each is going its way independently of the other. Even if we should decide to vaporize one of the fragments with a powerful laser, that would have no effect upon the probability of the other fragment finding its target. This example makes quite vivid, I believe, the distinction between the interactive fork, which characterizes direct physical interactions, and the conjunctive fork, which characterizes independent processes arising under special background conditions.

There is a further important point of contrast between conjunctive and interactive forks. Conjunctive forks possess a kind of temporal asymmetry which was described above. Interactive forks do not exhibit the same sort of temporal asymmetry. This is easily seen by considering a simple collision between two billiard balls. A collision of this type can occur in reverse; if a collision C precedes states of motion A and B in the two balls, then a collision C can occur in which states of motion just like A and B, except that the direction of motion is reversed, precede the collision. Causal interactions and causal processes do not, in and of themselves, provide a basis for temporal asymmetry.

Our ordinary causal language is infused with temporal asymmetry, but we should be careful in applying it to *basic* causal concepts. If, for example, we say that two processes are modified as a result of their interaction, the words suggest that we have already determined which are the states of the processes prior to the interaction, and which are the subsequent states. To avoid begging temporal questions, we should say that two processes intersect, and each of the processes has different characteristics on the two sides of the intersection. We do not try to say which part of the process comes earlier and which later. The same is true when we speak of marking. To erase a mark is the exact temporal reverse of imposing a mark; to speak of imposing or erasing is to presuppose a temporal direction. In many cases, of course, we know on other grounds that certain kinds of interactions are irreversible. Light filters absorb some frequencies, so that they transform white light into red. Filters do not furnish missing frequencies to turn red light into white. But until we have gone into the details of the physics of irreversible processes, it is best to think of causal interactions in temporally symmetric terms, and to take the causal connections which are furnished by causal processes as symmetric connections. Causal processes and causal interactions do not furnish temporal asymmetry; conjunctive forks fulfil that function.

6. PERFECT FORKS

In dealing with conjunctive and interactive forks, it is advisable to restrict our attention to the cases in which $P(A|C)$ and $P(B|C)$ do not assume either of the extreme values zero or one. The main reason is that the relation

$$P(A.B|C) = P(A|C) \times P(B|C) = 1 \qquad (10)$$

may represent a limiting case of either a conjunctive or an interactive fork, even though (10) is a special case of equation (1) and it violates relation (9).

Consider the Annie Oakley example once more. Suppose that she returns to the special shooting-gallery time after time. Given that practice makes perfect (at least in her case), she improves her skill until she can invariably hit the knife-edge in the manner which results in the two fragments finding their respective bull's-eyes. Up until the moment that she has perfected her technique, the results of her trials exemplified interactive forks. It would be absurd to claim that, when she achieves perfection, the splitting of the bullet no longer constitutes a causal interaction, but must now be regarded as a conjunctive fork. The essence of the interactive fork is to achieve a high correlation between two results; if the correlation is perfect, we can ask no more. It is, one might say, an arithmetical accident that when perfection occurs, equation (1) is fulfilled while the inequality (9) must be violated. If probability values were normalized to some value other than 1, that result would not obtain. It therefore seems best to treat this special case as a third type of fork—the *perfect fork*.

Conjunctive forks also yield perfect forks in the limit. Consider the example of illness due to consumption of poisonous mushrooms. If we assume—what is by no means always the case—that anyone who consumes a significant amount of the mushroom in question is certain to become violently ill, then we have another instance of a perfect fork. Even when these limiting values obtain, however, there is still no direct interaction between the processes leading respectively to the two cases of severe gastro-intestinal distress.

The main point to be made concerning perfect forks is that, when the probabilities take on the limiting values, it is impossible to tell from the statistical relationships alone whether the fork should be considered interactive or conjunctive. The fact that relations (1)–(4), which are used in the characterization of conjunctive forks, are satisfied does not constitute a sufficient basis for making a judgement about the temporal orientation of the fork. Only if we can establish, on separate grounds, that the perfect fork is a limiting case of a conjunctive (rather than an interactive) fork, can we conclude that the event at the vertex is a common cause rather than a common effect. Perfect forks need to be distinguished from the other two types mainly to guard against this possible source of confusion.

7. THE CAUSAL STRUCTURE OF THE WORLD

In everyday life, when we talk about cause–effect relations, we think typically (though not necessarily invariably) of situations in which one event (which we call the cause) is linked to another event (which we call the effect) by means of a causal process. Each of the two events which stands in this relation is an interaction between two (or more) intersecting processes. We say, for example, that the window was broken by boys playing baseball. In this situation, there is a collision of a bat with a ball (an interactive fork), the motion of the ball through space (a causal process), and a collision of the ball with the window (an interactive fork). For another example, we say that turning a switch makes the light go on. In this case, an interaction between a switching mechanism and an electrical circuit leads to a process consisting of a motion of electric charges in some wires, which in turn leads to emission of light from a filament. Homicide by shooting provides still another example. An interaction between a gun and a cartridge propels a bullet (a causal process) from the gun to the victim, where the bullet then interacts with the body of the victim.

The foregoing characterization of causal processes and various kinds of causal forks provides, I believe, a basis for understanding three fundamental aspects of causality:

1. *Causal processes* are the means by which structure and order are *propagated* or transmitted from one space–time region of the universe to other times and places.

2. *Causal interactions*, as explicated in terms of interactive forks, constitute the means by which *modifications in structure* (which are propagated by causal processes) are *produced*.

3. Conjunctive *common causes*—as characterized in terms of conjunctive forks—play a vital role in the *production* of structure and order. In the conjunctive fork, it will be recalled, two or more processes, which are physically independent of one another and which do not interact directly with each other, arise out of some special set of background conditions. The fact that such special background conditions exist is the source of a correlation among the various effects which would be utterly improbable in the absence of the common causal background.

There is a striking difference between conjunctive common causes on the one hand and causal processes and interactions on the other. Causal processes and causal interactions seem to be governed by basic laws of nature in ways which do not apply to conjunctive forks. Consider two paradigms of causal processes, namely, an electromagnetic wave propagating through a vacuum and a material particle moving without any net external forces acting upon it. Barring any causal interactions in both cases, the electromagnetic wave is governed by Maxwell's equations and the material particle is governed by Newton's first law of motion (or its counterpart in relativity theory). Causal interactions are typified by various sorts of collisions. The correlations between the changes which occur in the processes involved are governed—in most, if not all, cases—by fundamental physical conservation laws. Although I am not prepared to argue the case in detail, it seems plausible to suppose that *all fundamental physical interactions* can be regarded as exemplifications of the interactive fork.

Conjunctive common causes are not nearly as closely tied to the laws of nature. It should hardly require mention that, to the extent that conjunctive forks involve causal processes and causal interactions, the laws of nature apply as sketched in the preceding paragraph. However, in contrast to causal processes and causal interactions, conjunctive forks depend crucially upon *de facto* background conditions. Recall some of the examples mentioned above. In the plagiarism example, it is a non-lawful fact that two members of the same class happen to have access to the same file of term papers. In the mushroom poisoning example, it is a non-lawful fact that the two participants sup together out of a common pot. In the twin quasar example, it is a *de facto* condition that the quasar and the elliptic galaxy are situated in such a way that light coming to us from two different directions arises from a source which radiates quite uniformly from extended portions of its surface. . . .

8. CONCLUDING REMARKS

There has been considerable controversy since Hume's time regarding the question of whether causes must precede their effects, or whether causes and effects might be simultaneous with each other. It seems to me that the foregoing discussion provides a reasonable resolution of this controversy. If we are talking about the typical cause–effect situation, which I characterized above in terms of a causal process joining two distinct interactions, then we are dealing with cases in which the cause must precede the effect, for causal propagation over a finite time interval is an essential feature of cases of this type. If, however, we are dealing simply with a causal interaction—an intersection of two or more processes which produces lasting changes in each of them—then we have simultaneity, since each process intersects the other at the same time. Thus, it is the intersection of the white light pulse with the red filter which produces the red light, and the light becomes red at the very time of its passage through the filter. Basically, propagation involves lapse of time, while interaction exhibits the relation of simultaneity.

Another traditional dispute has centred upon the question of whether statements about causal relations pertain to individual events, or whether they hold properly only with respect to classes of events. Again, I believe, the foregoing account furnishes a straightforward answer. I have argued that causal processes, in many instances, constitute the causal connections between cause and effect. A causal process is an individual entity, and such entities transmit causal influence. An individual process can sustain a causal connection between an individual cause and an individual effect. Statements about such relations need not be construed as disguised generalizations. At the same time, it should be noted, we have used statistical relations to characterize conjunctive and interactive forks. Thus, strictly speaking, when we invoke something like the principle of the common cause, we are implicitly making assertions which involve statistical generalizations. Causal relations, it seems to me, have both particular and general aspects.

Throughout this discussion of causality, I have laid particular stress upon the role of causal processes, and I have even suggested the abandonment of the so-called 'event ontology'. It might be asked whether it would not be possible to carry through the same analysis, within the framework of an event ontology, by considering processes as continuous series of events. I see no reason for supposing that this programme could not be carried through, but I would be inclined to ask why we should bother to do so. One important source of difficulty for Hume, if I understand him, is that he tried to account for causal connections between non-contiguous events by interpolating intervening events. This approach seemed only to raise precisely the same questions about causal connections between events, for one had to ask how the causal influence is transmitted from one intervening event to another along the chain. The difficulty is circumvented, I believe, if we look to processes to provide the causal connections.[16] Focusing upon processes rather than events has, in my opinion, enormous heuristic (if not systematic) value. As John Venn said in 1866, 'Substitute for the time honoured "chain of causation", so often introduced into discussions upon this subject, the phrase a "rope of causation", and see what a very different aspect the question will wear.'[17]

---

[16] See Salmon, 'An "At-At" Theory'.   [17] *The Logic of Chance* (London, 1866), 320.

X

CAUSATION: REDUCTIONISM VERSUS REALISM*

MICHAEL TOOLEY

Any adequate approach to causation must provide accounts of causal laws, and of causal relations between states of affairs, or events, and, in each case, one is confronted with the choice between reductionism and realism. With respect to causal laws, the relevant issue concerns the relation between causal laws and the totality of events. According to reductionism, causal laws are supervenient upon the total history of the world. According to realism, they are not. With respect to causal relations, the central issue is whether causal relations between events are reducible to other states of affairs, including the non-causal properties of, and relations between, events. The reductionist holds that they are; the realist that they are not.

These choices between reductionist and non-reductionist approaches to causal laws and causal relations are surely among the most fundamental in the philosophy of causation. But in spite of that fact, they have received very little discussion. For, although there have been exceptions, the history of the philosophy of causation since the time of Hume has been largely the history of attempts to offer reductionist accounts of causal laws and of causal relations, and most philosophers have been content simply to assume that a reductionist approach to causation must be correct.

In this paper, I shall argue that reductionist accounts of causation are exposed to decisive objections, and that the time has come to explore realist alternatives.

1. REDUCTIONIST AND REALIST ALTERNATIVES

1.1 Causation and Logical Supervenience

Some recent discussions of causation have been concerned with the question of what causation is *in this world*, and it has been proposed, for example,

---

* I am indebted to David Armstrong for detailed and very helpful comments on an earlier draft.

that causation in this world can be identified with the transference of energy and/or momentum.[1] Such contingent identity theses concerning the nature of causation clearly constitute one sort of reductionism. It is not, however, the sort that I shall be concerned with here. For I shall be focusing, instead, upon questions such as whether causal laws are reducible, as a matter of *logical* necessity, to facts about the total history of the world, and, similarly, whether facts about causal relations between events are reducible, as a matter of *logical* necessity, to facts about other states of affairs.

A traditional way of putting these questions is in terms of the *analysability*, in certain ways, of causal concepts. Perhaps a slightly preferable way of formulating the matter, however, is in terms of the concept of *logical supervenience*. Let us say that two worlds, W and W^*, agree with respect to all of the properties and relations in some set, S, if and only if there is some one-to-one mapping, f, such that (1) for any individual x in world W, and any property P in set S, x has property P if and only if the corresponding individual, x^*, in W^*, also has property P, and vice versa, and (2) for any n-tuple of individuals, $x_1, x_2, \ldots x_n$ in W, and any relation R in set S, $x_1, x_2, \ldots x_n$ stand in relation R if and only if the corresponding individuals, $x_1^*, x_2^*, \ldots x_n^*$, in W^*, also stand in relation R, and vice versa. Then to say that the properties and relations in set T are logically supervenient upon the properties and relations in set S is to say that, for any two worlds W and W^*, if W and W^* agree with respect to the properties and relations in set S, they must also agree with respect to the properties and relations in set T.

Given these concepts, the reductionist theses that I shall be considering may now be characterized as follows. First, reductionism with respect to causal relations. This comes in two forms, depending upon what the reduction base is claimed to be:

Strong Reductionism with Respect to Causal Relations. Any two worlds that agree with respect to all of the non-causal properties of, and relations between, particular events or states of affairs, must also agree with respect to all of the causal relations between states of affairs. Causal relations are, in short, logically supervenient upon non-causal properties and relations.

Weak Reductionism with Respect to Causal Relations. Any two worlds that agree both with respect to all of the non-causal properties of, and relations between, particular events or states of affairs, and with respect to all causal laws, must also agree with respect to all of the causal relations between states of affairs.

Secondly, reductionism with respect to causal laws. The central contention here is that what causal laws there are is fixed by the total history of the

---

[1] See e.g. David Fair, 'Causation and the Flow of Energy', *Erkenntnis*, 14 (1979), 219–50.

world. That contention can also take, however, a stronger form and a weaker form:

Strong Reductionism with Respect to Causal Laws. Any two worlds that agree with respect to all of the *non-causal* properties of, and relations between, particular events, must also agree with respect to causal laws.

Weak Reductionism with Respect to Causal Laws. Any two worlds that agree with respect to all of the *causal and non-causal* properties of, and relations between, particular events, must also agree with respect to causal laws.

There are some obvious interrelations here. Strong reductionism for causal relations, when combined with weak reductionism for causal laws, entails strong reductionism for causal laws. Similarly, strong reductionism for causal laws, combined with weak reductionism for causal relations, entails strong reductionism for causal relations.

Strong reductionism on either issue cannot, accordingly, be combined with only weak reductionism on the other. But what about being merely a weak reductionist with regard to both causal laws and causal relations? This combination also seems impossible. For, on the one hand, if causal laws are logically supervenient upon the non-causal properties of, and relations between, particular events, together with the causal relations between events, then causal laws would seem to be ontologically less basic than causal relations, while if causal relations are logically supervenient upon causal laws plus the non-causal properties of, and relations between, particular events, then causal laws are ontologically more basic than causal relations. It would seem impossible, therefore, to formulate a coherent ontology if one attempts to embrace only weak reductionism both with respect to causal laws and with respect to causal relations.

Accordingly, if one is going to be reductionist with respect to both causal laws and causal relations, it is the strong reductionist views that one must embrace, and it is precisely this combination of positions that has been the dominant one since the time of Hume. Not all philosophers who are thoroughgoing reductionists with respect to causation fall, however, within the Humean tradition. For in the case of philosophers who approach causation in a broadly Humean way, what is fundamental is the acceptance of strong reductionism with respect to causal laws and weak reductionism with respect to causal relations: strong reductionism with respect to causal relations is a further conclusion that is drawn from those more fundamental commitments. It is possible, however, to start instead from weak reductionism with respect to causal laws, together with strong reductionism with respect to causal relations, and then to accept strong reductionism with respect to causal laws as a further consequence.

C. J. Ducasse is a good example of a philosopher who rejected a Humean approach to causation, but who was a strong reductionist none the less. For consider, first, the following passage:

The supposition of recurrence is thus wholly irrelevant to the meaning of cause; that supposition is relevant only to the meaning of law. And recurrence becomes related at all to causation only when a law is considered which happens to be a generalization of facts themselves individually causal to begin with. A general proposition concerning such facts is, indeed, a causal law, but it is not causal because general. It is general, i.e. a law, only because it is about a class of resembling facts; and it is causal only because each of them already happens to be a causal fact individually and in its own right (instead of, as Hume would have it, by right of its co-membership with others in a class of pairs of successive events).[2]

As this passage makes clear, weak reductionism with respect to causal relations is not a starting-point for Ducasse, since he rejects the idea that causal relations presuppose causal laws. His fundamental commitment with respect to causal relations is, instead, to a strong reductionist view, for he holds that causation can be analysed in terms of relations which Hume granted are observable in the individual instance—the relations, namely, of spatial and temporal contiguity, and of temporal priority.[3] On the other hand, weak reductionism with respect to causal laws is a starting-point for Ducasse, for he believes that causal laws are simply uniformities involving causal relations between particular events. So Ducasse is led to a thoroughgoing reductionism, but by a non-Humean route.

What alternatives are open if one rejects strong reductionism with respect to either causal laws, or causal relations, or both? Essentially there are four. First, realism with respect to causal laws can be combined with weak reductionism with respect to causal relations. The result is what might be characterized as a Humean view of causation plus a non-Humean view of laws.

Secondly, realism with respect to causal laws can also be combined with strong reductionism with respect to causal relations. This is the sort of position that results when a singularist reductionist approach to causation—such as Ducasse's—is combined with a realist approach to laws.

Thirdly, one can opt instead for a realist approach to causal relations, while accepting a reductionist view of causal laws. In that case, however, one would need to adopt a weak reductionist view. For according to a strong reductionist view of causal laws, the latter are logically supervenient upon the non-causal properties of, and relations between, events, and it is hard to

---

[2] C. J. Ducasse, 'On the Nature and the Observability of the Causal Relation', *Journal of Philosophy*, 23 (1926), 57–67, and repr. as Ch. VII above. See p. 129.

[3] Ibid., p. 127 above.

see how this could be the case if causal relations were not supervenient upon the same ontological base.

Finally, one can abandon all forms of reductionism with respect to causation, and embrace realism with respect to both causal laws and causal relations. This is, I shall argue, the preferred alternative.

2. REDUCTIONISM WITH RESPECT TO CAUSAL LAWS

The distinction between strong and weak reductionism with respect to causal laws is important for understanding what options are open when one is setting out an account of the nature of causation. It is not, however, important with respect to the choice between reductionist and realist approaches to laws, since strong and weak reductionist views are exposed to precisely the same objections.

Since a number of philosophers have recently argued, and in a detailed way, that reductionist accounts of the nature of laws are exposed to very strong objections,[4] my discussion here will be brief. I shall simply mention some of the more important objections that have been raised to reductionist accounts of the nature of laws.

First, then, there is the familiar problem of distinguishing between laws and accidental regularities. For example, there may well be some number N such that, at no time or place in the total history of the universe will there ever be a sphere of radius N centimetres that contains only electrons. But if there is such a number, does that mean that it is a *law* that no sphere of radius N centimetres can contain only electrons? Might it not, instead, be merely an accident that no such sphere exists? But if so, what serves to differentiate laws from mere cosmic regularities?[5]

A second objection concerns the possibility of basic, uninstantiated laws, and may be put as follows. For sake of illustration, let us suppose that our world involves psychophysical laws connecting different sorts of stimulation with emergent properties of experiences, so that it is a causal law, for example, that when a normal human looks at something that is a specific shade of purple, under standard conditions, that gives rise to an experience with some specific emergent property. Let us suppose, further, that at least

---

[4] Fred I. Dretske, 'Laws of Nature', *Philosophy of Science*, 44 (1977), 248–68; David M. Armstrong, *What is a Law of Nature?* (Cambridge, 1983), esp. chs. 1–5; and my own discussions in 'The Nature of Laws', *Canadian Journal of Philosophy*, 7/4 (1977), 667–98, and in *Causation: A Realist Approach* (Oxford, 1987), sect. 2. 1. 1.

[5] For a much fuller discussion of the problem of distinguishing between laws and accidental uniformities, see Armstrong, *What is a Law of Nature?*, ch. 2.

some of these psychophysical laws are basic laws—that is, incapable of being derived from any other laws, psychophysical or otherwise. Finally, let us assume that, for at least some of those basic psychophysical laws, the only instances of them at any time in the history of the universe involve sentient beings on our earth. Given these assumptions, consider what would have been the case if our world had been different in certain respects. Suppose, for example, that the earth had been destroyed by an explosion of the sun just before the point when, for the first time in history, a sentient being would have observed a purple flower, and so would have had an experience with the corresponding emergent property. What counterfactuals are true in the alternative possible world just described? In particular, what would have been the case if the sun had not gone supernova when it did? Would it not have been the case that a sentient being would have looked at a purple flower, and therefore have been stimulated in such a way as to have had an experience with the relevant emergent property?

It seems to me very plausible to hold that the counterfactual in question is true in that possible world. But that counterfactual cannot be true unless the appropriate psychophysical law obtains in that world. But in the world where the sun explodes before any sentient being has looked at a purple flower, the law in question will not have any instances. So if the counterfactual is true in that world, it follows that there can be basic causal laws that lack all instances. But if that is so, then causal laws cannot be logically supervenient upon the total history of the universe.[6]

A third objection concerns a problem posed by probabilistic laws. Consider a world where it is a law that the probability that an event with property P has property Q is equal to one-half. It does not follow that precisely one-half of the events with property P will have property Q. Indeed, the proportion that have property Q need not be anywhere near one-half: it can be absolutely any value whatever.

The existence of the law in question does have, of course, *probabilistic* implications with respect to the proportion that will have property Q. In particular, as the number of events with property P becomes larger and larger, the *probability* that the proportion of events with property P which also have property Q will be within any specified interval around the value one-half approaches indefinitely close to one. But this fact is, of course, perfectly compatible with the fact that the existence of the law in question does not *entail* any restrictions upon the proportion of events with property P that have property Q.

[6] I have discussed the question of the possibility of uninstantiated basic laws in more detail in *Causation*, 47–51.

More generally, any probabilistic law is compatible with *any* distribution of properties over events. In this respect, there is a sharp difference between probabilistic laws and non-probabilistic laws. Any non-probabilistic law imposes a constraint upon the total history of any world containing that law—namely, the corresponding regularity must obtain. But a probabilistic law, in contrast, imposes no constraint upon the total history of the world. Accordingly, unless one is prepared to supplement one's ontology in a very un-Humean way, by postulating something like objective, *single-case* chances, there would not seem to be even a potential reduction base in the case of probabilistic laws.[7]

The fourth and final objection that I shall mention concerns an epistemological problem that arises if one attempts to identify laws either with cosmic regularities in general, or with regularities that satisfy certain additional constraints. On the one hand, the evidence for any law consists of a finite number of observations. On the other, any law has a potentially infinite number of instances. Can such a finite body of evidence possibly justify one in believing that some law obtains, if laws are essentially just regularities? For if laws are merely certain kinds of regularities, with no further ontological backing, is it not in fact likely that the regularities that have held with respect to the cases that have been observed so far will break down at some point?

This objection can be formulated in a more rigorous way by appealing to some general, quantitative account of confirmation, according to which any generalization of the sort that expresses a possible law has probability zero relative to any finite body of evidence. Carnap's system of confirmation, for example, has that property.[8] It might be suggested, of course, that any system with this property is necessarily defective, but I have argued elsewhere that that is not the case.[9] . . .

But how is the realist any better placed with respect to this epistemological problem? The answer is that a realist can view the existence of a causal law as constituted by a single, atomic state of affairs, rather than as a potentially infinite conjunction of states of affairs. On the view that I favour, for example, laws are to be identified with certain second-order, atomic states of affairs involving irreducible relations between universals, and I have tried to show elsewhere, in a detailed way, that the adoption of this sort of realist

---

[7] A fuller account of the problem posed by probabilistic laws can be found in my *Causation*, 142–7.

[8] For a discussion of this, see Rudolf Carnap, *Logical Foundations of Probability*, 2nd edn. (Chicago, 1962), 570–5.

[9] *Causation*, 135.

account enables one to prove that quite a limited body of evidence may make it very probable that a given law obtains.[10]

To sum up. Reductionist accounts of causal laws face at least four serious objections. First, they appear unable to draw a satisfactory distinction between laws and accidental uniformities. Secondly, they cannot allow for the possibility of basic, uninstantiated laws. Thirdly, probabilistic laws seem to pose an intractable problem. And finally, it is difficult to see how one can ever be justified in believing that there are laws, if one adopts a reductionist account. A realist approach, in contrast, can provide satisfactory answers to all of these problems.

3. REDUCTIONISM WITH RESPECT TO CAUSAL RELATIONS

Philosophers have gradually become more aware of the seriousness of the problems confronting a reductionist approach to laws. Much less well known, however, is the fact that reductionist approaches to causal relations are also exposed to very strong objections.

The latter fall into two groups. First, there are objections that centre upon the problem of giving an account of the direction of causal processes, and which claim that there are possible causal worlds where reductionist accounts of the direction of causation either do not apply at all, or else do apply, but give the wrong answers.

Secondly, there are objections involving what may be referred to as problems of under-determination. For what these objections attempt to establish is that there can be worlds that agree with respect to, first, all of the non-causal properties of, and relations between, events, secondly, all causal laws, and thirdly, the direction of causation, but which disagree with respect to the causal relations between corresponding events.

3.1. Direction of Causation Objections

I shall consider two objections which focus upon the direction of causation. The thrust of the first is that there are possible causal worlds to which reductionist accounts of the direction of causation do not apply, while that

---

[10] *Causation*, 129–37. For criticisms of this approach to laws of nature, see D. H. Mellor, 'Necessities and Universals in Natural Laws', in Mellor (ed.), *Science, Belief and Behaviour* (Cambridge, 1980), 105–25; L. Jonathan Cohen, 'Laws, Coincidences and Relations between Universals', in Philip Pettit, Richard Sylvan, and Jean Norman (eds.), *Metaphysics and Morality: Essays in Honour of J. J. C. Smart* (Oxford, 1987), 16–34; and Bas C. van Fraassen, *Laws and Symmetry* (Oxford, 1989).

of the second is that there are other possible causal worlds for which reductionist accounts yield wrong answers with respect to the direction of causal processes.

3.1.1. *Simple Worlds*   Our world is a complex one, with a number of features that might be invoked as the basis of a reductionist account of the direction of causation. First of all, it is a world where the direction of increase in entropy is the same in the vast majority of isolated or quasi-isolated systems. Secondly, the temporal direction in which order is propagated—such as by the circular waves that result when a stone strikes a pond, or by the spherical wavefronts associated with a point source of light—is invariably the same. Thirdly, consider the causal forks that are involved when two events have either a common cause, or a common effect. A fork may be described as open if it does not involve both a common cause and a common effect. Then it is a fact about our world that all, or virtually all, open forks are open in the same direction—namely, towards the future.[11]

Can such features provide a satisfactory account of the direction of causation? One objection arises out of possible causal worlds that are much simpler than our own. In particular, consider a world that contains only two uncharged particles, of the same type, that rotate endlessly about one another, on circular trajectories, in accordance with the laws of Newtonian physics. Each particle will undergo acceleration of a constant magnitude, due to the force of gravity exerted on it by the other particle. So the world is certainly a causal one. But it is also a world that is utterly devoid of changes of entropy, of propagation of order, and of open forks. So there is no hope of basing an account of the direction of causation upon any of those features.

What account can a reductionist give, then, of the direction of causation? The answer is that there is only one possibility. For, given that the simple world just described is completely symmetrical in time, events themselves do not exhibit any structure that serves to distinguish between the direction from cause to effect and the inverse one from effect to cause. So if the direction of causation is to be reduced to anything else, it can only be to the direction of time. But, then, in turn, one will have to be a realist with respect to the latter. There will be no possibility of reducing the direction of time to any structure present in the arrangement of events in time.

---

[11] For the first, see Hans Reichenbach, *The Direction of Time* (Berkeley, Calif., 1956), 117–43, and Adolf Grünbaum, *Philosophical Problems of Space and Time*, 2nd edn. (Dordrecht, 1973), 254–64. For the second, see Karl Popper, 'The Arrow of Time', *Nature*, 177 (1956), 538. For the third, see Reichenbach, *Direction of Time*, 161–3, and Wesley Salmon, 'Why Ask "Why?"?', *Proceedings and Addresses of the American Philosophical Association*, 51/6 (1978), 696.

3.1.2. *Inverted Worlds* It is the year 4004 BC. A Laplacean-style deity is about to create a world rather similar to ours, but one where Newtonian physics is true. Having selected the year AD 2000 as a good time for Armageddon, the deity works out what the world will be like at that point, down to the last detail. He then creates two spatially unrelated worlds: the one just mentioned, together with another whose initial state is a flipped-over version of the state of the first world immediately prior to Armageddon—i.e. the two initial states agree exactly, except that the velocities of the particles in the one are exactly opposite to those in the other.

Consider, now, any two complete temporal slices of the first world, A and B, where A is earlier than B. Since the worlds are Newtonian ones, and since the laws of Newtonian physics are invariant with respect to time reversal, the world that starts off from the reversed, AD 2000 type state will go through corresponding states, B^* and A^*, where these are flipped-over versions of B and A respectively, and where B^* is earlier than A^*. So while the one world goes from a 4004 BC, Garden of Eden state to an AD 2000, pre-Armageddon state, the other world will move from a reversed, pre-Armageddon type state to a reversed, Garden of Eden type state.

In the first world, the direction of causation will coincide with such things as the direction of increase in entropy, the direction of the propagation of order in non-entropically irreversible processes, and the direction defined by most open forks. But in the second world, whereas the direction of causation runs from the initial state created by the deity—that is, the flipped-over AD 2000 type state—through to the flipped-over 4004 BC type state, the direction in which entropy increases, the direction in which order is propagated, and the direction defined by open forks will all be the opposite one. So if any of the latter were used to define the direction of causation, it would generate the wrong result in the case of the second world.

As with the "simple universes" argument, it is open to a reductionist to respond by holding that the direction of causation is to be defined in terms of the direction of time. But here, as before, this response is only available if one is prepared to adopt a realist view of the direction of time. For any reductionist account of the latter in terms of the structure exhibited by events in time cannot possibly generate the right results in both cases for two worlds that are "inverted twins"—such as the two worlds just described.

3.2. Under-determination Objections

A reductionist approach to causal relations is exposed to at least four other objections, which I shall now describe. The thrust of all four is that fixing all of the non-causal properties of, and relations between, events, all of the laws, both causal and non-causal, and, finally, the direction of causation for all possible causal relations that might obtain, does not always suffice to fix what causal relations there are between events.

The first three arguments are, in effect, variations on a single theme—all of them focusing upon problems that arise concerning causal relations in indeterministic worlds. They do differ slightly, however, in their assumptions. The first argument assumes only that indeterministic causal laws are logically possible. The second argument, on the other hand, incorporates the further assumption that there is nothing incoherent in the idea of an uncaused event, while the third argument also involves that assumption, together with the additional assumption that probabilistic laws are logically possible.

The final argument, in contrast, does not appeal to the possibility of indeterministic worlds. Its thrust is that, even in a fully deterministic world, causal relations between events need not be logically supervenient upon the direction of causation, the totality of laws, both causal and non-causal, and the non-causal properties of, and relations between, events.

3.2.1. *The Argument from the Possibility of Indeterministic Laws* A world with at least some basic probabilistic laws is necessarily an indeterministic world, so this first argument might equally well start from the assumption that probabilistic laws are logically possible. But there can be indeterministic laws that are not probabilistic. For example, it might be a law that an instance of property P will give rise *either* to an instance of property Q *or* to an instance of property R, without its being the case that there is any number k such that it is a law that an instance of property P will give rise, with probability k, to an instance of property Q. Accordingly, since indeterministic laws need not be probabilistic, and since the concept of a probabilistic law has been thought by some to be more problematic than that of a non- probabilistic law, it seems preferable to start from the slightly more modest assumption.

Given that probabilistic laws are indeterministic, and that quantum physics seems to lend strong support to the idea that the basic laws of nature may well be probabilistic, the assumption that indeterministic causal laws are logically possible is surely very plausible—though by no means indubitable. Let us consider, then, a world with only the following two basic causal laws—both of which, though not probabilistic, are indeterministic:

> For any object x, x's having property P for a temporal interval of length Δt either causes x to acquire property Q, or else causes x to acquire property R, but does not do both;

For any object x, x's having property S for a temporal interval of length Δt either causes x to acquire property Q, or else causes x to acquire property R, but does not do both.

Suppose now that a is an object in such a world, that a has property P, but not property S, throughout some interval of length Δt, and then acquires property Q, but not property R. In view of the first of the above laws, it must be the case that a's acquisition of property Q was caused by its possession of property P. Similarly, if a had property S, but not property P, throughout some interval of length Δt, and then acquired property Q, but not property R, it would have to be the case, given the second law, that a's acquisition of property Q was caused by its possession of property S. But what if a had acquired properties P and S at the same time, and had retained both throughout an interval of length Δt? If a then acquired only property Q, there would be no problem: it would simply be a case of causal over-determination. Similarly, if it acquired only property R. But what if the situation were as follows:

Time t through time $(t + \Delta t)$	Time $(t + \Delta t)$
Pa and Sa	Qa and Ra

Here, a has acquired *both* property Q *and* property R, and, as a result, there are two possibilities concerning the relevant causal relations:

Possibility 1	Possibility 2
Pa causes Qa, and Sa causes Ra	Pa causes Ra, and Sa causes Qa

One is therefore confronted with the question of what the relevant causal relations are. Was it the possession of property P, for the appropriate interval, that caused the acquisition of property Q, and the possession of S that caused the acquisition of R? Or was it, instead, the other way around? Given a reductionist view, however, no answer is possible. For the causal laws in question, together with the non-causal properties of the object, and its non-causal relations to other objects, plus facts about the direction of causation in all potential causal processes, do not entail that it was one way rather than the other.

How might a reductionist respond to this argument? One try would be to say that where an object acquires property P and property S at the same time, and then, after the relevant interval, acquires both property Q and property R, there are *no* causal relations at all involved. But given that, for example, the first of the above laws can only obtain if the possession of property P *always* causes an event that is of one of two sorts, this response would seem to entail that indeterministic laws of the above sort are not really logically possible—a claim that surely needs to be supported by some independent argument. Moreover, given that the present argument can easily be formulated in terms of probabilistic laws, the latter would also have to be rejected as incoherent.

Another response would be to argue that, although there are causal relations in the situation, they are not quite as determinate as one might initially assume. The idea here would be that, in the crucial situation where the object has both P and S, and then acquires both Q and R, it is not the case either that the possession of P for the relevant interval causes the acquisition of Q, or that it causes the acquisition of R. What is true, rather, is simply that the possession of property P for the relevant interval causes the state of affairs which involves either the acquisition of property Q, or the acquisition of property R.

But this response is also very dubious, since it appears to involve a confusion between, on the one hand, certain non-linguistic, non-conceptual entities which are the relata of causal relations—namely, states of affairs—and, on the other, certain linguistic expressions that may be used to designate states of affairs. Thus, in referring to states of affairs, one may certainly use disjunctive expressions to pick them out—such as the expression 'the state of affairs that involves either a's acquisition of property Q, or a's acquisition of property R'. But while states of affairs can be referred to in that way, it makes no sense to speak of states of affairs as themselves disjunctive in nature. The only states of affairs that can be picked out by the disjunctive expression in question are the state of affairs that consists of a's acquiring property Q, and the state of affairs that consists of a's acquiring property R. Accordingly, if the situation described above is to involve causal relations falling under the relevant laws, it must be the case either that the possession of property P for the relevant interval caused the acquisition of property Q, or that it caused the acquisition of property R, and similarly for property S.

3.2.2. *The Argument from the Possibility of Uncaused Events*   The second argument is, in a sense, a simpler version of the previous one. It does involve, however, one additional assumption—namely, that there is nothing incoherent in the idea of an uncaused event.

Given that further assumption, one can consider a world where objects sometimes acquire property Q without there being any cause of their doing so, and similarly for property R, and where, in addition, the following two statements are true:

(1) It is a law that, for any object x, x's having property P for a temporal interval of length Δt either causes x to acquire property Q, or else causes x to acquire property R;

(2) It can *never* be the case, for any object x, that x's having property P for a temporal interval of length Δt causes x to acquire both property Q *and* property R.

Suppose, finally, that an object a in such a world, having had property P for the appropriate interval, acquires both Q and R. In view of the law described in statement (1), either the acquisition of Q was caused by the possession of P for the relevant interval, or else the acquisition of R was so caused. But, given statement (2), it cannot be the case that the possession of P for the relevant interval caused *both* the acquisition of Q *and* the acquisition of R. So once again, it must be the case that one of two causal states of affairs obtains, but the totality of facts concerning, first, the non-causal properties of, and relations between, events, secondly, what laws there are, and thirdly, the direction of causation in all potential causal processes, does not suffice to fix which causal state of affairs obtains.

A possible reductionist response is that if it is a law that objects always acquire either property Q or property R, after having had property P for a relevant interval, and if, in addition, they sometimes acquire both property Q and property R in such circumstances, then the following must be the case:

(3) It is a law that, for any object x, x's having property P for a temporal interval of length Δt either causes x to acquire property Q, or causes x to acquire property R, or, finally, causes x to acquire both property Q and property R.

But if the latter is the case, then statement (2) cannot be true.

This response, however, does not seem satisfactory. For in the first place, the claim that, in the situation described, statement (3) must be true, surely calls for support. What sort of argument might be offered? The only possibility, I think, is to appeal to a reductionist view of causal laws, according to which they are to be identified with certain sorts of regularities.

In the second place, even if the contention in question is granted, for the sake of discussion, the underlying difficulty is only shifted. For now when an object acquires both Q and R, after having had P for the appropriate interval, we can say that it *may* have been the case that the latter state of affairs caused both the acquisition of Q and the acquisition of R. But, equally, it may instead have been the case that, say, only the acquisition of Q was so caused, and that the acquisition of R was an uncaused event. Or perhaps it was the other way around. There are, in short, three distinct possibilities with respect to the causal relations involved, and which of these obtains in any given case is not fixed by the facts in the proposed reductionist base.

3.2.3. *The Argument from the Possibility of Uncaused Events plus Prob-abilistic, Causal Laws*   The argument just set out can be reinforced, more-over, if one replaces the assumption that there can be indeterministic causal laws with the slightly stronger assumption that it is logically possible for there to be basic, probabilistic, causal laws. Given that assumption, the argument runs as follows. Imagine a world where objects sometimes acquire property Q without there being any cause of that occurrence. Suppose, fur-ther, that the following is a law:

> For any object x, x's having property P for a time interval Δt causally brings it about, with probability 0.75, that x has property Q.

If objects sometimes acquire property Q without there being any cause of their doing so, why shouldn't this also take place in cases where an object happens to have had property P for the relevant time interval, Δt? Indeed, might there not be excellent reason for thinking that there were such cases? For suppose that objects that have property P for the relevant interval go on to acquire property Q 76 per cent of the time, rather than 75 per cent of the time, and that this occurs even over the long term. Other things being equal, this would be grounds for doubting whether the above law obtained, and for thinking that the relevant law was rather that:

> For any object x, x's having property P for a time interval Δt causally brings it about, with probability 0.76, that x has property Q.

But other things might not be equal. In particular, it might be the case that the first of the above possible laws was derivable from a very powerful, simple, and well-confirmed theory, whereas competing possibilities were not.

If that were the case, one would have reason for believing that, over the long term, of the 76 cases out of a 100 where an object that has had property P for the relevant interval acquires property Q, 75 of those will be ones where the acquisition of property Q is caused by the possession of property P, while the other case will be one where property Q is spontaneously acquired.

There can, in short, be situations where there would be good reason for believing that not all cases where an object has property P for an interval Δt, and then acquires Q, are causally the same. There is, however, no hope of making sense of this, given a reductionist approach to causal relations. For the cases do not differ with respect to relevant non-causal properties and relations, nor with respect to causal laws, nor with respect to the direction of causation in any potential causal relations.

3.2.4. *The Argument from the Possibility of Exact Replicas of Causal Situ-ations*   The three arguments just set out all appeal to the possibility of indeterministic worlds. The thrust of this final argument, in contrast, is that

a reductionist approach to causation is exposed to counter-examples even in the case of deterministic worlds.

Suppose that event P causes event M. In general, there will certainly be nothing impossible about there also being an event, M^*, which has precisely the same properties[12] as M, both intrinsic and relational, but which is not caused by P. But what about relations? Is it logically possible for it also to be the case that either (1) the only relation between P and M is that of causation, or else (2) any other relation that holds between P and M also holds between P and M^*?

If either situation obtained, one would have a counter-example to a reductionist approach to causal relations. For on a reductionist view, P's causing M is logically supervenient upon the non-causal properties of, and the non-causal relations between, P and M, together with the causal laws. So if M^* has precisely the same non-causal properties as M, and also stands to P in the same non-causal relations as M does, then it follows, on a reductionist view, that P must also cause M^*, contrary to hypothesis.

But are such situations possible? In support of the claim that they are, I want to mention two considerations.[13] The first appeals to the logical possibility of there being immaterial minds that are not located in space. If that possibility is granted, the argument runs as follows. First, though the contrary view has been defended, it is hard to see why there could not be two immaterial minds, existing simultaneously, whose mental contents were the same at every instant—either by a grand accident, or because of identical initial conditions in a world with deterministic laws governing mental events. Secondly, a plausible case can be made out, I believe, for the view that identity over time must be analysed in terms of causal relations between different events in the history of the enduring entity in question. But if this is right, then consider any two qualitatively indistinguishable immaterial minds, A and A^*. Let P and M be any two temporal slices of mind A, and P^* and M^* be the corresponding temporal slices of A^*. Then P will be causally related to M but not to M^*, even though M does not differ from M^*, either with respect to its properties, or with respect to the non-causal relations in which it stands to P.

A similar sort of case, which also turns upon the idea that it is causal relations between the temporal parts of an object that unite those parts into a single, enduring entity, can be constructed for physical objects, given a

---

[12] The only restriction upon properties here is that they must not involve particulars—so that e.g. being 5 miles from the Grand Canyon does not count as a property.

[13] I have offered additional support for this claim in 'Laws and Causal Relations', in *Midwest Studies in Philosophy*, 9, ed. P. A. French, T. E. Uehling, and H. K. Wettstein (Minneapolis, 1985), 93–112. See pp. 99–107.

world that satisfies two conditions. First, it must be a world where the only *basic* external relations between different temporal slices of the world, or between parts of different temporal slices, are temporal relations and causal relations. Secondly, it must possess an appropriate sort of symmetry—specifically, rotational symmetry, such as characterized the simple Newtonian world, described earlier, which consisted of only two uncharged particles, of the same type, rotating endlessly about one another on circular trajectories.

Consider, then, that very simple Newtonian world, and assume, further, that the only basic, external relations obtaining between things existing at different times are temporal relations and causal relations. Let P be the extended temporal part, of one particle, which consists of all temporal parts of that particle which exist at times prior to some time t, and let M be the extended temporal part that consists of all the temporal parts of it existing at t or later. Similarly, let P^* and M^* be the corresponding parts of the other particle. Then, in view of the above assumption about identity over time, P is causally related to M in a way that it is not to M^*.

Can a reductionist approach to causal relations cope with this sort of case? Since M and M^* do not differ with respect to their non-causal properties, a reductionist needs to point to some non-causal relation in which one of them stands to P, while the other does not. What might that relation be? A natural suggestion is the relation of spatio-temporal continuity, given that M is spatio-temporally continuous with P, whereas M^* is not. But this suggestion assumes, of course, that causal relations do not enter into spatio-temporal continuity.

One way of attempting to support the latter assumption is by offering an analysis of spatio-temporal continuity in terms of a generalized betweenness relation that, rather than being restricted to locations at a given time, can hold between space–time points belonging to different temporal slices, and then maintaining, as some philosophers do, that such a generalized betweenness relation can properly be treated as primitive.[14] My own view is that the latter contention is unsound, and that, on the contrary, a generalized betweenness relation, rather than being analytically basic, stands in need of analysis. But even if that were to turn out not to be so, the strategy just sketched would still not provide the reductionist with any reply to the present argument, since spatio-temporal betweenness is not a basic relation *in the possible world in question*. For there the only basic external relations between things existing at different times are temporal relations and causal relations.

Moreover, it is not only an account of spatio-temporal continuity in terms of generalized spatio-temporal betweenness that is precluded for the world

[14] Cf. Hartry Field's formulation of the theory of Newtonian space–time in his *Science Without Numbers* (Princeton, NJ, 1980), 52–3.

in question: no account that does not involve causal relations will do. For there is a simple, general argument, which runs as follows, and which shows that *any* external relation which obtains between P and M, but not between P and M^*, must involve causation. Consider any such relation. In view of the fact that the world is one where the only basic external relations holding between things existing at different times are temporal relations and causal relations, a relation that did not involve causation could hold between P and M, while not holding between P and M^*, only if there were some temporal relation that obtained between P and M, but not between P and M^*, or vice versa. But the latter is impossible, given that M and M^* are simultaneous. Accordingly, there cannot be any non-causal relation that holds between P and M, but not between P and M^*, or vice versa.

This in turn means that a reductionist account cannot be given for the causal relations in question. For, by hypothesis, M and M^* do not differ with respect to their properties, and we have just seen that there cannot be any non-causal relation that obtains between P and M, but not between P and M^*, or vice versa. Nevertheless, P causes M, but not M^*. So we have another counter-example to any reductionist approach to causation.

4. CAUSAL RELATIONS, SINGULARISM, AND SINGULARIST REDUCTIONISM

One issue that needs to be addressed, at least very briefly, is that of the relation between the case against reductionism and the case for a singularist conception of causation. For while the two arguments concerned with the problem of the direction of causation have no bearing upon the question of whether there can be causal relations that do not fall under causal laws, the four arguments set out in Section 3. 2, on the other hand, are variants of arguments that I have used elsewhere in support of a singularist conception of causation.[15]

Essentially, there are two points that need to be made. The first is that the arguments set out in Section 3. 2 are basically arguments against reductionism. They need to be supplemented, before they will lend any support to a singularist conception of causation. In particular, one needs to appeal to considerations of simplicity, if one is to move on from an anti-reductionist conclusion to the view that there can be causal relations that do not fall under causal laws.

[15] Most recently in 'The Nature of Causation: A Singularist Account', in David Copp (ed.), *Canadian Philosophers: Celebrating Twenty Years of the CJP*, Canadian Journal of Philosophy, suppl. 16 (1990), 271–322.

The second point is that although those arguments can be supplemented in order to generate support for a singularist conception of causation, the singularist conception in question must be a realist one. For the under-determination arguments in Section 3. 2, no less than the direction of causation arguments in Section 3. 1, are arguments against any form of reductionism with respect to causal relations, including singularist reductionism.[16]

5. REALISM WITH REGARD TO CAUSAL RELATIONS

If reductionism must be abandoned, what form should a realist approach to causation take? The basic choice here is between two views: first, the view that causal relations are observable, not only in the everyday sense of that term, but in a much stronger sense which entails that concepts of causal relations are analytically basic; and secondly, the view that causal concepts are theoretical concepts, so that causal relations can only be characterized, indirectly, as those relations that satisfy some appropriate theory.

A number of philosophers have favoured the former view, but their arguments in support of it have sometimes been very weak. Elizabeth Anscombe appeals, for example, to the fact that one often acquires observational knowledge of causal states of affairs: one sees the stone break the window, or the knife cut through the butter.[17] But observational knowledge, in this broad, everyday sense, would not seem to provide adequate grounds for concluding that the relevant concepts are analytically basic. One can, for example, quite properly speak of physicists as seeing electrons when they look into cloud chambers, even though the concept of an electron is certainly capable of being analysed in terms of simpler concepts.

More sophisticated arguments have, however, been offered. David Armstrong, for example, distinguishes very carefully between perceptual knowledge in a broad sense, which may involve inference, and perceptual knowledge in a narrow sense, which is completely free of all inference, and he contends that we do have non-inferential knowledge of causal states of affairs, such as the fact that something is pressing against one's body.[18] More recently, Evan Fales has offered a very detailed and careful defence of the view that one can have non-inferential knowledge of causal facts.[19]

---

[16] Singularist reductionism is also exposed to other objections, including a very strong Humean-style argument. See e.g. sect. 2 of 'The Nature of Causation: A Singularist Account'.

[17] G. E. M. Anscombe, *Causality and Determination: An Inaugural Lecture* (Cambridge, 1971), repr. as Ch. V above.

[18] David M. Armstrong, *A Materialist Theory of the Mind* (New York, 1968), 97.

[19] Evan Fales, *Causation and Universals* (London and New York, 1990).

This issue is not, I believe, easily resolved, for it seems to me that whether one can have non-inferential knowledge of causal relations between events depends upon what the correct account of non-inferential knowledge is. If, as Armstrong holds, direct realism is correct, then I think it can be plausibly held that one has non-inferential knowledge of causal states of affairs. If, on the other hand, a satisfactory account of non-inferential knowledge requires a strong notion of direct acquaintance, according to which what properties one is directly acquainted with is logically supervenient upon the phenomenological content of one's experience, then there would seem to be an argument for the conclusion that causal relations cannot be immediately perceived. The argument in question would turn upon the idea that there could be worlds—call them Berkeleian worlds—where the contents of one's experiences would be as they are now, but where the events that one observed did not stand in causal relations to one another. I shall not, however, attempt to develop that argument in a detailed way at this point.

If this is right, and there is no epistemologically neutral way of showing either that one can, or that one cannot, have non-inferential knowledge of causal relations between events, are there any other grounds that can be offered for preferring one form of realism to the other? I believe that there are. In the first place, causal relations would seem to have certain formal properties. For even if it is true, as some have argued, that there could be causal loops, it is surely impossible for any event to be the *immediate* cause of itself. I have argued elsewhere, however, that a satisfactory explanation of the formal properties of causation can be given if causal relations are treated as theoretical relations.[20] A realist view that holds, on the other hand, that the intrinsic nature of causal relations (or of some causal relations) is given in immediate perception is forced, in contrast, to treat the relevant formal properties as brute facts, incapable of any explanation.

In the second place, although the direction of causation is not, I have argued, to be reduced to features such as the direction of increase in entropy, or the direction of the transmission of order in non-entropic, irreversible processes, or the direction of open forks, it is surely true that these and other facts often provide evidence concerning how events are causally connected. Again, if causal relations are treated as theoretical relations, then it is possible to show that the features in question do provide evidence for causal connections[21]—something which cannot, I believe, be done, if one assumes that causal relations are basic and unanalysable.

[20] *Causation*, 274–87.   [21] Ibid. 299–302.

6. SUMMING UP

I have argued that reductionist accounts, both of causal laws and of causal relations, are open to very serious objections. In the case of laws, I mentioned the problems posed by cosmic, but accidental uniformities, by uninstantiated basic laws, and by probabilistic laws, together with the difficulty of showing that one is justified in believing that laws obtain, if one holds that laws are, basically, cosmic uniformities. In the case of causal relations, I advanced two sorts of objections. First, there were the objections that focused upon the problem of explaining the direction of causation. I argued that a reductionist approach is unable to provide a satisfactory account of the direction of causation either for certain very simple universes, or for inverted universes, unless one is prepared both to define the direction of causation in terms of the direction of time, and to adopt a realist view of the latter. Secondly, there were the under-determination objections, the thrust of which was that causal relations between events are not logically supervenient even upon the totality of all non-causal facts, together with all laws, both causal and non-causal, plus the direction of causation in all potential causal processes.

For a long time, reductionist approaches to laws and to causal relations were the only ones on offer. This is not, of course, surprising, for it is only comparatively recently that satisfactory realist accounts of the semantics of theoretical terms have been available. What is rather curious, however, is that while the emergence of such accounts has resulted in realism being quite widely espoused in philosophy of science, the philosophy of causation has remained largely untouched by that development. But if the arguments set out above are sound, the time has come to abandon reductionist approaches to causal relations and causal laws, and to explore realist alternatives, for only the latter offer any hope of success.

XI

CAUSATION*

DAVID LEWIS

Hume defined causation twice over. He wrote 'we may define a cause to be *an object followed by another, and where all the objects, similar to the first, are followed by objects similar to the second.* Or, in other words *where, if the first object had not been, the second never had existed.*'[1]

Descendants of Hume's first definition still dominate the philosophy of causation: a causal succession is supposed to be a succession that instantiates a regularity. To be sure, there have been improvements. Nowadays we try to distinguish the regularities that count—the 'causal laws'—from mere accidental regularities of succession. We subsume causes and effects under regularities by means of descriptions they satisfy, not by overall similarity. And we allow a cause to be only one indispensable part, not the whole, of the total situation that is followed by the effect in accordance with a law. In present-day regularity analyses, a cause is defined (roughly) as any member of any minimal set of actual conditions that are jointly sufficient, given the laws, for the existence of the effect.

More precisely, let C be the proposition that c exists (or occurs) and let E be the proposition that e exists. Then c causes e, according to a typical regularity analysis,[2] iff (1) C and E are true; and (2) for some non-empty set $\mathcal{L}$ of true law-propositions and some set $\mathcal{F}$ of true propositions of particular fact, $\mathcal{L}$ and $\mathcal{F}$ jointly imply $C \supset E$, although $\mathcal{L}$ and $\mathcal{F}$ jointly do not imply E and $\mathcal{F}$ alone does not imply $C \supset E$.[3]

Much needs doing, and much has been done, to turn definitions like this one into defensible analyses. Many problems have been overcome. Others remain: in particular, regularity analyses tend to confuse causation itself with

* I thank the American Council of Learned Societies, Princeton University, and the National Science Foundation for research support.

[1] *An Enquiry Concerning Human Understanding*, sect. 7.

[2] Not one that has been proposed by any actual author in just this form, so far as I know.

[3] I identify a *proposition*, as is becoming usual, with the set of possible worlds where it is true. It is not a linguistic entity. Truth-functional operations on propositions are the appropriate Boolean operations on sets of worlds; logical relations among propositions are relations of inclusion, overlap, etc. among sets. A sentence of a language *expresses* a proposition iff the sentence and the proposition are true at exactly the same worlds. No ordinary language will provide sentences to express all propositions; there will not be enough sentences to go around.

various other causal relations. If c belongs to a minimal set of conditions jointly sufficient for e, given the laws, then c may well be a genuine cause of e. But c might rather be an effect of e: one which could not, given the laws and some of the actual circumstances, have occurred otherwise than by being caused by e. Or c might be an epiphenomenon of the causal history of e: a more or less inefficacious effect of some genuine cause of e. Or c might be a pre-empted potential cause of e: something that did not cause e, but that would have done so in the absence of whatever really did cause e.

It remains to be seen whether any regularity analysis can succeed in distinguishing genuine causes from effects, epiphenomena, and pre-empted potential causes—and whether it can succeed without falling victim to worse problems, without piling on the epicycles, and without departing from the fundamental idea that causation is instantiation of regularities. I have no proof that regularity analyses are beyond repair, nor any space to review the repairs that have been tried. Suffice it to say that the prospects look dark. I think it is time to give up and try something else.

A promising alternative is not far to seek. Hume's 'other words'—that if the cause had not been, the effect never had existed—are no mere restatement of his first definition. They propose something altogether different: a counterfactual analysis of causation.

The proposal has not been well received. True, we do know that causation has something or other to do with counterfactuals. We think of a cause as something that makes a difference, and the difference it makes must be a difference from what would have happened without it. Had it been absent, its effects—some of them, at least, and usually all—would have been absent as well. Yet it is one thing to mention these platitudes now and again, and another thing to rest an analysis on them. That has not seemed worth while.[4] We have learned all too well that counterfactuals are ill understood, wherefore it did not seem that much understanding could be gained by using them to analyse causation or anything else. Pending a better understanding of counterfactuals, moreover, we had no way to fight seeming counter-examples to a counterfactual analysis.

But counterfactuals need not remain ill understood, I claim, unless we cling to false preconceptions about what it would be like to understand them. Must an adequate understanding make no reference to unactualized possibilities? Must it assign sharply determinate truth conditions? Must it connect counterfactuals rigidly to covering laws? Then none will be forthcoming. So much the worse for those standards of adequacy. Why not take counterfactuals at

---

[4] One exception: Aardon Lyon, 'Causality', *British Journal for Philosophy of Science*, 18.1 (May 1967), 1–20.

face value: as statements about possible alternatives to the actual situation, somewhat vaguely specified, in which the actual laws may or may not remain intact? There are now several such treatments of counterfactuals, differing only in details.[5] If they are right, then sound foundations have been laid for analyses that use counterfactuals.

In this paper, I shall state a counterfactual analysis, not very different from Hume's second definition, of some sorts of causation. Then I shall try to show how this analysis works to distinguish genuine causes from effects, epiphenomena, and pre-empted potential causes.

My discussion will be incomplete in at least four ways. Explicit preliminary settings-aside may prevent confusion.

1. I shall confine myself to causation among *events*, in the everyday sense of the word: flashes, battles, conversations, impacts, strolls, deaths, touchdowns, falls, kisses, and the like. Not that events are the only things that can cause or be caused; but I have no full list of the others, and no good umbrella-term to cover them all.

2. My analysis is meant to apply to causation in particular cases. It is not an analysis of causal generalizations. Presumably those are quantified statements involving causation among particular events (or non-events), but it turns out not to be easy to match up the causal generalizations of natural language with the available quantified forms. A sentence of the form 'C-events cause E-events,' for instance, can mean any of

   (a) For some c in C and some e in E, c causes e,
   (b) For every e in E, there is some c in C such that c causes e,
   (c) For every c in C, there is some e in E such that c causes e,

not to mention further ambiguities. Worse still, 'Only C-events cause E-events' ought to mean

   (d) For every c, if there is some e in E such that c causes e, then c is in C

if 'only' has its usual meaning. But no; it unambiguously means (b) instead! These problems are not about causation, but about our idioms of quantification.

3. We sometimes single out one among all the causes of some event and call it 'the' cause, as if there were no others. Or we single out a few as the 'causes', calling the rest mere 'causal factors' or 'causal conditions'. Or we speak of the 'decisive' or 'real' or 'principal' cause. We may select the abnormal or extraordinary causes, or those under human control, or those we

[5] See e.g. Robert Stalnaker, 'A Theory of Conditionals', in Nicholas Rescher (ed.), *Studies in Logical Theory* (Oxford, Blackwell, 1968), repr. in F. Jackson (ed.), *Conditionals* (Oxford, OUP, 1991), 28–45; and my *Counterfactuals* (Oxford, Blackwell, 1973).

deem good or bad, or just those we want to talk about. I have nothing to say about these principles of invidious discrimination.[6] I am concerned with the prior question of what it is to be one of the causes (unselectively speaking). My analysis is meant to capture a broad and non-discriminatory concept of causation.

4. I shall be content, for now, if I can give an analysis of causation that works properly under determinism. By determinism I do not mean any thesis of universal causation, or universal predictability-in-principle, but rather this: the prevailing laws of nature are such that there do not exist any two possible worlds which are exactly alike up to some time, which differ thereafter, and in which those laws are never violated. Perhaps by ignoring indeterminism I squander the most striking advantage of a counterfactual analysis over a regularity analysis: that it allows undetermined events to be caused.[7] I fear, however, that my present analysis cannot yet cope with all varieties of causation under indeterminism. The needed repair would take us too far into disputed questions about the foundations of probability.

COMPARATIVE SIMILARITY

To begin, I take as primitive a relation of *comparative overall* similarity among possible worlds. We may say that one world is *closer to actuality* than another if the first resembles our actual world more than the second does, taking account of all the respects of similarity and difference and balancing them off one against another.

(More generally, an arbitrary world w can play the role of our actual world. In speaking of our actual world without knowing just which world is ours, I am in effect generalizing over all worlds. We really need a three-place relation: world w_1 is closer to world w than world w_2 is. I shall henceforth leave this generality tacit.)

I have not said just how to balance the respects of comparison against each other, so I have not said just what our relation of comparative similarity is to be. Not for nothing did I call it primitive. But I have said what *sort* of relation it is, and we are familiar with relations of that sort. We do make judgements of comparative overall similarity—of people, for instance—by

---

[6] Except that Morton G. White's discussion of causal selection, in *Foundations of Historical Knowledge* (New York, Harper & Row, 1965), 105–81, would meet my needs, despite the fact that it is based on a regularity analysis.

[7] That this ought to be allowed is argued in G. E. M. Anscombe, *Causality and Determination: An Inaugural Lecture* (Cambridge, CUP, 1971), repr. as Ch. V above; and in Fred Dretske and Aaron Snyder, 'Causal Irregularity', *Philosophy of Science*, 39.1 (Mar. 1972), 69–71.

balancing off many respects of similarity and difference. Often our mutual expectations about the weighting factors are definite and accurate enough to permit communication. I shall have more to say later about the way the balance must go in particular cases to make my analysis work. But the vagueness of overall similarity will not be entirely resolved. Nor should it be. The vagueness of similarity does infect causation; and no correct analysis can deny it.

The respects of similarity and difference that enter into the overall similarity of worlds are many and varied. In particular, similarities in matters of particular fact trade off against similarities of law. The prevailing laws of nature are important to the character of a world; so similarities of law are weighty. Weighty, but not sacred. We should not take it for granted that a world that conforms perfectly to our actual laws is *ipso facto* closer to actuality than any world where those laws are violated in any way at all. It depends on the nature and extent of the violation, on the place of the violated laws in the total system of laws of nature, and on the countervailing similarities and differences in other respects. Likewise, similarities or differences of particular fact may be more or less weighty, depending on their nature and extent. Comprehensive and exact similarities of particular fact throughout large spatio-temporal regions seem to have special weight. It may be worth a small miracle to prolong or expand a region of perfect match.

Our relation of comparative similarity should meet two formal constraints. (1) It should be a weak ordering of the worlds: an ordering in which ties are permitted, but any two worlds are comparable. (2) Our actual world should be closest to actuality, resembling itself more than any other world resembles it. We do *not* impose the further constraint that for any set A of worlds there is a unique closest A-world, or even a set of A-worlds tied for closest. Why not an infinite sequence of closer and closer A-worlds, but no closest?

COUNTERFACTUALS AND COUNTERFACTUAL DEPENDENCE

Given any two propositions A and C, we have their *counterfactual* $A \ \Box \rightarrow C$: the proposition that if A were true, then C would also be true. The operation $\Box \rightarrow$ is defined by a rule of truth, as follows. $A \ \Box \rightarrow C$ is true (at a world w) iff either (1) there are no possible A-worlds (in which case $A \ \Box \rightarrow C$ is *vacuous*), or (2) some A-world where C holds is closer (to w) than is any A-world where C does not hold. In other words, a counterfactual is non-vacuously true iff it takes less of a departure from actuality to make the consequent true along with the antecedent than it does to make the antecedent true without the consequent.

We did not assume that there must always be one or more closest A-worlds. But if there are, we can simplify: $A \ \square \rightarrow C$ is non-vacuously true iff C holds at all the closest A-worlds.

We have not presupposed that A is false. If A is true, then our actual world is the closest A-world, so $A \ \square \rightarrow C$ is true iff C is. Hence $A \ \square \rightarrow C$ implies the material conditional $A \supset C$; and A and C jointly imply $A \ \square \rightarrow C$.

Let $A_1, A_2, \ldots$ be a family of possible propositions, no two of which are compossible; let $C_1, C_2, \ldots$ be another such family (of equal size). Then if all the counterfactuals $A_1 \square \rightarrow C_1$, $A_2 \square \rightarrow C_2, \ldots$ between corresponding propositions in the two families are true, we shall say that the C's *depend counterfactually* on the A's. We can say it like this in ordinary language: whether C_1 or C_2 or ... depends (counterfactually) on whether A_1 or A_2 or ....

Counterfactual dependence between large families of alternatives is characteristic of processes of measurement, perception, or control. Let $R_1, R_2, \ldots$ be propositions specifying the alternative readings of a certain barometer at a certain time. Let $P_1, P_2, \ldots$ specify the corresponding pressures of the surrounding air. Then, if the barometer is working properly to measure the pressure, the R's must depend counterfactually on the P's. As we say it: the reading depends on the pressure. Likewise, if I am seeing at a certain time, then my visual impressions must depend counterfactually, over a wide range of alternative possibilities, on the scene before my eyes. And if I am in control over what happens in some respect, then there must be a double counterfactual dependence, again over some fairly wide range of alternatives. The outcome depends on what I do, and that in turn depends on which outcome I want.[8]

CAUSAL DEPENDENCE AMONG EVENTS

If a family $C_1, C_2, \ldots$ depends counterfactually on a family $A_1, A_2, \ldots$ in the sense just explained, we will ordinarily be willing to speak also of causal dependence. We say, for instance, that the barometer reading depends causally on the pressure, that my visual impressions depend causally on the scene before my eyes, or that the outcome of something under my control depends causally on what I do. But there are exceptions. Let $G_1, G_2, \ldots$ be alternative possible laws of gravitation, differing in the value of some numerical constant. Let $M_1, M_2, \ldots$ be suitable alternative laws of planetary

---

[8] Analyses in terms of counterfactual dependence are found in two papers of Alvin I. Goldman: 'Toward a Theory of Social Power', *Philosophical Studies*, 23 (1972), 221–68; and 'Discrimination and Perceptual Knowledge', presented at the 1972 Chapel Hill Colloquium.

motion. Then the M's may depend counterfactually on the G's, but we would not call this dependence causal. Such exceptions as this, however, do not involve any sort of dependence among distinct particular events. The hope remains that causal dependence among events, at least, may be analysed simply as counterfactual dependence.

We have spoken thus far of counterfactual dependence among propositions, not among events. Whatever particular events may be, presumably they are not propositions. But that is no problem, since they can at least be paired with propositions. To any possible event e, there corresponds the proposition $O(e)$ that holds at all and only those worlds where e occurs. Thus $O(e)$ is the proposition that e occurs.[9] (If no two events occur at exactly the same worlds—if, that is, there are no absolutely necessary connections between distinct events—we may add that this correspondence of events and propositions is one to one.) Counterfactual dependence among events is simply counterfactual dependence among the corresponding propositions.

Let $c_1, c_2, \ldots$ and $e_1, e_2, \ldots$ be distinct possible events such that no two of the c's and no two of the e's are compossible. Then I say that the family $e_1, e_2, \ldots$ of events *depends causally* on the family $c_1, c_2, \ldots$ iff the family $O(e_1), O(e_2), \ldots$ of propositions depends counterfactually on the family $O(c_1), O(c_2), \ldots$ As we say it: whether e_1 or e_2 or $\ldots$ occurs depends on whether c_1 or c_2 or $\ldots$ occurs.

We can also define a relation of dependence among single events rather than families. Let c and e be two distinct possible particular events. Then e *depends causally* on c iff the family $O(e), \sim O(e)$ depends counterfactually on the family $O(c), \sim O(c)$. As we say it: whether e occurs or not depends on whether c occurs or not. The dependence consists in the truth of two counterfactuals: $O(c) \;\Box\!\!\rightarrow O(e)$ and $\sim O(c) \;\Box\!\!\rightarrow \sim O(e)$. There are two cases. If c and

---

[9] Beware: if we refer to a particular event e by means of some description that e satisfies, then we must take care not to confuse $O(e)$, the proposition that e itself occurs, with the different proposition that some event or other occurs which satisfies the description. It is a contingent matter, in general, what events satisfy what descriptions. Let e be the death of Socrates—the death he actually died, to be distinguished from all the different deaths he might have died instead. Suppose that Socrates had fled, only to be eaten by a lion. Then e would not have occurred, and $O(e)$ would have been false; but a different event would have satisfied the description 'the death of Socrates' that I used to refer to e. Or suppose that Socrates had lived and died just as he actually did, and afterwards was resurrected and killed again and resurrected again, and finally became immortal. Then no event would have satisfied the description. (Even if the temporary deaths are real deaths, neither of the two can be *the* death.) But e would have occurred, and $O(e)$ would have been true. Call a description of an event e *rigid* iff (1) nothing but e could possibly satisfy it, and (2) e could not possibly occur without satisfying it. I have claimed that even such commonplace descriptions as 'the death of Socrates' are non-rigid, and in fact I think that rigid descriptions of events are hard to find. That would be a problem for anyone who needed to associate with every possible event e a sentence $\varphi(e)$ true at all and only those worlds where e occurs. But we need no such sentences—only propositions, which may or may not have expressions in our language.

e do not actually occur, then the second counterfactual is automatically true because its antecedent and consequent are true: so e depends causally on c iff the first counterfactual holds. That is, if e would have occurred if c had occurred. But if c and e are actual events, then it is the first counterfactual that is automatically true. Then e depends causally on c iff, if c had not been, e never had existed. I take Hume's second definition as my definition not of causation itself, but of causal dependence among actual events.

CAUSATION

Causal dependence among actual events implies causation. If c and e are two actual events such that e would not have occurred without c, then c is a cause of e. But I reject the converse. Causation must always be transitive; causal dependence may not be; so there can be causation without causal dependence. Let c, d, and e be three actual events such that d would not have occurred without c and e would not have occurred without d. Then c is a cause of e even if e would still have occurred (otherwise caused) without c.

We extend causal dependence to a transitive relation in the usual way. Let $c, d, e, \ldots$ be a finite sequence of actual particular events such that d depends causally on c, e on d, and so on throughout. Then this sequence is a *causal chain*. Finally, one event is a *cause* of another iff there exists a causal chain leading from the first to the second. This completes my counterfactual analysis of causation.

COUNTERFACTUAL VERSUS NOMIC DEPENDENCE

It is essential to distinguish counterfactual and causal dependence from what I shall call *nomic dependence*. The family $C_1, C_2, \ldots$ of propositions depends nomically on the family $A_1, A_2, \ldots$ iff there are a non-empty set $\mathcal{L}$ of true law-propositions and a set $\mathcal{F}$ of true propositions of particular fact such that $\mathcal{L}$ and $\mathcal{F}$ jointly imply (but $\mathcal{F}$ alone does not imply) all the material conditionals $A_1 \supset C_1$, $A_2 \supset C_2, \ldots$ between the corresponding propositions in the two families. (Recall that these same material conditionals are implied by the counterfactuals that would comprise a counterfactual dependence.) We shall say also that the nomic dependence holds *in virtue of* the premise sets $\mathcal{L}$ and $\mathcal{F}$.

Nomic and counterfactual dependence are related as follows. Say that a proposition B is *counterfactually independent* of the family $A_1, A_2, \ldots$ of alternatives iff B would hold no matter which of the As were true—that is,

iff the counterfactuals $A_1 \square \rightarrow B$, $A_2 \square \rightarrow B$ . . . all hold. If the C's depend
nomically on the A's in virtue of the premise sets $\mathscr{L}$ and $\mathscr{F}$, and if in addition
(all members of) $\mathscr{L}$ and $\mathscr{F}$ are counterfactually independent of the A's, then
it follows that the C's depend counterfactually on the A's. In that case, we may
regard the nomic dependence in virtue of $\mathscr{L}$ and $\mathscr{F}$ as explaining the counterfactual dependence. Often, perhaps always, counterfactual dependences may
be thus explained. But the requirement of counterfactual independence is
indispensable. Unless $\mathscr{L}$ and $\mathscr{F}$ meet that requirement, nomic dependence in
virtue of $\mathscr{L}$ and $\mathscr{F}$ does not imply counterfactual dependence, and, if there is
counterfactual dependence anyway, does not explain it.

Nomic dependence is reversible, in the following sense. If the family C_1,
C_2, . . . depends nomically on the family A_1, A_2, . . . in virtue of $\mathscr{L}$ and $\mathscr{F}$, then
also A_1, A_2, . . . depends nomically on the family AC_1, AC_2, . . . , in virtue of $\mathscr{L}$
and $\mathscr{F}$, where A is the disjunction $A_1 \vee A_2 \vee \ldots$. Is counterfactual dependence
likewise reversible? That does not follow. For, even if $\mathscr{L}$ and $\mathscr{F}$ are independent of A_1, A_2, . . . and hence establish the counterfactual dependence of
the C's on the A's, still they may fail to be independent of AC_1, AC_2, . . . ,
and hence may fail to establish the reverse counterfactual dependence of the
A's on the AC's. Irreversible counterfactual dependence is shown below: @
is our actual world, the dots are the other worlds, and distance on the page
represents similarity 'distance'.

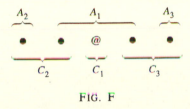

FIG. F

The counterfactuals $A_1 \square \rightarrow C_1$, $A_2 \square \rightarrow C_2$, and $A_3 \square \rightarrow C_3$ hold at the actual
world; wherefore the C's depend on the A's. But we do not have the reverse
dependence of the A's on the AC's, since instead of the needed $AC_2 \square \rightarrow A_2$ and
$AC_3 \square \rightarrow A_3$ we have $AC_2 \square \rightarrow A_1$ and $AC_3 \square \rightarrow A_1$.

Just such irreversibility is commonplace. The barometer reading depends
counterfactually on the pressure—that is as clear-cut as counterfactuals ever
get—but does the pressure depend counterfactually on the reading? If the
reading had been higher, would the pressure have been higher? Or would the
barometer have been malfunctioning? The second sounds better: a higher
reading would have been an incorrect reading. To be sure, there are actual

laws and circumstances that imply and explain the actual accuracy of the barometer, but these are no more sacred than the actual laws and circumstances that imply and explain the actual pressure. Less sacred, in fact. When something must give way to permit a higher reading, we find it less of a departure from actuality to hold the pressure fixed and sacrifice the accuracy, rather than vice versa. It is not hard to see why. The barometer, being more localized and more delicate than the weather, is more vulnerable to slight departures from actuality.[10]

We can now explain why regularity analyses of causation (among events, under determinism) work as well as they do. Suppose that event c causes event e according to the sample regularity analysis that I gave at the beginning of this paper, in virtue of premise sets $\mathscr{L}$ and $\mathscr{F}$. It follows that $\mathscr{L}$, $\mathscr{F}$, and $\sim O(c)$ jointly do not imply $O(e)$. Strengthen this: suppose further that they do imply $\sim O(e)$. If so, the family $O(e)$, $\sim O(e)$, depends nomically on the family $O(c)$, $\sim O(c)$ in virtue of $\mathscr{L}$ and $\mathscr{F}$. Add one more supposition: that $\mathscr{L}$ and $\mathscr{F}$ are counterfactually independent of $O(c)$, $\sim O(c)$. Then it follows according to my counterfactual analysis that e depends counterfactually and causally on c, and hence that c causes e. If I am right, the regularity analysis gives conditions that are almost but not quite sufficient for explicable causal dependence. That is not quite the same thing as causation; but causation without causal dependence is scarce, and if there is inexplicable causal dependence we are (understandably!) unaware of it.[11]

EFFECTS AND EPIPHENOMENA

I return now to the problems I raised against regularity analyses, hoping to show that my counterfactual analysis can overcome them.

The *problem of effects*, as it confronts a counterfactual analysis, is as follows. Suppose that c causes a subsequent event e, and that e does not also cause c. (I do not rule out closed causal loops *a priori*, but this case is not to be one.) Suppose further that, given the laws and some of the actual

---

[10] Granted, there are contexts or changes of wording that would incline us the other way. For some reason, 'If the reading had been higher, that would have been because the pressure was higher' invites my assent more than 'If the reading had been higher, the pressure would have been higher.' The counterfactuals from readings to pressures are much less clear-cut than those from pressures to readings. But it is enough that some legitimate resolutions of vagueness give an irreversible dependence of readings on pressures. Those are the resolutions we want at present, even if they are not favored in all contexts.

[11] I am not here proposing a repaired regularity analysis. The repaired analysis would gratuitously rule out inexplicable causal dependence, which seems bad. Nor would it be squarely in the tradition of regularity analyses any more. Too much else would have been added.

circumstances, c could not have failed to cause e. It seems to follow that if the effect e had not occurred, then its cause c would not have occurred. We have a spurious reverse causal dependence of c on e, contradicting our supposition that e did not cause c.

The *problem of epiphenomena*, for a counterfactual analysis, is similar. Suppose that e is an epiphenomenal effect of a genuine cause c of an effect f. That is, c causes first e and then f, but e does not cause f. Suppose further that, given the laws and some of the actual circumstances, c could not have failed to cause e; and that, given the laws and others of the circumstances, f could not have been caused otherwise than by c. It seems to follow that if the epiphenomenon e had not occurred, then its cause c would not have occurred and the further effect f of that same cause would not have occurred either. We have a spurious causal dependence of f on e, contradicting our supposition that e did not cause f.

One might be tempted to solve the problem of effects by brute force: insert into the analysis a stipulation that a cause must always precede its effect (and perhaps a parallel stipulation for causal dependence). I reject this solution. (1) It is worthless against the closely related problem of epiphenomena, since the epiphenomenon e does precede its spurious effect f. (2) It rejects *a priori* certain legitimate physical hypotheses that posit backward or simultaneous causation. (3) It trivializes any theory that seeks to define the forward direction of time as the predominant direction of causation.

The proper solution to both problems, I think, is flatly to deny the counterfactuals that cause the trouble. If e had been absent, it is not that c would have been absent (and with it f, in the second case). Rather, c would have occurred just as it did but would have failed to cause e. It is less of a departure from actuality to get rid of e by holding c fixed and giving up some or other of the laws and circumstances in virtue of which c could not have failed to cause e, rather than to hold those laws and circumstances fixed and get rid of e by going back and abolishing its cause c. (In the second case, it would of course be pointless not to hold f fixed along with c.) The causal dependence of e on c is the same sort of irreversible counterfactual dependence that we have considered already.

To get rid of an actual event e with the least overall departure from actuality, it will normally be best not to diverge at all from the actual course of events until just before the time of e. The longer we wait, the more we prolong the spatio-temporal region of perfect match between our actual world and the selected alternative. Why diverge sooner rather than later? Not to avoid violations of laws of nature. Under determinism *any* divergence, soon or late, requires some violation of the actual laws. If the laws were held sacred, there would be no way to get rid of e without changing all of the past;

and nothing guarantees that the change could be kept negligible except in the recent past. That would mean that if the present were ever so slightly different, then all of the past would have been different—which is absurd. So the laws are not sacred. Violation of laws is a matter of degree. Until we get up to the time immediately before e is to occur, there is no general reason why a later divergence to avert e should need a more severe violation than an earlier one. Perhaps there are special reasons in special cases—but then these may be cases of backward causal dependence.

PRE-EMPTION

Suppose that c_1 occurs and causes e; and that c_2 also occurs and does not cause e, but would have caused e if c_1 had been absent. Thus c_2 is a potential alternative cause of e, but is pre-empted by the actual cause c_1. We may say that c_1 and c_2 overdetermine e, but they do so asymmetrically.[12] In virtue of what difference does c_1 but not c_2 cause e?

As far as causal dependence goes, there is no difference: e depends neither on c_1 nor on c_2. If either one had not occurred, the other would have sufficed to cause e. So the difference must be that, thanks to c_1, there is no causal chain from c_2 to e; whereas there is a causal chain of two or more steps from c_1 to e. Assume for simplicity that two steps are enough. Then e depends causally on some intermediate event d, and d in turn depends on c_1. Causal dependence is here intransitive: c_1 causes e via d even though e would still have occurred without c_1.

So far, so good. It remains only to deal with the objection that e does *not* depend causally on d, because if d had been absent then c_1 would have been absent and c_2, no longer pre-empted, would have caused e. We may reply by denying the claim that if d had been absent then c_1 would have been absent. That is the very same sort of spurious reverse dependence of cause on effect that we have just rejected in simpler cases. I rather claim that if d had been absent, c_1 would somehow have failed to cause d. But c_1 would still have been there to interfere with c_2, so e would not have occurred.

---

[12] I shall not discuss symmetrical cases of overdetermination, in which two overdetermining factors have equal claim to count as causes. For me these are useless as test cases because I lack firm naïve opinions about them.

XII

CAUSES AND COUNTERFACTUALS

JAEGWON KIM

A conditional of the form 'If it were the case that A, it would be the case that B' points to some sort of dependency relationship between the propositions A and B—and, by extension, between the facts, events, states, etc. expressed by A and B. An analysis of counterfactuals would tell us exactly what this dependency relationship comes to. The causal relation, too, appears to be such a relationship: if an event c is a cause of an event e, then the occurrence of e depends in some sense on the occurrence of c. We say: but for the cause the effect would not have occurred. It is thus that Lewis wants to explain causal dependency in terms of counterfactual dependency.

Speaking only of actual events and skirting issues concerning the analysis of counterfactuals, we can summarize Lewis's account in the following two statements:

(1) An event e causally depends on an event c just in case if c had not occurred e would not have occurred.

(2) An event c is a cause of an event e just in case there is a chain of events from c to e, each event in this chain being causally dependent on its predecessor.

It follows that the counterfactual conditional 'If c had not occurred, e would not have occurred' entails, under Lewis's analysis, the causal statement 'c caused e.'

It seems, however, that the sort of dependency expressed by counterfactuals is considerably broader than strictly causal dependency and that causal dependency is only one among the heterogeneous group of dependency relationships that can be expressed by counterfactuals. Let us look at a few cases:

1. First, there are cases that exemplify some sort of 'logical' or 'analytical' dependency. Consider:

If yesterday had not been Monday, today would not be Tuesday.

Should we say on the strength of this counterfactual that today's being Tuesday was caused by yesterday's being Monday? But perhaps these aren't *events*; but then consider:

If George had not been born in 1950, he would not have reached the age of 21 in 1971.

2. Second, there are cases in which one event is a constituent part of another, the two events satisfying the required counterfactual. For example, my writing the letter 'r' twice in succession is a constituent event in the event of my writing 'Larry'; and it is presumably true to say:

If I had not written 'r' twice in succession, I would not have written 'Larry'.

But I do not see a causal relation between these events.

3. Consider cases in which an agent does an action by doing another. Thus, by turning the knob, I open the window. The following counterfactual is true:

If I had not turned the knob, I would not have opened the window.

However, my turning the knob does not cause my opening the window (although it does cause the window's being open).

4. The kind of case that I find interesting is one in which one event 'determines' another without *causally* determining it. The second event depends asymmetrically on the first for its occurrence, but is not a *causal* consequence of it. When my sister gave birth to her first child, I became an uncle. My becoming an uncle was determined by, was dependent on, the birth of the child, but was not a causal effect of it. And the two events sustain the required counterfactual:

If my sister had not given birth at t, I would not have become an uncle at t.

If these examples are plausible, counterfactual dependency is too broad to pin down causal dependency. And as Lewis himself points out, cases of over-determination raise special difficulties for his analysis; they constitute prima-facie evidence that counterfactual dependency is also too narrow to capture causal dependency.

Lewis says that his account explains why the regularity analysis of causal relations works as well as it does. Lewis is surely right in attending to this problem: obviously, considerations involving law-like regularities are important in ascertaining causal relations, and any adequate theory of causation should explain that epistemological aspect of causal relations. I am not certain, however, that Lewis in fact provides an explanation here. His argument depends crucially on a lemma established earlier in his paper to the effect that if the family of propositions $C_1, \ldots, C_n$ depends nomically on $A_1, \ldots, A_n$ in virtue of $\mathcal{L}$ and $\mathcal{F}$, then $C_1, \ldots, C_n$ counterfactually depends on $A_1, \ldots, A_n$ provided that $\mathcal{L}$ and $\mathcal{F}$ are counterfactually independent of $A_1, \ldots, A_n$. However, the proof of this lemma nowhere makes use of the fact that $\mathscr{L}$ is a set of *laws*. (One conjectures, though, that the nomological nature of $\mathscr{L}$ may have something to do with $\mathscr{L}$'s counterfactual independence of $A_1, \ldots, A_n$.) It would seem that Lewis must show in greater detail how considerations of laws enter into our judgements of similarity between possible worlds, and hence how laws relate to counterfactuals, before we can properly understand how his counterfactual account relates to the classical regularity theory.

What is the function of causal statements? Why do we make causal judgements? The following are some of the more common contexts in which we engage in causal talk: (1) we make causal judgements to *explain* the occurrence of particular events; (2) we seek causal knowledge because of its *predictive* usefulness; (3) knowledge of causal connections often gives us power to *control* events; (4) causal attributions involving agents are important in the attribution of *moral responsibility*, *legal liability*, and so on; (5) causal concepts are often used in special technical senses in physical theory. In assessing the comparative merits of rival accounts of causation, we should consider not only the alleged counter-examples (e.g. over-determination, pre-emption, etc.) but also, and more importantly, how well the proposed analyses account for those aspects of causal judgements just mentioned, among others. If we compare the classical regularity theory with Lewis's account with this in mind, it is by no means clear that the latter fares significantly better than the former. But a final judgement would be premature; more would have to be known, for example, about the role of laws in Lewis's account of counterfactuals.

XIII

LEWIS'S PROGRAMME

PAUL HORWICH

In reaction to the two classic difficulties in Goodman's treatment of counterfactuals—the contenability problem and the explication of law—a radically different approach was instigated by Stalnaker[1] and has been developed by Lewis into a broad account of temporally asymmetric phenomena. I would like to end this chapter by looking carefully at Lewis's theory. We shall find that it is faced with a variety of criticisms—avoidable, if at all, only at the cost of cumbersome, *ad hoc* modifications. Therefore we shall get further support for the point of view developed earlier—in which counterfactual conditionals are analysed in terms of causation.

Lewis's theory of causation and counterfactual dependence splits into four stages. In the first place, he says that causation consists in a chain of counterfactual dependence:[2]

> *C* caused *E* *if and only if* there was a sequence of events $X_1, X_2, \ldots, X_n$, such that:
>
> > if *C* had not occurred, then X_1 would not have occurred, if X_1 had not occurred, then X_2 would not have occurred, ... if Xn had not occurred, then *E* would not have occurred.

(Lewis subsequently generalizes the account to accommodate indeterministic causation.[3])

Second, this analysis is supplemented[4] with a semantic theory of the counterfactual conditional:

> If *p* were true, then *q* would be true *if and only if*
>
> > there is a possible world in which *p* and *q* are true that is more similar to the actual world than any possible world in which *p* is true and *q* is false.

[1] Robert Stalnaker, 'A Theory of Conditionals', in Nicholas Rescher (ed.), *Studies in Logical Theory* (Oxford, 1968), and id., *Inquiry* (Cambridge, Mass., 1984).
[2] David Lewis, 'Causation', *Journal of Philosophy*, 70 (1973), 556–67; repr. as Ch. XI above.
[3] David Lewis, *Philosophical Papers*, ii (Oxford, 1986).
[4] David Lewis, *Counterfactuals* (Cambridge, Mass., 1973).

Third, Lewis fills out the picture with an account of the features of possible worlds that make them more or less similar to actuality.[5] The most similar worlds are said to be those in which our laws of nature are rarely violated. But exact similarity with respect to particular facts in some large region of space–time is also a major factor and will promote similarity even at the cost of minor violations of law. A significant element in this account is that there is no built-in time bias. Concepts of temporal order are not employed at all in the principles describing the determinants of similarity.

Finally, Lewis's fourth assumption[6] introduces the time asymmetry that provides the ultimate basis for the directionality of counterfactual dependence and hence of causation. He makes the empirical claim that (almost) every event is grossly over-determined by subsequent states of the world, but is not so over-determined by its history. Or, in other words, that the future of every event contains many independent definite traces of its occurrence, although before hand there need have been little or no conclusive indication that it would happen.

These four ingredients work together as follows. Let us imagine a hypothetical change in the course of the world—specifically, that some actual event C at time t did not occur at that time. It would be hard to reconcile this supposition with what actually happened after t, for in fact C brought about many phenomena that determine that C did occur at t. On the other hand, it would be relatively easy to square the supposition that C did not happen with the course of the world before t. Because although that history may have determined that C would occur, events are not substantially over-determined by what preceded them. Thus at the cost of a small violation of our laws of nature, we can reconcile the non-occurrence of C with the actual history of the world before t. But we cannot, without much greater cost, reconcile this with the actual future of the world after t. Consequently, among possible worlds without C, those that are just like ours until t and then diverge are more similar to the actual world than those that are just like the actual world after t, or those that differ from the actual world before t. Thus from the asymmetry of over-determination it follows that if the present were different from the way it is, then the future would be different, but not the past. Counterfactuals of the form, 'If C had not occurred, then E would not have occurred', where C was later than E, will be false. Consequently there will normally be no chain of counterfactually dependent events leading backward in time. Therefore effects will not precede their causes.

Difficulties with Lewis's theory of causal direction emerge at each of the four stages. Let us consider some of these problems beginning with objec-

[5] David Lewis, 'Counterfactual Dependence and Time's Arrow', *Noûs*, 13 (1979), 455–76.
[6] Ibid.

tions to the very idea that causation should be analysed in terms of counter-factual dependence regardless of how such dependence is itself to be construed.

1. *Causal over-determination.* This occurs when an event is the product of more than one causal chain which would each have been sufficient to produce the event. For example, a man's death may be causally over-determined if he is shot in the head simultaneously by two people Smith and Bloggs, acting independently of one another. In such a case the effect is not counterfactually dependent on its causes. The man would have died even if Smith had not shot him. Nevertheless, I think we would say that Smith's shot was a cause of his death. Therefore, contrary to Lewis's analysis, the presence of a chain of counterfactual dependence is not necessary for causation.

Lewis is perfectly aware of such cases but does not regard them as counter-examples to his view.[7] For he believes that it is unclear how to apply causal terminology to instances of over-determination. However, even if he is right about this (which seems doubtful), it is still a mark against his analysis that it yields a *definitely* negative answer to the question of whether Smith's shot was a cause of death. For if our conception of causation neither clearly applies nor clearly fails to apply, then an accurate analysis should reflect this indeterminacy. Note that no such difficulty with over-determination confronts our causal theory of counterfactuals. That theory will correctly *deny* that if Smith had not fired, the victim would still be alive. For, since the shots were causally independent of one another, the occurrence of Bloggs's shot will be among the circumstances in which the absence of Smith's shot is supposed.

2. *Non-causal determination.* A counterfactual dependence between events is often associated, as Lewis says, with a causal relation between them. But it need not be. There are other alternatives.[8] For example,

If John had not been killed, his wife would not have been widowed.

If the last chapter had not been written, the book would not have been completed.

Thus, counterfactual dependence does not imply causal connection.

3. *Directionality.* Even when the counterfactual dependence of E on C *does* reflect some sort of causal connection between them, this need not be because C causes E. As we have seen, it may be, rather, that C is an *effect* of E. For example,

---

[7] Lewis, 'Causation'.

[8] Jaegwon Kim, 'Causes and Counterfactuals', *Journal of Philosophy*, 70 (1973), 570–2, repr. as Ch. XII above; and David H. Sanford, 'The Direction of Causation and the Direction of Condition-ship', *Journal of Philosophy*, 73 (1976), 193–207.

If the match had lit, it would have been struck.

If I had jumped, there would have been a net outside the window.

To handle this problem, Lewis is forced to postulate a special 'back-tracking' sense of counterfactual dependence, associated with special rules for measuring the similarity of possible worlds. But I argued earlier[9] that there is little pre-theoretical rationale for this multiplication of senses.

4. *Causal pre-emption.* This takes place when the cause of an event prevents something else from causing that event. For example, Smith's shooting a man pre-empts Bloggs's shooting him if Bloggs is frightened off before firing by the sound of Smith's gun. If C's causing E pre-empts G's causing E, then, on the face of it, E is not counterfactually dependent on C because, even if C hadn't occurred, E would have been caused by G instead. Thus pre-emption might seem to present a problem for the counterfactual theory of causation.

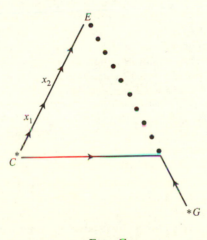

FIG. G

But, as Lewis points out, his analysis can nevertheless be satisfied, for there may be a chain of causal dependence $(x_1, x_2, \ldots)$ connecting C and E, as shown in the figure. One might still be tempted to deny that E depends on x_2, arguing that if x_2 had not occurred, then neither would x_1 nor C, so G

---

[9] [Ed. note] The relevant discussion, which has not been reprinted here, is found in *Asymmetries in Time* (Cambridge, Mass., 1987), ch. 10, sect. 3.

would not have been pre-empted from causing E. However, says Lewis, since we are not employing "back-tracking conditionals", x_2's non-occurrence would not have made any difference to prior members of the chain; so C would still have been there and would have still pre-empted G's causing E.

One way of criticizing this strategy is to repeat the complaint made in point 3 regarding the alleged distinction between normal and back-tracking conditionals. Another objection emerges if we consider cases where C causes E *directly*—without there being any intermediate event X such that C causes X and X causes E. If we now suppose that C pre-empts G's causing E, we then have a case in which Lewis's escape will not work, and his counterfactual analysis breaks down. Suppose, for example, that ball A rolls into ball B, causing B to move out of the way of ball D, which would have caused exactly the motion of B that A actually causes. This is a case of pre-emption. A's striking B causes B's motion; however, if A had not struck B, B would nevertheless have been set into motion by D. Therefore B's motion is not counterfactually dependent on A's hitting B. Moreover there are no events that mediate the causal connection between A's hitting B and B's motion. So there is no event that depends on A's hitting B and that B's motion depends on. Thus Lewis's counterfactual condition seems to be too strong.

Again, the alternative approach is not subject to this difficulty. When C pre-empts G from causing E, our theory will say, as it should, that if C had been absent, then E would have been caused by G. Moreover the account of causation set out earlier[10] entails correctly that G is not actually a cause of E. For a cause must be *essential*, given surrounding circumstances, for the determination of its effect. But the only antecedent conditions that in combination with G will determine E are conditions that include C (or its causes or effects), and such conditions determine E without the help of G.

Admittedly, none of these arguments constitutes a knockdown argument against Lewis's approach. With enough cleverness it will no doubt be possible to save the theory from counter-examples. Indeed, Lewis does have ingenious ways of elaborating and extending his approach to deal with the problems just discussed.[11] However, one cannot help but have the sinking feeling that we are heading for an interminable series of objections and modifications, and that even if there is an end result, it will not have the simplicity and intuitive appeal that recommended the original version. Thus, even though no irrebuttable objection to Lewis's programme may be at hand, there are grounds for dissatisfaction, and reason to cast around for an alter-

---

[10] [Ed. note] Horwich's account of causation, which has not been reprinted here, is found in *Asymmetries in Time*, ch. 8.
[11] Lewis, *Philosophical Papers*, ii.

native. These concerns are compounded as we go on to consider objections to the further stages of Lewis's theory. Let us now look at a problem that emerges when the analysis of causation is supplemented with the theory of counterfactual conditionals.

5. *Psychological implausibility.* According to Lewis, a counterfactual holds when the consequent is true in possible worlds very like our own except for the fact that the antecedent is true. But it is vital that the degree of similarity not be assessed by intuitive pre-theoretical criteria. Rather, the relative importance of various factors in determining how similar some world is to our own must be retrieved from our views about which conditionals are true and which are false. For example, it has often been objected against Lewis that on his view

If the president had pressed the button, a nuclear war would have ensued

must be false, since a world in which the circuit fails and there is no war would be more like actuality than a world in which all life is destroyed. Lewis's reply, as I have indicated, is to maintain that we should infer from the truth of the conditional that the intuitive standards of similarity are not relevant. We should recognize that the appropriate standard of similarity will include something like the following ranking of how important various forms of differences are: first (most substantial), the existence of many miracles (violations of our laws), second, the absence of an exact matching of particular facts over large regions of space–time, and third, the occurrence of a small number of miracles.

Now these criteria of similarity may well engender the right result in each case. However, it seems to me problematic that they have no pre-theoretical plausibility and are derived solely from the need to make certain conditionals come out true and others false. For it is now quite mysterious *why* we should have evolved such a baroque notion of counterfactual dependence. Why did we not, for example, base our concept of counterfactual dependence on our ordinary notion of similarity? As long as we lack answers to these questions, it will seem extraordinary that we should have any use for the idea of counterfactual dependence, given Lewis's description of it; and so that account of our conception of the counterfactual conditional must seem psychologically unrealistic.

Finally, let us examine some further difficulties that arise when the a priori component of Lewis's theory is supplemented by the addition of his vital a posteriori hypothesis.

6. *Over-sophistication.* The predominantly future orientation of counterfactual dependence, and causation, fall out as consequences of Lewis's theory

only relative to a contingent, empirical assumption regarding the asymmetry of over-determination. He assumes that given a hypothetical change in the actual course of events, it would require many miracles to preserve the actual future, but it would be relatively easy to reconcile that hypothetical change with the actual history of the world. True, some miracle would have to be supposed (assuming determinism) in order to preserve the past, but not on the scale of what would be needed to perfectly shield the future from that change.

It may seem, contrary to this assertion, that many contexts may be found in which it would be just as easy to shield the future from a hypothetical change as to shield the past. Consider, for example, the counterfactual conditional

> If his chair had been one foot to the left at 3 p.m. then the rock would have hit him.

The antecedent may be reconciled with our actual history before 3 p.m. by imagining a miraculous sudden jump in the chair's position just before 3 p.m. But can we not similarly square the supposition with our actual future by imagining a miraculous sudden jump by the chair back to its original position just after 3 p.m? No, says Lewis. Such a jump would not do the trick, for the chair at 3 p.m. in its hypothetical, temporary position emitted light waves and gravitational forces that are not exactly like the waves and forces it would have emitted if it had not been there then. Therefore, to obtain an exact match with the future, we need to imagine not only the chair jumping back but also many further miracles in order to transform the waves and forces emitted from one position into waves and forces that seem to have come from another position. But the presence of so many miracles would make for a world that is very unlike our own. That is why, if the present were different, the future would have to be different.

My quarrel with this strategy is that it is too scientifically sophisticated. We have presumably been using counterfactuals for thousands of years and have always regarded the future as counterfactually dependent on the past. It cannot be that the ground for such a view lies in the province of contemporary physics. If it were, as Lewis contends,[12] a matter of plain observational fact that the future grossly over-determines every event, then it would be legitimate to employ an awareness of that fact in the explanation of our linguistic behaviour. But it seems to me that as things are, the fact (if, indeed, it is a fact)˙is fairly inaccessible—unknown to most people, even today, let alone to our ancestors. Consequently the evaluation of counterfactual conditionals cannot be conducted on the basis of such knowledge.

---

12 Ibid.

ething to the effect that if there hadn't

for the *counterfactual* theory of *event*
have three options. (1) We can focus
sing these not as counterfactuals but
events fall under causal laws. (2) We
se them only to relate whole states of
vidual event out of it. (3) We can retreat
d counterfactuals, and analysing causal
t how pairs of facts, or pairs of states of
al laws.

ACTUAL ANALYSIS

t causation is one of the two offered by
rm it says that

s, means that *e* depended counterfactually

d not have occurred.

it is to square with certain things we firmly
he most obvious refinement is to equate '*c*
that *e* depended counterfactually on *c* but
vents from *c* to *e* each member of which
mmediate predecessor. (You may think that
ch member depends counterfactually on its
it follow that the last depends counterfac-
s No. The relation expressed by counterfac-
not to be transitive.) Other refinements are
in happen that *c* caused *e* but if *c* had not
ld have caused *e*; and the analysis must be
. Those matters are skilfully handled by the
counterfactual analysis, David Lewis, in his
', and I need not spend time on them.[3]

wever, which seems not to have been noticed
with by minor repairs. It implies that no version

f Philosophy, 70 (1973), 556–67 (repr. in his *Philosophical*
I above), in which 'Events' makes its first appearance.

Lewis does attempt to provide support for his contention, but the argument is not convincing. He points out that detective stories written for the general public presuppose that crimes leave traces. However, it seems clear, in the first place, that we do not take for granted that a "perfect" crime is impossible (although, not surprisingly, such an event would not be good material for a detective story). And, in the second place, even if clues are presented that do point unambiguously to the criminal, it is not generally supposed that his identity must be *over*-determined by the clues.

7. *Empirical implausibility*. Moreover it is not at all obvious that Lewis's empirical assumption is even correct, let alone common knowledge. No doubt there is at least a grain of truth in it, provided by the fork asymmetry: the fact that correlated events have characteristic common causes but not always a typical common effect. But what Lewis needs is a very extreme version of this phenomenon. He must assume that *every* event is one of the later endpoints of a normal fork. This is not merely the trivial claim that every event has "siblings" (i.e. other events with the same cause). It claims, in addition, that the common cause is determined by, and may be inferred from, each of the effects on its own. Lewis does not, however, give grounds for a thesis of such generality, and I see no reason to accept it.

8. *Backward causation*. Causal over-determination is, as we noted earlier, the production of an event by more than one causal chain, each of which would have been sufficient on its own for that outcome. Now, according to Lewis, it is the nomological over-determination of the present by the future that leads to the conclusion that if the present were different, the future would be too, which leads in turn to the future direction of causation. This idea, however, has the following counter-intuitive consequence. Consider an event that happens to be very heavily causally over-determined: for example, a collision caused by several particles simultaneously reaching the same point in space. If that collision had not occurred, then the course of history leading up to it may nevertheless have been as it actually was, but only provided that numerous miracles occur to prevent each of the particles from arriving at that spot when it did. But, as Lewis has argued in connection with the future consequences of an event, this is too high a price to pay. A closer possible world is one in which the miracles are not needed, since the recent history of the world is different and does not involve those particles moving in that way. Thus we have a past-oriented counterfactual and therefore a case of backward causation. But this is not a welcome result. Surely not every case we would normally describe as substantial causal over-determination is really a case of backward causation! . . .

This completes my discussion of Lewis's programme. His account of causation began with a critical appraisal of its main competition, namely, the sort of regularity theory that I have been advocating here:

It remains to be seen whether any regularity analysis can succeed in distinguishing genuine causes from effects, epiphenomena, and pre-empted potential causes—and whether it can succeed without falling victim to worse problems, without piling on the epicycles and without departing from the fundamental idea that causation is instantiation of regularities. I have no proof that regularity analyses are beyond repair, nor any space to review the repairs that have been tried. Suffice it to say that the prospects look dark. I think it is time to try something else.[13]

It seems to me that the pendulum has swung. What Lewis said about regularity analyses is now a fair assessment of the counterfactual approach.

[13] Lewis, 'Causation', 557.

hand, say that 'x caused y' means som
been x there wouldn't have been y.

This paper will present a difficulty
causation. If the difficulty is fatal, w
on event causation statements, anal
rather as saying that ordered pairs o
can stay with counterfactuals but u
affairs, keeping the concept of an ind
still further, dropping both events a
statements as saying something abou
affairs, can be subsumed under caus

THE COUNTERF

The counterfactual analysis of eve
Hume. In its roughest, strongest fo

c caused e,

where c and e are individual event
on c, that is, that

If c had not occurred, e woul

This obviously has to be refined if
believe about what causes what.
caused e' with the statement not
rather that there is a series of e
depended counterfactually on its
this is no refinement at all: if ea
immediate predecessor, doesn't
tually on the first? The answer i
tual conditionals is well known
also needed. For example, it c
occurred some other event wou
modified so as to allow for tha
principal recent advocate of the
papers 'Causation' and 'Events

There is another difficulty, he
before and which cannot be dealt

[3] David Lewis, 'Causation', Journal
Papers, ii (Oxford, 1986), and as Ch.

of the counterfactual analysis of event causation can be squared with our ordinary ways of thinking: a defensible analysis along these lines would have to be radically revisionary—addressed not to the conceptual scheme we have, but to one that we could have—which is not what Hume and Lewis intended.

ESSENCES OF EVENTS

As Lewis's work brings out very clearly, any counterfactual about a particular event implies or presupposes something about the event's essence. If we are to counterfactualize about particulars we must be able to distinguish worlds at which a given event does not occur at all from ones at which it occurs but is somewhat unlike the way it actually was. Suppose that at noon precisely I wave my right hand, and someone makes the statement S:

> If that hand-wave had not occurred, the auctioneer wouldn't have thought you were bidding.

Now, if I had waved my right hand a fraction faster than I actually did, or raised it an inch higher, the auctioneer would still have thought I was bidding; so if S is to come out true, those possible waves must count as the wave I actually did. That implies that my actual wave could have been a bit faster or higher than it was, which means that its actual speed and trajectory are not of its essence.

But suppose that at each of the nearest worlds where I don't wave my right hand at all at that moment I wave my left hand, and the auctioneer thinks I am bidding. Is S true in this case? You might think it isn't, because at those worlds my actual hand-wave doesn't occur and yet the auctioneer still thinks I am bidding. But *doesn't* my hand-wave occur at the left-hand-wave worlds also? What is wrong with the idea that a single event which was in fact a right-handed wave could have been a left-handed one, so that the person who says 'If that hand-wave had not occurred . . .' is not pointing to worlds where at that moment I wave with my left rather than with my right hand? This raises the question of whether my right-handed wave was *essentially* right-handed. I don't want to answer it—just to illustrate its crucial relevance to counterfactuals about events.

There is not much literature on this. It comes under four headings.

(1) Some of it, including all that Davidson has said on the topic, is based directly on the fact that things like this are sometimes said:

> Every Wednesday morning, the members of the squad vote on what practical joke to play on the corporal that day. Last Wednesday's joke

was a hotfoot, but if Private Jones had voted the other way it would have been a fake air-raid alarm.[4]

If we take that as a datum, without processing or digesting it in any way, we shall conclude that a certain event which was a hotfoot could instead have been a fake air-raid alarm. This, in my opinion, amounts to refusing to take the notion of event-essence seriously; and I think that is how Davidson intended it—he was showing his contempt for counterfactuals about events, having been urged by Chisholm to say something about them.

It is pretty clear, anyway, that those standards assign wrong truth-values to many counterfactuals about events. In some circumstances we would want the counterfactual

> If no member of the squad had had any matches, that hotfoot would not have occurred

to come out true. But it won't do so if the hotfoot could have been a fake air-raid alarm.

And there is an easy way of avoiding that unwanted result. We need only suppose that when the speaker says ' . . . *it* would have been a fake air-raid alarm' he is using 'it' as a pronoun of laziness, to save himself from uttering 'last Wednesday's joke' again, and does not mean to refer to the same item as was first referred to by that phrase. Analogously, some say that in

> John takes his family to a good restaurant every Christmas, and Henry does it every Thanksgiving,

the 'it' is clearly a pronoun of laziness. I shall say no more about this matter. It seems clear that if we are to get a useful view about the essences of events, it must have its roots in theory, and cannot be casually skimmed off the surface of our talk.

(2) Peter van Inwagen has likened the essences of events to the essences of substances.[5] We are inclined these days to believe that a substance's origin is essential to it: I could have become a farmer, but I could not have had parents other than my actual ones. Analogously, van Inwagen suggests, perhaps it is impossible that an event should have had a causal history different from the one that it actually had.

Van Inwagen's thesis clearly entails that if c caused e then if c had not occurred e would not have occurred; and this is also entailed by the simplest,

---

[4] See Donald Davidson, 'Eternal vs. Ephemeral Events', in his *Essays on Actions and Events* (Oxford, 1980), at 197 f.

[5] Peter van Inwagen, 'Ability and Responsibility', *Philosophical Review*, 87 (1978), 201–24, at 208 f.

boldest form of the counterfactual analysis of event causation, though not by the analysis in its final, cautious version. Apart from that partial overlap, I have not sorted out the relations between the two. Anyway, I can't see how to put van Inwagen's idea to work in evaluating the counterfactual analysis, so I now set it aside without further discussion.

(3) Lawrence Lombard has argued that an event's time of occurrence is essential to it.[6] Given that I waved my right hand at noon precisely, I could have kept my hand in my pocket at that time and waved my right hand five seconds later, but that would necessarily have been a different wave. Lombard's one argument for this is unsound, I believe, but in any case we shall soon see that this view about the essences of events cannot be combined with the counterfactual analysis of event causation.

(4) David Lewis, in his paper 'Events', says a lot about the essences of events. But rather than offering an independent theory about event essences, and then checking it against the counterfactual analysis of event causation, he works in the opposite direction. He starts with our ordinary careful beliefs about what causes what, interprets them in accordance with the counterfactual analysis, and draws conclusions about what the essences of events must be like if we are not to be convicted of too much error in our views about what causes what. In the absence of any secure independent grounds for judgements about the essences of events, this modest procedure is acceptable, and may indeed be the best that can be managed.

AN EXAMPLE AND A RESULT

Here is an example; it is mine, but it illustrates Lewis's procedure: I fall onto a lamp at midnight, knocking it to the floor so that it breaks. I stipulate that this happens in such a way as to make the statement

(i) My fall caused the lamp's destruction

clearly true. I am not merely saying that my falling caused the lamp to be destroyed, or that the lamp was destroyed because I fell; those are fact-causation statements, and are quite irrelevant to my present topic. I am asserting that a certain particular fall caused a certain particular destruction, which is an event-causation statement. According to the counterfactual analysis, (i) is equivalent (near enough) to

(i) If my fall hadn't occurred, the lamp's destruction wouldn't have occurred either.

---

[6] Lawrence Lombard, *Events* (London, 1986), 206–16.

Now, suppose as is quite possible that (i) is true but that no conduct of mine could possibly have prevented the lamp from being destroyed within the next year: at all the physically possible worlds which are like ours up to just before midnight the lamp is destroyed within a year of that time. In that case, this counterfactual:

(ii) If my fall hadn't occurred the lamp would never have been destroyed

is clearly false. Now, if (i) is true while (ii) is false, it follows that the lamp's actual destruction—a particular event that I shall call D—has a richer essence than merely being a destruction of that lamp, or merely occurring when and where that lamp is destroyed.. For if that were D's whole essence then D would exist at every world where the lamp is ever destroyed, including ones where I don't fall at midnight and the lamp is destroyed five years later. If some of those worlds are 'close' to the actual world, the statement that if my fall hadn't occurred D wouldn't have occurred comes out false, because at some of those close worlds my fall doesn't occur but D does occur five years later. And if that conditional is false, then—according to the counterfactual analysis—it is false after all that my fall caused the destruction of the lamp.

That gives us a negative result about the essences of events. There is more to the essence of any lamp's destruction than merely its occurring when and where that lamp is destroyed; there is more to the essence of any particular death than just its occurring when and where that person dies; and so on.

THE ASYMMETRY FACT

Now, Lombard's theory about event essences has just this consequence: there is more to the essence of the destruction of a lamp than its being the destruction of that lamp. It says that every event essentially occurs when it actually occurs, so that if D occurred at midnight any possible destruction of the lamp at any other time would have been a different event. So far, so good: but the theory has other consequences which cannot be safely combined with the counterfactual analysis of event causation. Take a case where this is true:

There was heavy rain in April and electrical storms in the following two months; and in June the lightning took hold and started a forest fire. *If it hadn't been for the heavy rain in April, the forest would have caught fire in May.*

Add Lombard's thesis to that, and you get

If the April rain hadn't occurred the forest fire wouldn't have occurred.

Interpret that in terms of the counterfactual analysis and you get

The April rains caused the forest fire.

That is unacceptable. A good enough theory of events and of causation might give us reason to accept some things that seem intuitively to be false, but no theory should persuade us that delaying a forest's burning for a month (or indeed for a minute) is causing a forest fire.

But although you cannot cause a fire by delaying something's burning, you can cause a fire by hastening something's burning. When we judge that lightning caused this fire, we don't ask whether the forest would in any case have burned at some future time; and so the way is open for many events that we take to be causes of fires to be merely causes of something's burning earlier rather than later. Similarly, many causes of falls merely cause the thing to fall earlier than it otherwise would have, and so on through causes of quarrels, reconciliations, thefts, slumps, recoveries, outbursts, landslides, floods, traffic jams, adjournments, and so on.[7]

So perhaps we can combine the counterfactual analysis with half of Lombard's thesis, the half saying that if an event actually occurs at T then it essentially occurs no later than T. For then we can say, with respect to a hillside that slid at T and of which it is true that

If c had not occurred it would have slid later than T,

that

If c had not occurred the (actual) landslide would not have occurred

which lets us infer that

c caused the landslide.

That looks about right: we treat as causes of landslides those events that speed up the land's sliding, but not those that delay it.

Actually, it is not quite as simple as that, because in special circumstances an event that stopped the forest from burning in May could also cause it to burn in June, and that event would be both a delayer of burning and a cause of the fire; similarly with the landslide. Here is another example: My disturbance in the church prevents John and Jane from marrying today; but it also affects one of the witnesses in a manner that leads him, months later, to bring John and Jane together again. In this case, my disturbance delays their marrying at T and is a cause of their subsequent marriage. A final example: a massage dislodges a blood clot that would have killed the patient within

---

[7] The point is especially clear in connection with causes of deaths. *No* event ever brings it about that someone dies whereas otherwise she wouldn't have died at all. But I keep deaths out of my illustrations because I find that lethal examples make philosophers suspect that I am trading unfairly on the special fact about deaths, namely that each of us undergoes exactly one of them.

ten minutes, but also starts another chain of events that kills him two hours later.

Such complications are unimportant, however, and do not detract from my central thesis, which is that there is a strong asymmetry in this part of our conceptual scheme. Here it is in a nutshell:

You are informed that a movement of mine affected *when* a certain stone fell from the top of a wall; but for my movement, the stone would have fallen earlier than it actually did, or would have fallen later than it actually did; I'm not telling you which. I do tell you that fully informed observers of the scene agree about whether my movement caused the stone's fall, and I invite you to guess what their opinion is, i.e. to guess whether the movement *did* cause the fall. You have no basis for guessing.[8] Now consider: would it help you if I told you that but for my movement the stone would have fallen earlier than it actually did, or told you that but for my movement the stone would have fallen later than it actually did? Clearly that would help you. That reflects what I call *the asymmetry fact* about this part of our conceptual scheme.

IS IT A CONCEPTUAL FACT?

I think that this is a conceptual fact. I contend that what we mean by ' . . . is a cause of *e*' or ' . . . causes *e*' is something of the form ' . . . causes it to be the case that P_e at a certain time rather than later or never', where P_e is a temporally unsaturated proposition that is appropriately related to the event *e*. Thus, for example, to cause a fire is to cause it to be the case that the thing burns at a certain time rather than later or never, to cause a riot is to cause it to be the case that some people behave riotously at a certain time rather than later or never, and so on.

If that is not right, then what is?

(1) The linguistic data might be explained in terms of pragmatics rather than semantics. That is, it might be said that if a misunderstanding between two people delays their getting reconciled, the statement

The misunderstanding caused their reconciliation

is, strictly speaking, true, but people are uncomfortable about assenting to it because it *suggests* something false, and this leads them to talk as though they could see it to be false.

---

[8] If you think you have, that is because you are nourishing your imagination on a one-sided diet of examples, arbitrarily picturing me as pushing the stone off the wall, rather than protecting it from being pushed off.

It can happen that a statement is true in what it says and false in what it implies or suggests, and this can lead people to treat it as though it were false. And indeed this possibility can legitimately be used to defend a semantic thesis against apparent counter-examples. But we should never accept it in a particular case without asking how, why, the true statement comes to make the false suggestion; and in the present case there seems to be no decent answer.

Here is one try. 'Take a case where the cause delays the obtaining of a bad state of affairs: because of the nurse's therapy the patient did not have a stroke that morning though he did have one a month later. It is literally true that her therapy caused the patient's stroke, but we don't like saying this because it suggests something false, namely that *the nurse did something bad*.' But why should the statement suggest this if not because that is what it means? If the sentence 'The nurse's therapy caused the patient's stroke' means only that the therapy made a difference to when the patient suffered a stroke, why should that carry any suggestion at all that she did something bad, that is, that she hastened his having a stroke rather than delaying it? Possible answer: 'Because hasteners are much more common than delayers. Given that the therapy made some difference to the time, it is statistically more likely to have brought it forward than to have pushed it back.' That would be an excellent answer if it were true. But it is blatantly false.

(2) Dropping the pragmatic approach, and conceding that the truth-value of 'c caused e' is pretty tightly tied to that of 'c caused it to be the case that P_e at a certain time rather than later or never', someone might suggest that what links them is not an immediate semantic connection but rather a fact about how the actual world is causally structured.[9] The suggestion is that there is a relation R such that: (1) it is a conceptual truth that c causes e only if $R(c, e)$, and (2) it is a contingent truth that $R(c, e)$ is seldom or never true when c delays the obtaining of P_e and usually or always true when it hastens it.

One could hardly accept this without being given some account of what R is, and I have no suggestions about that. Nor do I need to pursue the matter further. It is important for anyone wanting comprehensively to understand our concept of event causation, but for my purposes here it makes no difference whether the asymmetry fact is purely conceptual or whether it is contingent. Either way, it will cause just as much trouble for the counterfactual analysis of event causation, as I shall show in due course.

[9] I owe this suggestion to Kit Fine, who has greatly helped me to clarify and focus my thinking in this paper.

TROUBLE FROM THE ASYMMETRY FACT

I shall pretend that the asymmetry fact is the fact that *all* hasteners and *no* delayers are causes. That is stronger than the truth, of course, but it will help to keep the discussion simple, and nothing in my argument will depend on that extra strength.

Let me be a little more exact about that. I shall first give my basic argument for the view that as long as our concept of event causation is sensitive in *any* degree to the difference between hasteners and delayers, the counterfactual analysis of event causation is fatally flawed. Then I shall expound a possible way of escaping from its conclusion: it relies upon the notion of a 'counterpart', which will lead many to reject it out of hand; but I have no quarrel with counterparts, and will give two other reasons for disliking the suggested escape route. The more important of those reasons would fail if the asymmetry to which I have called attention were extremely weak—that is, if there were only a mild tendency for hasteners to be causes or for delayers not to be. But, although the truth of the matter is not as strong as I shall (for expository purposes) pretend, it is nowhere near weak enough to undercut that final argument of mine. Here now is my basic argument against the counterfactual analysis.

The misunderstanding delayed their getting reconciled, so it did not cause their reconciliation. So, by the counterfactual analysis, it is not the case that

> If the misunderstanding had not occurred, the reconciliation would not have occurred.

That means that the very same reconciliation occurred at some of the worlds where the misunderstanding did not occur. The only way of making sense of this is to suppose that at those worlds the reconciliation occurred earlier than it did at the actual world. In general, *necessarily, any event could have occurred earlier than it did occur.*

The intervention by the marriage counsellor hastened their getting reconciled, so it caused their reconciliation. So, by the counterfactual analysis,

> If the intervention had not occurred, the reconciliation would not have occurred.

But there are plenty of nearby worlds where the intervention didn't occur and yet they did get reconciled weeks or months later; so we must say that their actual reconciliation is not to be identified with any of those later reconciliations. In general, *necessarily, no event could have occurred later than it did occur.*

Putting these two results together, we get an incoherent position. Start with an event e^* at a world W^*, and ask which events at other worlds can be identified with it. By the former of our results, e^* can be identified with many events that occur earlier at other worlds—for example e at W. But now let us ask which events at worlds other than W we can identify e with. By the latter of our results, e cannot be identified with any events occurring later than it occurs at W—for example event e^* at W^*. And so, putting the two together: e^* is e, but e is not e^*.

To reinforce this, I shall work it out in terms of an example.

A CONCRETE EXAMPLE

Consider two worlds, at each of which you and I are standing on top of a wall which is being demolished by a wrecker's ball; just in front of me there is a pebble, which I try to kick off the wall before the wrecker's ball gets to it. At world W I do kick the stone, with the result that it falls at t rather than a few seconds later; call that fall of the stone e. At world W^* you push me so that my kick goes awry and the stone is undisturbed until the wrecker's ball knocks it off the wall a little after t; call that fall of the stone e^*. I add the further stipulation S, that the closest no-kick world to W is W^* and the closest no-push world to W^* is W. S doesn't follow from the rest of the description, but it is a consistent addition with it, and that is all we need.

Now, informed and competent speakers of English will agree that at W my kick causes e; by the counterfactual analysis, that entails that if the kick had not occurred e would not have occurred; but by S the closest no-kick world is W^* where e^* occurs; so e is not e^*. But competent speakers will also agree that at W^* your push does not cause e^*; by the counterfactual analysis it follows that it is false that if your push had not occurred e^* would not have occurred; by S it follows that if your push had not occurred e^* would still have occurred; the only possible candidate for the role of e^* at W is e; so e^* is e. Thus we have a flat-out contradiction.

A COUPLE OF DISCLAIMERS

I haven't reached this result through illegitimately streamlining and strengthening the asymmetry fact. If there is any temporal asymmetry in this part of our causal thinking, there is trouble for the counterfactual analysis of event causation. We are looking at a pair of worlds, W where e occurs at time t, and W^* where e^* occurs at time t^*. And we are being forced—by the counterfactual analysis of event causation, combined with the temporal asymmetry in this part of our conceptual scheme—to say that whether e is e^* depends in part on whether the pair $\{t, t^*\}$ exemplifies the later-than relation or rather the earlier-than relation. But this is absurd, because any pair that exemplifies one also exemplifies the other. And, as I said, the absurdity remains so long as there is any asymmetry, however hedged in by conditions, in this part of our conceptual scheme.

Furthermore, the trouble is just as bad if the asymmetry is not purely conceptual but reflects the fact that at the actual world hasteners tend to be causes while delayers tend not to be. Anyone who thinks there is such a contingent fact presumably takes it to be a deep, broad one—more like the fact that there is no action at a temporal distance than like the fact that I went swimming this morning—and so it will obtain not only at our world but also at worlds that are close to ours, for example, worlds differing from ours only by a single kick or push and the fall of a pebble. That is all I need. In my kick–push example, for instance, the contradiction is reached just so long as the asymmetry fact obtains both at W and at W^*; it doesn't have to obtain at all worlds.

PRIVILEGE FOR THE ACTUAL WORLD

Perhaps there is a way out, however. Faced with a pair of event descriptions pertaining to two different worlds, we have been asking

> What is the temporal relation between the events-at-worlds referred to by these descriptions? Is it earlier-than or later-than?

And that is an idiot question because if either answer is right then both are. But we might do better if there were some special feature that was always possessed by one but not the other member of our pair of event descriptions. Then we could replace the idiot question by something of the form

> What temporal relation does the privileged one of these have to the other? Earlier-than or later-than?

and that might have either answer but cannot have both.

What could we mean here by 'privileged'? What is the special feature that is always possessed by just one member of the pair? The only remotely plausible answer is that the description involving the actual world is privileged. On that basis, then, the crucial question is something like this:

> How does the event at the actual world relate to the event at the non-actual world? Is it earlier or later than it?

If we order our pairs in that way, by attending to which of them pertains to the actual world, we may seem to be on our way to the intuitively right answers. And this is just what the asymmetry fact implies if it is taken to be the fact that

> No event could have occurred later than it *actually* did. Any event could have occurred earlier than it *actually* did.

But that is not the right way to express the asymmetry fact, and this proposed rescue of the counterfactual analysis is not acceptable.

Here is why. If we are to use the concept of event causation at all, we should be able to use it not only (i) in describing what actually happens but also (ii) in practical deliberation, where we don't yet know which of the worlds is actual, and (iii) in counterfactuals about what would have caused what if things had gone differently in some respect. But neither the second nor third of these would go right if we accepted the proposed rescue of the counterfactual analysis, according to which we can't say whether c causes e at world W without knowing whether W is the actual world.

That this is true about (ii) practical deliberation is perhaps too obvious to need to be spelled out in detail. As for (iii) counterfactuals about event causation: let us return to my kick–push example, and suppose that the actual world is W^* at which you push me and my kick misses the stone. Intuitively it seems reasonable to suppose that at that world we could truly say that

> If your push hadn't occurred, my kick would have caused a fall of the stone;

but by the counterfactual analysis, together with my stipulation S, that implies that

> At world W it is the case that: if my kick hadn't occurred e wouldn't have occurred.

But the proposed rescue won't let us say this. It requires that none of the later falls at nearby worlds be identified with e, but now we are not assured of that because e does not occur at the actual world and the 'it couldn't have occurred later' principle is now being applied only to actual events.

COUNTERPART THEORY TO THE RESCUE?

So far I have assumed that we are dealing with the *identity* relation between events at different worlds, but if instead we employ a *counterpart* relation we may after all be able to reconcile the asymmetry fact with the counterfactual analysis of event causation. I shall explain this by first sketching Lewis's (and Leibniz's) counterpart theory for *substances*.[10]

---

[10] See David Lewis, 'Counterpart Theory and Quantified Modal Logic', originally published in 1968 and repr. in his *Philosophical Papers*, i (Oxford, 1983), 26–39, with a 1983 Postscript, 39–46.

For simplicity's sake, let's narrow it down to *people*. The very same person cannot occur at more than one world, according to Lewis and Leibniz, but we can still divide counterfactuals about named people into true and false. Someone meditating on Nelson Rockefeller's handling of the Attica prison incident might say:

> If Mario Cuomo had been in charge, there would have been no deaths or injuries;

and this has a chance of being non-vacuously true because it means something about possible men who qualify as *counterparts* of Mario Cuomo: they are sufficiently like him (in the right ways) for us to talk about how they are in the language of how he might have been. So the Cuomo counterfactual is true if, and only if, there are no deaths or injuries in the Attica prison incident at the closest world where a counterpart of Mario Cuomo is in charge.

For present purposes, the most important point to grasp is that identity is symmetrical whereas the counterpart relation need not be. In general, we expect the latter to go both ways: if possible person x is a counterpart of the actual Mario Cuomo, then Cuomo is probably a counterpart of x, so that some counterfactuals about x will get their truth-values from facts about Cuomo. But there is no necessity about this. Individual x at world W_x has as a counterpart y at world W_y if and only if the two are alike in ways that have a certain kind of significance from the standpoint of W_x; and y has x as a counterpart if and only if the two are alike in ways that have a certain kind of significance from the standpoint of W_y. The similarities are the same, whatever world you look at them from, but their kind or degree of significance may differ; and so the counterpart relation is not symmetrical.

This seems to open up a glittering way of escape from the difficulty which is my topic in this paper. For now we can say that at the world W where my kick causes the fall e of the stone, it is true that

> If my kick had not occurred e would not have occurred, because no event at the nearest no-kick world W^* is a counterpart of e, and in particular e^* *is not a counterpart of* e. But at W^* where your push spoils my kick, we are still free to say that your push does not cause e^*, implying that at the nearest no-push world some counterpart of e^* does occur, to wit, e *is a counterpart of* e^*. There is no contradiction in this, because being-a-counterpart-of is not a symmetrical relation.

AN ASIDE ON MODAL CONTINUANTS

David Lewis does not handle counterfactuals about events in the language of 'counterparts'. Rather than saying that the event we call the death of Socrates occurs only at the actual world though it has counterparts at other worlds, he treats the death of Socrates as what he has elsewhere called a 'modal continuant'—a class whose members belong to different worlds. An event, according to Lewis, is a class of spatio-temporal zones, no two existing at the same world. The class we designate by the phrase 'the death of Socrates' has one member at the actual world, namely the place–time at which Socrates died.

Suppose that the informal English sentence 'Socrates' death could have been less painful than it actually was' is true. According to counterpart theory it is true because

> Some counterpart of Socrates' death is less painful than the death itself was;

according to modal continuant theory, it is true because

> Some member of Socrates' death is less painful than its actual world member was.

As that example suggests, there is a simple route from counterpart theory to the other: if you have been confining x to one world and handling counterfactuals about it in terms of its counterparts, you can change gear and instead identify x with the class whose members are it and all its erstwhile counterparts. I need not draw a map of the route for the journey the other way. It is clear enough that Lewis is right in saying that the theory of modal continuants 'is an equivalent reformulation of counterpart theory'.[11]

Although the two do the same work, they do it differently. Applying counterpart theory to substances, the referent of the name 'Thomas Hobbes' is perfectly determinate, but there is some indeterminacy about which possible things are counterparts of it, and this makes counterfactuals containing the name 'Thomas Hobbes' somewhat indeterminate. Applying modal continuant theory, there is indeterminacy about which item (which class of things) is picked out by 'Thomas Hobbes', but once the referent is fixed it is also determinate which worlds it exists at, and so counterfactuals in which the name occurs suffer from no indeterminacy from that source. Lewis is on record as objecting to such promiscuous indeterminacy of reference in the names of substances,[12] but it could be an advantage where events are concerned, for it is plausible to suppose phrases like 'Thomas Hobbes's birth' and 'Thomas Hobbes's reconciliation with Cromwell' have referential slack that is not shared by the name 'Thomas Hobbes'. Perhaps that is why Lewis chose to handle events in terms of modal continuants and substances in terms of counterparts.

---

[11] Ibid. 41.   [12] Ibid.

Because the two theories are equivalent in power, the 'non-symmetry' escape route that would be opened up by counterpart theory is also available to Lewis in the context of his treatment of events as modal continuants. But it seems more complicated there, and harder to grasp intuitively,[13] which is why I have chosen to present it in terms of counterpart theory.

EVALUATING THE PROPOSED RESCUE

Someone who holds that counterpart theory is wrong, across the board, should think that I have already completed an adequate case against the counterfactual analysis of event causation. Someone who rejects counterpart theory for substances might nevertheless find it tolerable for events; but I cannot discuss that position, because I can think of no plausible reasons for it. What remains is the position of the person who is sympathetic to counterpart theory for particulars of every kind, including substances and events. Since that is my own position, I have a special reason for wanting to evaluate the proposed rescue of the counterfactual analysis from that standpoint.

One of Lewis's reasons for counterpart theory is his 'extreme' realism about worlds: given his view of what sort of item a world is, it's hard to see how a single substance could exist at more than one world. But even for those of us who do not confidently agree with him about that, there are pulls towards counterpart theory as applied to substances. For me the strongest pull comes from the fact that answers to questions about the essences of substances seem not to fall sharply into the objectively true and objectively false, but rather to lie on a smooth scale from undeniable to intolerable, with much of the middle ground being sensitive to needs, interests, and contexts. If counterpart theory is true, that is just what one would expect; but if it is false—that is, if questions of the form 'Could x, which is not actually F, have been F?' have objectively right answers—it is puzzling that we should be so lost and adrift in our attempts to find out what the answers are.[14]

This reason for favouring counterparts (i) rests on a general view about what is going on when in ordinary thought and talk we counterfactualize about particular substances, and (ii) owes nothing to the special needs of any philosophical theory in which counterfactuals are used or mentioned.

In sharp double contrast with that, the proposed invocation of counterparts in connection with events (i) cannot be motivated by reflection on our

---

[13] I am indebted to Kit Fine for a tutorial on how to do it.

[14] For some related remarks, see David Lewis's *Counterfactuals* (Cambridge, Mass., 1973), 38–43. Thomas McKay's remarkable 'Against the Constitutional Sufficiency Principle', in *Midwest Studies in Philosophy*, 11 (1986) can be, though it is not by its author, used as a basis for a different, though equally powerful, case for counterpart theory.

untutored untheoretical talk about how particular events might have been different, because we don't engage in any such talk (or, if we do, we have no pre-theoretic way of telling when we are talking in that way; consider the 'practical joke' example which I adapted from Davidson); and (ii) it owes everything to the fact that without it the counterfactual analysis of event causation comes to grief. The difference between the two situations should, I submit, make us suspicious of the proposed treatment of events, inclining us to think it an *ad hoc* rescue of a theory which should be allowed to fall.

A still weightier consideration is the following. If event e occurs at world W at a certain time, and e^* occurs at W^* at the same time, it may well be that each has the other as a counterpart. But for each such contemporaneous counterpart that e has, it has astronomically many earlier counterparts of most of which it is not a counterpart. Thus, if the counterfactual analysis of event causation is to be squared with the asymmetry fact, we need a counterpart relation that is *drastically* non-symmetrical—a relation R such that on the information that $R(x, y)$ the proposition that $R(y, x)$ is highly improbable.

I submit that this degree of non-symmetry makes the proposed rescue implausible. Our counterpart relation has to be induced through theory from the data concerning which counterfactuals we accept and which we reject, and that leaves room for the possibility that it is a non-symmetrical relation. But let us bear in mind what the role of this relation is supposed to be: it is a relation R such that

> if $R(x, y)$ then the proposition that Fx can properly be expressed by saying that *it could be the case that Fy*.

It is not credible that a relation's holding between x and y could have that effect—making us willing to say things about x in sentences that don't name x—unless the relation approximated to identity, so to speak. So although strict symmetry should not be insisted upon, it is hard to believe that any counterpart relation should be as extravagantly non-symmetrical as the one we have been looking at.

So the counterpart relation cannot come to the rescue after all. The counterfactual theory of event identity cannot be squared with the asymmetry fact.

XV

VARIETIES OF CAUSATION[*]

ERNEST SOSA

1

It is an essential feature of 'nomological' accounts of causation that according to them

> (N) an event or state of affairs P (partially) causes (or is 'a cause' or 'causal factor' of) another Q only if there are actual ('initial') conditions I and a law of nature L such that, by necessity, if P and I and L all obtain then Q must obtain, where the law L is essential in that P and I alone do *not* necessitate Q.

(Various refinements might now be introduced to deal with sundry difficulties, but that much is surely a basic tenet of the tradition.)

It is further commonly assumed, especially by Humeans (regularists), (i) that laws make no essential reference to any particulars: that laws are purely general, and (ii) that laws are not necessary truths.

Suppose that by making a certain board B come to stand in a certain relation R to a certain stump S I create a certain table T. Presumably table T comes into existence *because* board B comes to have relation R to stump S, and B's bearing R to S is a cause (a causal factor) of T's coming into existence. Surely such generation is a paradigm of ordinary causation. The source of the existence of the table is the joining of the board and the stump. The source of the existence of a certain zygote is the union of a particular sperm and a particular ovum. And so on. But what law of nature or, even, what quasi-law or law-like principle could possibly play in such a case of generation the role required by nomological accounts?

There is of course the following principle:

> (L) If a board of type β comes to bear relation R to a stump of type σ in a certain place at a certain time, then a table comes into existence at that place and time.

* This paper was read at the Oberlin Colloquium of April 1977. A later version was delivered as part of the Oaxtepec Conference of August 1978, organized by the Instituto de Investigaciones Filosóficas of the Universidad Nacional Autónoma de Mexico.

Suppose further that we are given the following initial conditions:

(I) Board B is of type β and stump S is of type σ.

We can now perhaps see a way to account for the fact that the source of the existence of a table is the joining of the board and the stump, a way to account for that fact without violating N, the tenet common to nomological accounts of causation. For,

> let Q be the coming into being of a table at location l and time t, and let P be board B's coming to bear R to stump S at location l and time t. It now follows that, by necessity, if P and I and L all obtain, then Q must obtain.

But that takes us at best only part of the way and does not fully answer our question, for the question is not only how the nomological model can account for the fact that the joining of the board and stump causes the existence of a table. Our question is really how the nomological model can account for the fact that the joining of the board and stump causes the existence of *this* table, of table T. Besides, if for simplicity 'table' is defined simply by reference to geometrical properties, then it seems likely that any plausible candidate for the status of principle L would be a necessary truth.

It is not particularity *per se* that is the source of the trouble, however, for the nomological model does not have the same difficulty explaining *changes* in this very table. Thus if it rains on table T that causes the very table in question to be wet. And this presents no special difficulty for tenet N of nomological accounts. The source of trouble is thus not that the effect essentially involves a particular—this table—but rather that it involves the generation of a particular. *Changes* in the properties or relations of particulars present no special difficulty for N, but the *generation* of particulars does. And yet, again, generation does seem a variety of causation.

Our problem can be solved only by broadening our outlook. For, so far as I can see, generation is not just an anomaly for the nomological model—something to be worked on and solved in due course. It seems clear that there is no hope of modifying the nomological model in any way that preserves its basic identity while providing a solution to the problem of generation. What has to go is at the heart of the nomological model, for it is the idea that contingent and purely general principles are essentially involved in any case of causation. We must broaden our outlook to encompass types of causation that do not thus essentially involve such principles. For instance, the fact of generation apparently requires what we might properly call 'material causation'.

Our particular board B could not possibly have been joined by relation R to our particular stump S at the time t, while the board remained a board of type β and the stump remained a stump of type σ without our particular table T coming into existence at that time. This is a necessary connection involving particulars. (And it is not fully parasitic on necessary connections among their properties, in the way the entailment of Fa by $(Fa \,\&\, Ga)$ is parasitic on the necessity of $(x)(Fx \,\&\, Gx \supset Fx)$. It is however a necessary connection that does give rise to a causal relation in the strictest sense: i.e. to the causal relation of generation.

2

So far we have considered a difficulty for the nomological model deriving from the fact that people make things, bring them into existence, by bringing it about that certain materials with certain properties come to be interrelated in certain ways, so that the things come into existence *because* the materials come to be interrelated thus. Let us now consider a more general argument designed to show that the nomological model is incompatible with anything's coming into existence as a result of its components coming to be interrelated in the way required for their composing the thing. The argument is presented in part (a) of this section, below, and discussed in part (b).

(a) If an entity is caused to come into being then presumably there is a truth of the following sort: (1) E comes into being at t because of the fact P. Now according to the nomological model what underlies this truth must be the existence of some general law or principle L such that the conjunction of L with P and with some initial conditions I (which hold in the circumstances) logically implies that E comes into being at t. And L will presumably have the following form: if an entity meets conditions C at a time t', then it does not exist before t but does exist at t, where tRt'. And this in turn amounts to the following conjunction $(L_1$ and $L_2)$: L_1 (If an entity meets conditions C at a time t', then it does not exist before t, where tRt') $\&\, L_2$ (If an entity meets conditions C at a time t' then it does exist at t, where tRt').

If such a conjunctive law is to be causal it must be in virtue of the second conjunct. For consider the first conjunct. Since no entity could meet conditions C at a time when it did not exist, t' cannot be earlier than t. But then if the first conjunct were causal it would assure us that an entity fails to exist up to a time t *as a result* of meeting conditions C at that time or later. And that is surely absurd.

Consider next the second conjunct, L_2. Again of course the time t' cannot be earlier than the time t, for no entity can meet conditions C at a time when it does not exist. And the time t' cannot be later than the time t, for no entity could come into existence at a certain time as a result of meeting certain conditions at a *later* time. So the time t' must be the same as the time t. But then, given the nature of L_2, $(L_2 \,\&\, P \,\&\, I)$ cannot logically imply that an entity E exists at a certain time unless $(P \,\&\, I)$ logically implies that E meets conditions C at that very time. But then $(P \,\&\, I)$ alone already logically implies that E exists at that same time. And this violates the requirements of the nomological model.

(b) It may be replied that the law required for explaining the coming into existence of E at t need not have the form required above, provided we can assume a kind of mereological essentialism. For the law could then take the following form:

$$L' \, (x) \, (y) \, [(Fx \,\&\, Gy \,\&\, Rxy) \supset (\exists z) \, (z = CR \, (x, y))]$$

where '$CR(x, y)$' is short for 'the entity composed of x and y by x bearing R to y'.

Thus if F stands for being a board and G stands for being a stump and R stands for the relation of lying on, we can use L' above in conjunction with the fact that B is a board, S is a stump and B comes to lie on S at t to explain how the entity composed of B and S (when and only when B lies on S) comes into existence at t.

But that only gives us an explanation of how it is that something causes there to exist at t a unique entity composed of B and S by B lying on S. We do not yet have an explanation concerning the very thing that is such a unique entity, of how it is that something causes *that* very thing to come into being. For might not some other thing have been the unique entity composed of B and S by B lying on S? Here we may be told, in accordance with mereological essentialism, that nothing else could possibly have been the unique entity composed of B and S by B lying on S except the very thing that is in fact composed of B and S by B lying on S.

That reply is of no use to the defender of the nomological model, however, for it makes the law L' derivable from the mereological principle that, necessarily, for any x and any y, if x is a board and y is a stump and x is lying on y, then there exists a z such that it is necessarily the case that z is identical with the entity composed of x and y by x lying on y—or, in symbols:

$$(M) \, \Box \, (x) \, (y) \, [(Fx \,\&\, Gy \,\&\, Rxy) \equiv (\exists z) \, \Box \, (z = CR(x,y))]$$

And if so, then the 'law' L' turns out to be a necessary truth, which violates one of the essential requirements of the nomological model.

Against this, however, there is the following rejoinder. All we need to know now in order to explain how our table T is caused to come into existence at t is some explanation of how board B comes to lie on (to bear R to) stump S. For this last will then mereologically entail that $CR(B, S)$ comes into existence. And, as we have seen, nothing but our table T could possibly be $CR(B, S)$—i.e. the R-compound of B and S, the compound of B and S that is the thing composed of B and S by B bearing R to S. Thus as soon as we have an account of how something causes B to bear R to S, that will explain how something causes T to come into existence. And it will be recalled that the nomological model has no special difficulty accounting for the causation of changes, such as board B coming to lie on stump S.

I conclude that it may well be possible for the nomological model to help account for how *some* causes bring about the coming into being of something. So far as we have been able to determine, however, the nomological model can accomplish that only at the cost of accepting a kind of mereological essentialism.

Moreover, from the fact that the nomological model can account for the operation of *some* causes in generation (by appealing to mereological essentialism), we may not conclude that generation no longer gives it any difficulty. May it not be that there are *other* generational causes which the nomological model is unable to accommodate? This is suggested already in Section 1 above and is spelled out in Section 3.

3

Have we exaggerated the nomological model's predicament? Let us reconsider our simple example of the board B and the stump S. And let us suppose (a) that B could not possibly lie on S without there being our particular table T in existence, (b) that at time t, B comes to lie on S, and (c) that it is placed there then (i.e. it is moved to that position then).

It seems reasonable to derive the following from (a)–(c): (d1) T exists at time t because B lies on S at t, and (d2) B lies on S at t because B is placed on S at t.

T exists at t as a result of or in consequence of the fact that B lies on S at t. It has already been argued above that the nomological model *can* account for this type of causation if it is combined with mereological essentialism. For whenever a board x (such as B) lies on a stump y (such as S) there is the R-compound of x and y: $CR(x, y)$. Furthermore, if $z = CR(x, y)$ then z is *necessarily* identical with $CR(x, y)$ and $CR(x, y)$ could not have been anything other than z. Thus our table T could not possibly have failed to be an R-compound of our board and stump, could not have failed to be the result of B lying on S. And in no possible world could the R-compound of our board and stump possibly have been anything other than our particular table T.

But none of that is really of any help to the nomological model. For the connection between B lying on S at t and the existence of the R-compound of B and S is a *necessary* connection and thus useless to the nomological model. What purely general and *contingent* principle underlies the truth of (d1)?

Are we perhaps guilty of a process–result confusion? What is involved in generation is a *process* and what generates the table at t is perhaps *not* the board B's lying on the stump S at t. Let us suppose that a carpenter makes the table by placing B on S at t. Then what brings the table into existence is his work, and what constitutes his work is his placing of B on S by moving B to S. So (d3) B is placed on S at t because the carpenter places B on S at t (by moving it there from a nearby position).

That is all very well, but it is hardly of any help to the nomological model in accounting for the causal relation expressed by (d1). What is more, we must now account not only for (d1) but also for (d2) and (d3). Our attempt to solve the difficulty raised by (d1) for the nomological model has only compounded the difficulty by bringing out (d2) and (d3), each of which is a further case of causation that the nomological model is apparently unable to accommodate. Thus we need to be told what contingent and purely general principles bear to any of the following the relation required by the nomological model:

(d1) there is such a thing as table T in existence at t because (as a result of or in consequence of the fact that) at t board B lies on stump S;

(d2) board B is placed on stump S at t because (as a result of or in consequence of the fact that) it is placed there then (i.e. it is moved there then); and

(d3) board B is placed on stump S at t because (as a result of or in consequence of the fact that) the carpenter places it there then (by moving it there from a nearby position).

4

Part of the foregoing argument may be put as follows. If there is now an aggregate A, then there are now entities $C1$ and $C2$ and a relation R such that (i) necessarily, if $C1$ now bears R to $C2$, then A now exists, and (ii) $C1$ *could* now come to bear R to $C2$. But if $C1$ did now come to bear R to $C2$, then A would come into existence now as a (mereological) result or in (mereological) consequence of that. Hence if there is now an aggregate then there is a possible case of causation (the generation of the aggregate) that could not be accounted for by the nomological model. Thus for the nomological model aggregates cannot really exist but must be at best mere shadows or fictions.

That reveals a fundamental connection in the logical atomist programme between its reductionist atomism and its Humean nomological model of causation.

5

Material causation—the type of causation involved in mereological generation—has now been admitted as a basic form of causation not parasitic on truths that are either general or contingent. This prompts the question of whether there are other forms of causation not accounted for by the nomological model. *If the root causal relation is being a 'source', whose converse is being a result or consequence*, then there do appear to be other prima-facie forms of causation such that the cause does entail the result or consequence.

If an apple is red then it is coloured as a result of being red; it is coloured *because* it is red. If Tom is alone in the room, then it is a fact that there is someone in the room as a result of (in consequence of, because of) the fact that Tom is in the room. If there is no one in the room but Peter, Paul, and Mary, each of whom is tall, then it is a fact that everyone in the room is tall as a result of (in consequence of, because of) the fact that both there is no one in the room but Peter, Paul, and Mary and each of these is tall.

These examples demand that we acknowledge a form of necessary causation to be distinguished from its more familiar contingent counterpart. It is not obvious how to analyse this form of necessary causation, but it does seem a genuine form of causation. . . . In each of the examples given, the consequence somehow derives necessarily from the cause and not conversely. One is reminded of the consequentialist properties of value theory, and indeed these can reasonably be taken to provide further examples of consequentialist causation. Thus if an apple is sweet, juicy, etc., then it is a *good* apple *because* it is sweet, juicy, etc. It is a good apple as a result or as a consequence of being sweet, juicy, etc., and that is what makes it so good.

But there are forms of necessary causation other than consequentialist causation. Why does that pipe move that way over the surface of the water? Because it is the periscope of a submarine moving thus. Why is board B on stump S at t? Because it is placed there just then by the carpenter. Let us call the type of causation involved here inclusive causation.

Unlike consequentialist causation, this latter type of causation does not involve a consequence deriving necessarily from a cause that is somehow more basic. Here I do not pretend to have an account of what it is for a state of affairs or a property to be more basic than another. That is part of the problem of analysing consequentialist causation. . . . In appealing to the notion that consequentialist results derive from causes that are somehow more basic, therefore, I am simply appealing to what seems intuitively right and a proper object of analysis.

In the cases of inclusive causation cited above it is arguable that the *result* is more basic than the cause! Thus the motion of the whole submarine may be said to derive from a plurality of more basic facts that includes the motion of its periscope. The process brought about by the carpenter that eventuates in the board's being on the stump at t may be said to derive from a (possibly infinite) plurality of more basic facts that includes the board's being on the stump at t. Hence a state of affairs $S1$ may be an *inclusive* cause of something $S2$ that is in turn one of the *consequentialist* causes of $S1$.

6

It would be very surprising if after all these years it turned out that there was *nothing* to the nomological model. And surely that is not an inescapable conclusion. For the nomological model may still give us a good account of *nomological* causation. One of the pitfalls on the way of analysis is, however, a too facile use of the motto: divide and conquer. When confronted with a purported counter-example the analyst may be tempted to reject it as not relevant to the specific concept under analysis. 'It seems superficially to be so relevant' he may say, 'but only because it is really relevant only to a *different* concept that happens to have the same label in our language.' The facile use of this strategy is a cheap stratagem that secures analysis against failure—and precludes success. In defence of my suggestion that it be used in support of the nomological model, I can only voice the belief that an interesting form of causation is amenable to a nomological account. After all, the history of the analysis of causation since Hume is to a significant extent a history of improved approximations to this concept. . . .

But that does not rule out other forms of bona fide causation, . . . such as material causation, consequentialist causation, and inclusive causation. I have argued that these are distinct from one another and distinct also from the nomological causation that is parasitic on contingent general principles. At the same time these all seem to be types of causation in that most proper sense in which causes are sources of results or consequences that derive from them.

What there is in common to all forms of causation is, it appears, necessitation. At least we may think of it thus if we can conceive of basic nomological causation as a relation between a state of affairs C that *includes* a causal law and a result R, where C now does necessitate R (by logical implication). This is of course compatible with the elliptical talk that we allow ourselves, as when we say that the striking of a match caused its ignition, when the ignition was *really* the result or consequence not just of the striking but of some broader state of affairs that includes a law (of the right sort). If this is acceptable, then in every case where R is a result or consequence of C, it is a necessary truth that C obtains only if R obtains, i.e. C necessitates R. But the necessitated is not always a result or consequence of the necessitator. When it is a fact that p & q, that p & q necessitates that p, but the fact that p is not always a result or consequence of the fact that p & q. It is a task for analysis to find the special features that distinguish causal from non-causal necessitation.

It might be objected that much of the foregoing is a mere terminological manœuvre, that it simply takes what philosophers have long called causation, relabels it 'nomological causation', and goes on to classify it with certain wholly other relations that philosophers have not heretofore called causal relations. And it might perhaps be that the word 'cause' and its cognates have been so closely and so persistently associated with nomological causation by philosophers that they must be surrendered. But even then the basic point would remain, for nomological causation is a relation between a source and a consequence or result, and so is material causation (e.g. generation), so is consequentialist causation (e.g. the apple is chromatically coloured as a result of being red), and so is inclusive causation (e.g. the board is on the stump at t in consequence of the fact that the carpenter places it there then). These are all source–consequence relations or result-yielding relations. My suggestion has been that the underlying reason for this intuition of homogeneity is that they are all cases of necessitation, each with its own distinguishing features. If this is right then even nomological causation is basically a type of necessitation, where the real source of the effect is not just the mentioned partial cause but a fuller situation that includes a law of nature.[1]

---

[1] A more ambitious defence of my proposal would reject the nomological model's requirement that laws of nature must be contingent. This is a more satisfyingly simple and coherent strategy which has been occasionally (but rarely) defended.

NOTES ON THE CONTRIBUTORS

G. Elizabeth M. Anscombe was, until her retirement, Professor of Philosophy at Cambridge University. She has been translator and co-editor of the posthumous works of Wittgenstein, and among her publications are *Intentions* (1957), *An Introduction to Wittgenstein's Tractatus* (1959), and (with Peter Geach) *Three Philosophers* (1961).

Jonathan Bennett is Professor of Philosophy at Syracuse University, and the author of *Rationality* (1964), *Kant's Analytic* (1964), *Locke, Berkeley, and Hume: Central Themes* (1971), *Linguistic Behaviour* (1976), *A Study of Spinoza's Ethics* (1984), and *Events and their Names* (1988).

Donald Davidson has held appointments at Stanford, Princeton, Rockefeller, and Chicago, and is now Professor of Philosophy at the University of California at Berkeley. He is the author of *Essays on Actions and Events* (1980), and *Inquiries into Truth and Interpretation* (1984).

Curt John Ducasse was head of the Philosophy Department at Brown University. His many publications include *Causation and the Types of Necessity* (1924), *The Philosophy of Art* (1927), *Philosophy as a Science: Its Matter and Method* (1941), *Nature, Mind, and Death* (1951), *A Philosophical Scrutiny of Religion* (1953), and *Truth, Knowledge, and Causation* (1969).

Paul Horwich is Professor of Philosophy at MIT, and the author of *Probability and Evidence* (1982), *Asymmetries in Time* (1987), and *Truth* (1990).

Jaegwon Kim has held appointments at Cornell and Michigan, and is now Professor of Philosophy at Brown University. He has published a number of articles in areas such as metaphysics and philosophy of mind, and was co-editor of *Values and Morals: Essays in Honor of William Frankena, Charles Stevenson, and Richard Brandt* (1978).

David Lewis is Professor of Philosophy at Princeton University. His publications include *Convention* (1969), *Counterfactuals* (1973), *On the Plurality of Worlds* (1986), and *Philosophical Papers* (1983 and 1986).

John L. Mackie was Reader in Philosophy at Oxford University and Fellow of University College, Oxford. Among his many publications are *Truth, Probability and Paradox* (1973), *The Cement of the Universe* (1974), *Problems from Locke* (1976), *Ethics: Inventing Right and Wrong* (1977), *Hume's Moral Theory* (1980), and *The Miracle of Theism* (1982).

Wesley Salmon is Professor of Philosophy at the University of Pittsburgh. His many publications in philosophy of science include *The Foundations of Scientific Inference* (1967), *Statistical Explanation and Statistical Relevance*

(1971), *Space, Time, and Motion: A Philosophical Introduction* (1975), *Scientific Explanation and the Causal Structure of the World* (1984), and *Four Decades of Scientific Explanation* (1990).

MICHAEL SCRIVEN has been Professor of Philosophy at the University of California at Berkeley and at the University of San Francisco, and Professor of Education at the University of Western Australia. His many publications include *Primary Philosophy* (1966), *Reasoning* (1976), and *Logic of Evaluation* (1981).

ERNEST SOSA is Professor of Philosophy at Brown University. His publications include *Knowledge in Perspective* (1991), as well as papers in epistemology, philosophy of mind, and metaphysics.

MICHAEL TOOLEY is Professor of Philosophy at the University of Colorado at Boulder. He is the author of *Abortion and Infanticide* (1983) and *Causation: A Realist Approach* (1987).

GEORG HENRIK VON WRIGHT was Professor of Philosophy at the University of Cambridge, and a Research Professor in the Academy of Finland. He has been a co-editor of the posthumous works of Wittgenstein, and among his many publications are *An Essay on Modal Logic* (1951), *Logical Studies* (1957), *The Logical Problem of Induction* (1957), *The Logic of Preference* (1963), *The Varieties of Goodness* (1963), *Norm and Action* (1963), *Explanation and Understanding* (1971), and *Causality and Determinism* (1974).

SELECT BIBLIOGRAPHY

(Not including material in this volume.)

1. BOOKS

Armstrong, David M., *What Is a Law of Nature?* (Cambridge, 1983).

Beauchamp, Tom L. (ed.), *Philosophical Problems of Causation* (Encino and Belmont, Calif., 1974).

—— and Rosenberg, Alexander, *Hume and the Problem of Causation* (New York and Oxford, 1981).

Bunge, Mario, *Causality* (Cambridge, Mass., 1959).

Burks, Arthur W., *Chance, Cause, and Reason: An Inquiry into the Nature of Scientific Evidence* (Chicago, 1977).

Ducasse, Curt John, *Causation and the Types of Necessity* (Seattle, 1924; Dover paperbacks, 1969).

Eells, Ellery, *Rational Decision and Causality* (Cambridge, 1982).

Fales, Evan, *Causation and Universals* (London and New York, 1990).

Hart, Herbert Lionel Adolphus, and Honoré, Anthony Maurice, *Causation in the Law* (Oxford, 1959).

Hume, David, *A Treatise of Human Nature*, i and ii (London, 1739), iii (London, 1740).

—— *An Enquiry Concerning Human Understanding* (London, 1748).

Inwagen, Peter van (ed.), *Time and Cause: Essays Presented to Richard Taylor* (Dordrecht, 1980).

Körner, Stephan (ed.), *Explanation* (Oxford, 1975).

Mackie, John L., *The Cement of the Universe* (Oxford, 1974).

Madden, Edward H., and Harré, Rom, *Causal Powers* (Totowa, NJ, 1975).

Michotte, Albert, *The Perception of Causality* (New York, 1963).

Reichenbach, Hans, *The Direction of Time* (Berkeley, Calif., and Los Angeles, 1956).

Salmon, Wesley C., *Scientific Explanation and the Causal Structure of the World* (Princeton, 1984).

Skyrms, Brian, *Causal Necessity* (New Haven, Conn., and London, 1980).

Strawson, Galen, *The Secret Connexion: Causation, Realism, and David Hume* (Oxford, 1989).

Suppes, Patrick, *A Probabilistic Theory of Causality* (Amsterdam, 1970).

Tooley, Michael, *Causation: A Realist Approach* (Oxford, 1987).

van Fraassen, Bas C., *Laws and Symmetry* (Oxford, 1989).

von Wright, Georg Henrik, *Explanation and Understanding* (Ithaca, NY, 1971).

2. ARTICLES AND CHAPTERS IN BOOKS

Anderson, John, 'The Problem of Causality', *Australasian Journal of Philosophy*, 2 (1938), 127–42; repr. in his *Studies in Empirical Philosophy* (Sydney, 1962), 126–36.

Anglin, William S., 'Backwards Causation', *Analysis*, 41 (1981), 86–91.

Anscombe, G. Elizabeth M., 'Causality and Extensionality', *Journal of Philosophy*, 66 (1969), 152–9.

Armstrong, David M., and Heathcote, Adrian, 'Causes and Laws', *Noûs*, 25 (1991), 63–73.

Aronson, Jerrold, 'The Legacy of Hume's Analysis of Causation', *Studies in the History and Philosophy of Science*, 7 (1971), 135–56.

Ayer, Alfred J., 'Why Cannot Cause Succeed Effect?', *The Problem of Knowledge* (Harmondsworth, 1956), 170–5.

Bennett, Jonathan, 'Counterfactuals and Possible Worlds', *Canadian Journal of Philosophy*, 4 (1974), 391–402.

—— 'Counterfactuals and Temporal Direction', *Philosophical Review*, 93 (1984), 57–91.

Black, Max, 'Why Cannot an Effect Precede its Cause?', *Analysis*, 16 (1955–6), 49–58.

Blackburn, Simon, 'Hume and Thick Connexions', *Philosophy and Phenomenological Research*, suppl. 50 (1990), 237–50.

Brand, Myles, 'Simultaneous Causation', in Peter van Inwagen (ed.), *Time and Cause* (Dordrecht, 1980), 137–53.

—— and Swain, Marshall, 'On the Analysis of Causation', *Synthèse*, 21 (1970), 222–7.

Bretzel, Philip von, 'Concerning a Probabilistic Theory of Causation Adequate for the Causal Theory of Time', *Synthèse*, 35 (1977), 173–90.

Bromberger, Sylvain, 'What Are Effects?', in *Analytical Philosophy*, 1st ser., ed. Ronald J. Butler (Oxford, 1962), 15–20.

Burks, Arthur W., 'The Logic of Causal Propositions', *Mind*, 60 (1951), 363–82.

Cartwright, Nancy, 'Causal Laws and Effective Strategies', *Noûs*, 13 (1979), 419–38; repr. in *How the Laws of Physics Lie* (Oxford, 1983).

Castañeda, Hector-Neri, 'Causes, Causality, and Energy', *Midwest Studies in Philosophy*, 9, ed. Peter A. French, Theodore E. Uehling, and Howard K. Wettstein (Minneapolis, 1984), 17–27.

Chisholm, Roderick M., 'The Agent as Cause', in Myles Brand and Douglas Walton (eds.), *Action Theory* (Dordrecht, 1976), 199–211.

—— and Taylor, Richard, 'Making Things to Have Happened', *Analysis*, 20 (1960), 73–82.

Cohen, L. Jonathan, 'Laws, Coincidences and Relations between Universals', in Philip Pettit, Richard Sylvan, and Jean Norman (eds.), *Metaphysics and Morality: Essays in Honour of J. J. C. Smart* (Oxford, 1987), 16–34.

Collingwood, Robin George, 'On the So-Called Idea of Causation', *Proceedings of the Aristotelian Society*, 38 (1938), 85–112.

Collins, Arthur W., 'Explanation and Causality', *Mind*, 75 (1966), 482–500.

Davis, Wayne, 'Probabilistic Theories of Causation', in James H. Fetzer (ed.), *Probability and Causation: Essays in Honor of Wesley Salmon* (Dordrecht, 1988), 133–60.

Dray, William H., 'Must Effects Have Causes?', *Analytical Philosophy*, 1st ser., ed. Ronald J. Butler (Oxford, 1962), 20–5.

Dretske, Fred I., 'Laws of Nature', *Philosophy of Science*, 44 (1977), 248–68.

—— and Snyder, Aaron, 'Causal Irregularity', *Philosophy of Science*, 39 (1972), 69–71.

Dummett, Michael, 'Can an Effect Precede its Cause?', *Proceedings of the Aristotelian Society*, suppl. 28 (1954), 27–44.

—— 'Bringing about the Past', *Philosophical Review*, 73 (1964), 338–59; repr. in *Truth and Other Enigmas* (London, 1978), 333–50.

Dupré, John, and Cartright, Nancy, 'Probability and Causality: Why Hume and Indeterminism Don't Mix', *Noûs*, 22 (1988), 521–36.

Earman, John, 'Causation: A Matter of Life and Death', *Journal of Philosophy*, 73 (1976), 5–25.

Eells, Ellery, 'Probabilistic Causal Interaction', *Philosophy of Science*, 53 (1986), 52–64.

—— and Sober, Elliott, 'Probabilistic Causality and the Question of Transitivity', *Philosophy of Science*, 50 (1983), 35–57.

Ewing, Alfred Cyril, 'Causation and Induction', *Philosophy and Phenomenological Research*, 12 (1962), 465–85.

—— 'A Defence of Causality', in W. E. Kennick and Morris Lazerowitz (eds.), *Metaphysics* (Englewood Cliffs, NJ, 1966), 258–75.

Fair, David, 'Causation and the Flow of Energy', *Erkenntnis*, 14 (1979), 219–50.

Fales, Evan, 'Causation and Induction', *Midwest Studies in Philosophy*, 9, ed. Peter A. French, Theodore E. Uehling, and Howard K. Wettstein (Minneapolis, 1984), 113–34.

Flew, Antony, 'Can an Effect Precede its Cause?', *Proceedings of the Aristotelian Society*, suppl. 28 (1954), 45–62.

—— 'Effects before their Causes — Addenda and Corrigenda', *Analysis*, 16 (1955–6), 104–10.

—— 'Causal Disorder Again', *Analysis*, 17 (1956–7), 81–6.

Foster, John, 'Induction, Explanation, and Natural Necessity', *Proceedings of the Aristotelian Society*, 83 (1982–3), 87–101.

Gale, Richard M., 'Why a Cause Cannot be Later than its Effect', *Review of Metaphysics*, 19 (1965), 209–34.

Gasking, Douglas, 'Causation and Recipes', *Mind*, 64 (1955), 479–87.

Giere, Ronald N., 'Causal Systems and Statistical Hypotheses', in L. Jonathan Cohen and Mary Hesse (eds.), *Applications of Inductive Logic* (Oxford, 1980), 251–70.

Good, I. J., 'A Causal Calculus I–II', *British Journal for the Philosophy of Science*, 11 (1961), 305–18, and 12 (1962), 43–51.

Gorovitz, Samuel, 'Leaving the Past Alone', *Philosophical Review*, 73 (1964), 360–71.

—— 'Causal Judgments and Causal Explanations', *Journal of Philosophy*, 62 (1965), 695–711.

Hanson, Norwood Russell, 'Causal Chains', *Mind*, 64 (1955), 289–311.

Healey, Richard, 'Temporal and Causal Asymmetry', in Richard G. Swinburne (ed.), *Space, Time and Causality* (Dordrecht, 1983), 79–105.

Heathcote, Adrian, 'A Theory of Causality: Causality = Interaction (As Defined by a Suitable Quantum Field Theory)', *Erkenntnis*, 31 (1989), 77–108.

Hesslow, Germund, 'Two Notes on the Probabilistic Approach to Causation', *Philosophy of Science*, 43 (1976), 290–2.

Horwich, Paul, 'Backward Causation' and 'Causation', *Asymmetries in Time* (Cambridge, Mass., 1987), 91–109 and 129–45.

Humphreys, Paul, 'Cutting the Causal Chain', *Pacific Philosophical Quarterly*, 61 (1980), 305–14.

—— 'Probabilistic Causality and Multiple Causation', in Peter D. Asquith and Ronald N. Giere (eds.), *PSA 1980* (East Lansing, Mich., 1981), 25–37.

Jackson, Frank, 'A Causal Theory of Counterfactuals', *Australasian Journal of Philosophy*, 55 (1977), 3–21.

Jackson, Frank and Pettit, Philip, 'Program Explanation: A General Perspective', *Analysis*, 50 (1990), 107–17.

Kim, Jaegwon, 'Causation, Nomic Subsumption and the Concept of Event', *Journal of Philosophy*, 70 (1973), 217–36.

Lewis, David, 'Counterfactual Dependence and Time's Arrow', *Noûs*, 13 (1979), 455–76; repr. with postscripts in his *Philosophical Papers*, ii (Oxford, 1986), 32–66.

—— 'Postscripts to "Causation" ', in his *Philosophical Papers*, ii (Oxford, 1986), 173–213.

Lucas, John Randolph, 'Causation', in *Analytical Philosophy*, 1st ser., ed. Ronald J. Butler (Oxford, 1962), 32–65.

Mackie, John L., 'Counterfactuals and Causal Laws', in *Analytical Philosophy*, 1st ser., ed. Ronald J. Butler (Oxford, 1962), 65–80.

Madden, Edward H., 'A Third View of Causality', *Review of Metaphysics*, 23 (1969), 67–84.

Mandelbaum, Maurice, 'Causal Analysis in History', *Journal of the History of Ideas*, 3 (1942), 30–50.

Marc-Wogau, Konrad, 'On Historical Explanation', *Theoria*, 28 (1962), 213–33.

Martin, Raymond, 'The Sufficiency Thesis', *Philosophical Studies*, 23 (1972), 205–11.

Mellor, D. Hugh, 'Necessities and Universals in Natural Laws', in Mellor (ed.), *Science, Belief and Behaviour* (Cambridge, 1980), 105–25.

—— 'Fixed Past, Unfixed Future', in Barry Taylor (ed.), *Contributions to Philosophy: Michael Dummett* (The Hague, 1986), 166–86.

—— 'On Raising the Chances of Effects', in James H. Fetzer (ed.), *Probability and Causation: Essays in Honor of Wesley Salmon* (Dordrecht, 1988), 229–39.

Menzies, Peter, 'A Unified Account of Causal Relata', *Australasian Journal of Philosophy*, 67 (1989), 59–83.

—— 'Probabilistic Causation and Causal Processes: A Critique of Lewis', *Philosophy of Science*, 56 (1989), 642–63.

Otte, Richard, 'A Critique of Suppes' Theory of Probabilistic Causality', *Synthèse*, 48 (1981), 167–90.

Pap, Arthur, 'Philosophical Analysis, Translation Schemas, and the Regularity Theory of Causation', *Journal of Philosophy*, 49 (1952), 657–66.

Papineau, David, 'Causal Asymmetry', *British Journal for the Philosophy of Science*, 36 (1985), 273–89.

Pears, David F., 'The Priority of Causes', *Analysis*, 17 (1956–7), 54–63.

Putnam, Hilary, 'Is the Causal Structure of the Physical itself Something Physical?', *Midwest Studies in Philosophy*, 9, ed. Peter A. French, Theodore E. Uehling, and Howard K. Wettstein (Minneapolis, 1984), 3–16.

Railton, Peter, 'Probability, Explanation, and Information', *Synthèse*, 48 (1981), 233–56.

Ramsey, Frank Plumpton, 'General Propositions and Causality', in Richard Bevan Braithwaite (ed.), *The Foundations of Mathematics* (Paterson, NJ, 1960), 237–55.

Rosen, Deborah A., 'In Defense of a Probabilistic Theory of Causality', *Philosophy of Science*, 45 (1978), 368–86.

—— 'A Probabilistic Theory of Causal Necessity', *Southern Journal of Philosophy*, 18 (1980), 71–86.

Ruddick, William, 'Causal Connection', *Synthèse*, 18 (1968), 46–67.

Russell, Bertrand, 'On the Notion of Cause', *Proceedings of the Aristotelian Society*, 13 (1912–13), 1–26; repr. in *Mysticism and Logic* (Harmondsworth, 1953), 171–96.

Salmon, Wesley, 'Theoretical Explanation', in Stephan Körner (ed.), *Explanation* (Oxford, 1975), 118–43.

—— 'An "At-At" Theory of Causal Influence', *Philosophy of Science*, 44 (1977), 215–24.

—— 'Why Ask "Why?"?', *Proceedings and Addresses of the American Philosophical Association*, 51/6 (1978), 683–705.

Sanford, David H., 'The Direction of Causation and the Direction of Conditionship', *Journal of Philosophy*, 73 (1976), 193–207.

Schlick, Moritz, 'Causality in Contemporary Physics, I and II', *Philosophical Studies*, 12 (1962), 177–93, and 281–98.

Scriven, Michael, 'Randomness and the Causal Order', *Analysis*, 17 (1956–7), 5–9.

—— 'Causes, Connections, and Conditions in History', in William H. Dray (ed.), *Philosophical Analysis and History* (New York, 1966), 238–64.

—— 'Causation as Explanation', *Noûs*, 9 (1975), 3–16.

Shoemaker, Sydney, 'Properties, Causation and Projectibility', in L. Jonathan Cohen and Mary Hesse (eds.), *Applications of Inductive Logic* (Oxford, 1980), 291–312.

—— 'Causality and Properties', in Peter van Inwagen (ed.), *Time and Cause* (Dordrecht, 1980), 109–35.

Shorter, J. M., 'Causality and a Method of Analysis', *Analytical Philosophy*, 2nd ser., ed. Ronald J. Butler (Oxford, 1965), 145–57.

Simon, Herbert Alexander, and Rescher, Nicholas, 'Cause and Counterfactual', *Philosophy of Science*, 33 (1966), 323–40.

Skyrms, Brian, 'Resiliency, Propensities, and Causal Necessity', *Journal of Philosophy*, 74 (1977), 704–13.

Sober, Elliott, 'Two Concepts of Cause', in Peter D. Asquith and Philip Kitcher (eds.), *PSA 1984*, ii (East Lansing, Mich., 1984), 405–24.

Suppes, Patrick, 'Conflicting Intuitions about Causality', *Midwest Studies in Philosophy*, 9, ed. Peter A. French, Theodore E. Uehling, and Howard K. Wettstein (Minneapolis, 1984), 151–68.

Swoyer, Chris, 'The Nature of Natural Laws', *Australasian Journal of Philosophy*, 60/3 (1982), 203–23.

Taylor, Richard, 'Causation', *The Monist*, 47 (1962–3), 287–313.

—— 'Causation and Action', *Action and Purpose* (Englewood Cliffs, NJ, 1966), 3–96.

Tooley, Michael, 'The Nature of Laws', *Canadian Journal of Philosophy*, 7/4 (1977), 667–98.

—— 'Laws and Causal Relations', *Midwest Studies in Philosophy*, 9, ed. Peter A. French, Theodore E. Uehling, and Howard K. Wettstein (Minneapolis, 1984), 93–112.

—— 'The Nature of Causation: A Singularist Account', in David Copp (ed.), *Canadian Philosophers: Celebrating Twenty Years of the CJP*, Canadian Journal of Philosophy, suppl. 16 (1990), 271–322.

Vendler, Zeno, 'Effects, Results and Consequences', *Analytical Philosophy*, 1st ser., ed. Ronald J. Butler (Oxford, 1962), 1–15.

—— 'Causal Relations', *Journal of Philosophy*, 64 (1967), 704–13.

Warnock, Geoffrey J., 'Every Event Has a Cause', in Antony Flew (ed.), *Logic and Language* (Oxford, 1951), 107–9.

INDEX OF NAMES